Language of the Land

ISBN 0-8444-0963-4

Language of the Land

THE LIBRARY OF CONGRESS BOOK OF LITERARY MAPS

Martha Hopkins
Interpretive Programs Office

and

Michael Buscher
Geography and Map Division

LIBRARY OF CONGRESS   WASHINGTON   1999

♾ The paper used in this publication meets the requirements for permanence established by the American National Standard for Information Sciences "Permanence of Paper for Printed Library Materials" (ANSI Z 39.48–1984).

Cover
The Adventures of Huckleberry Finn from the Book by Mark Twain, illustratrated by Everett Henry. *(See pages 180 and 256.)*

Endpapers
Detail from *An Ancient Mappe of Fairyland, Newly Discovered and Set Forth,* illustrated by Bernard Sleigh. *(See pages 181 and 271.)*

Library of Congress Cataloging-in-Publication Data

Hopkins, Martha E.
    Language of the land : The Library of Congress book of literary
maps / Martha Hopkins and Michael Buscher.
      p. cm.
    Includes bibliographical references and index.
    ISBN 0–8444–0963–4
    1. Literary landmarks—Maps—Bibliography. I. Buscher, Michael.
II. Title.
Z6026.L57H66   1998
[G1046.E65]
016.809—dc21   98–21591
                                                    CIP

For sale by the
U.S. Government Printing Office
Superintendent of Documents
P.O. BOX 371954
Pittsburgh, PA 15250–7954

Contents

Preface

The Library of Congress, America's oldest national cultural institution, will be two hundred years old in the year 2000. With generous support from the U.S. Congress, it has become the largest repository of recorded knowledge in the world and a symbol of the vital connection between knowledge and democracy. The Library's diverse collections include more than 113 million items and encompass most languages and most formats. In addition to seventeen million books, it contains incomparable collections of pamphlets, manuscripts, music, maps, prints, photographs, motion pictures, sound recordings, and other research materials.

The Library of Congress is unique among the world's national libraries in that we allow all adults, without special permission or accreditation, to use the institution's collections for research purposes. Moreover, through our commitment to making our key American history collections available in digital form on the Internet, the Library now shares portions of its unique Americana collections with students and researchers throughout the United States and the world.

Maps and atlases have been an important part of the Library's collections since their beginning in 1800, when a joint congressional committee purchased three maps and an atlas from a London dealer. The copyright laws of the nineteenth century greatly strengthened the Library's cartographic collections. To this day, copyright is a major source of commercially produced U.S. maps; in fact, most of the literary maps in this book were acquired through copyright deposit.

Language of the Land is the result of a collaborative effort among several Library of Congress divisions, namely the Geography and Map Division, the Interpretive Programs Office, and the Center for the Book. The Library is pleased to share its remarkably diverse collection of literary maps with the world and invites educators in particular to join with us in finding creative ways of using these unique educational tools.

James H. Billington
The Librarian of Congress

Foreword

The Geography and Map Division, established in 1897 as the Hall of Maps to serve Congress and government agencies, has custody of the Library's cartographic collections. The division's holdings have grown during the past two centuries to more than 4,600,000 map sheets, 60,000 atlases, one million microfilm images, and 7,000 computer files. Approximately 100,000 items are acquired yearly thorough government deposits, domestic and international exchanges, purchases, and gifts. The holdings of the Geography and Map Division date from the fourteenth century and cover virtually every country and subject.

As the de facto National Map Library, the Geography and Map Division serves as a major center for research relating to cartography and geography. Maps acquired by the division since 1969 have been cataloged and their bibliographic records made available through the Library's MARC (Machine Readable Cataloging) Maps database, which is available electronically through the Internet. Recently the division has begun to scan and mount selected core map collections on the Internet as part of the Library's National Digital Library Program.

An essential element of the Geography and Map Division's effort to make its collections more accessible to scholars and the public during the past one hundred years has been the publication of more than one hundred major bibliographies, exhibition catalogs, map facsimiles, and guides such as the nine-volume *List of Geographical Atlases* (1909–1992), *Civil War Maps: An Annotated List of Maps and Atlases in the Library of Congress (1989)*, and *Panoramic Maps of Cities in the United States (1984)*. With the publication of this work, Martha Hopkins and Michael Buscher provide the first extensive survey of a little-known but fascinating cartographic genre.

Ralph E. Ehrenberg
Chief, Geography and Map Division

Acknowledgments

The authors wish to express their appreciation to Irene Chambers, Interpretive Programs Officer, and Ralph Ehrenberg, Chief, Geography and Map Division, for their generous support of this project. They also thank John Cole, Center for the Book, for his advice, patience, and encouragement.

We are especially grateful for the many helpful suggestions of the friends and colleagues who read portions of the manuscript: Cheryl Regan, Interpretive Programs Office, Alice Birney, Manuscript Division, and Ronald Grim, Geography and Map Division, Library of Congress; Barbara Tedford, Professor of English, Glenville State College; Susan Lowell; and Jane Lewin. Maurvene Williams, Center for the Book, helped obtain the many copyright permissions. Mikhail Levner, the Library's representative in Moscow, obtained the Russian copyright permissions. We also appreciate the skillful editing and expert handling of all the many details of turning the manuscript into a book provided by Iris Newsom, Editor, and Gloria Holmes, Production Manager, of the Publishing Office.

Others at the Library of Congress who contributed their time and talents are: Don Fusaro, ITS; Stephen Cranton and Eric Solsten, Federal Research Division; Enikö Molnár Basa and John Reynolds, Cataloging Division; Barbara Dash, Rare Book Division; Carl Eck, Congressional Research Service; Abby Smith, formerly of Library Services; Harry Leich, European Division; Georgia Higley, Serials and Government Publications Division; Margaret Coughlan, Children's Literature Center; Yusef El Amin, Marita Clance, and Jim Higgins, Photoduplication Service; Linda Martin, Patricia Rigsbee, and Joan Doherty, Copyright Office; and the Cataloging and the Collections Management teams of the Geography and Map Division.

We also benefitted from the generous assistance of Lorna Knight and Linda Hoad, National Library of Canada; John Robert Colombo; David Shaw; Molly Maguire and Aaron Silverman; Gary Jones, Onodaga County Public Library, New York; Henry Shuemaker; Joseph Morgan; Richard Foley; Peter Stevens, Embassy of Canada, Washington, D.C.; Pat Crohn, Cleveland Museum of Art; Pat Lynagh, National Museum of American Art, Smithsonian Institution; Walter Reed; Maryly Peck, Polk Community College, Florida; and Lillian Lewicki.

About the Authors

Martha Hopkins, Exhibit Director in the Interpretive Programs Office of the Library of Congress, curated the *Language of the Land* exhibit. She holds degrees in English from the College of William and Mary and the University of Virginia and has taught English at colleges in Virginia and West Virginia. Her next project is a literary map of Washington, D.C.

Michael Buscher holds a degree in history from the University of Maryland. He has worked with the cartographic collections of the Library of Congress for almost twenty years and is currently the head of the Geography and Map Division's Collections Management Team.

Authors' Note

This book is an annotated guide to the more than two hundred literary maps in the collections of the Geography and Map Division of the Library of Congress. We define a literary map as a map that records the location and identity of geographical places and features associated with authors and their works and serves as a guide to the worlds of novelists, poets, dramatists, and other authors of imaginative literature. Our definition also includes folklore maps and literary atlases.

The concept of literary maps as a distinct genre evolved during the authors' work on a Library of Congress exhibit, *Language of the Land: Journeys into Literary America,* displayed at the Library in 1993 and throughout the United States as a travelling exhibit between 1993 and 1996. Developed by the Library's Interpretive Programs Office in cooperation with the Geography and Map Division and the Library's Center for the Book, the exhibit was made possible by a generous grant from the Lila Wallace-Reader's Digest Fund. In Washington, the exhibit featured forty-seven maps locating places associated with authors and their literary works along with photographs of some of those places, rare books, and manuscript material.

While preparing the exhibit, the authors did not find any studies or bibliographies of literary maps and recognized the need for one. Also, we felt that, although *Language of the Land* displayed some of the most visually exciting examples of the Library's rich holdings, the large number of maps not exhibited should be made accessible to a wider audience.

The book is designed as a cartobibliography with an entry for each map that consists of a black-and-white photograph, bibliographic information, and a brief description. Selected maps are reproduced as full-color, full-page illustrations.

Because of the variety of ways these maps were produced, attributing authorship was often difficult. Wherever possible, we tried to distinguish between compilers, who prepared the content of the map; designers, who conceived the overall look of the map; and illustrators, who executed the drawings. In some cases the same person played more than one of these roles. In other cases it is clear that some people who played these roles were not credited on the map. Because information was not always available or clear, we may have made errors in assigning these categories. We tried to be consistent, but some of our classification was unavoidably arbitrary.

Library of Congress call numbers are given for most maps. However, some maps form part of two special pictorial map collections, the Ethel M. Fair and the Muriel H. Parry collections. Instead of call numbers, these maps are identified by individual numbers within each collection.

Maps are categorized into world literature maps; maps of individual regions and countries; American literature maps; maps showing regions and most states of the United States; British literature maps, which were numerous enough to merit a category of their own; maps related to specific authors or specific books; maps of imaginary worlds; and literary atlases and other compilations. Within each section entries are arranged alphabetically by title, and in the case of those with the same title, chronologically. Maps of individual cities follow maps of the country, region, or state in which they are located and are arranged alphabetically.

This book, like the exhibit, emphasizes poster-sized maps. Small maps that appeared in books or in magazines are included only if they exist in the collections as detached, separate items.

Readers may note that the maps described deal primarily with the American and British literary traditions. This focus occurs because the maps the Library has received through copyright deposit and other gifts happen to be in these areas. Comparative study of other collections may yield maps dealing with the literature of other cultures and lead to different conclusions about literary maps as a whole.

The Library hopes this volume will be a valuable aid to students of geography and literature and encourage further study of and creation of literary maps. The Geography and Map Division also wants to continue developing its collections in this genre and would welcome information about examples that are not represented here.

Introduction

"There ain't anything that is so interesting to look at as
a place that a book has talked about." **Mark Twain**
Tom Sawyer Abroad (1894)

Toward Defining A Literary Map

Considering the wealth of materials that constitute human knowledge, we need maps if
we are to cover the terrain successfully. Literary maps are one way of organizing an area
of that knowledge in a visually appealing way. Specifically, a literary map records the location of places associated with authors and their literary works or serves as a guide to
their imaginative worlds. It may present places associated with a literary tradition, an individual author, or a specific work. Some maps highlight an entire country's literary heritage; others feature authors identified with a particular city, state, or region. Maps can
feature real places connected with an individual author, literary character, or book, such
as those featuring Jane Austen's England, Sherlock Holmes's London, or the settings in
Moby Dick, or they may show wholly imaginary landscapes such as Oz, Middle Earth, or
Neverland.

Although they may depict actual places, literary maps generally portray them with
the power of imagination rather than with precise, geographic accuracy. They differ from
most reference maps in the kind and quantity of information provided. Because there is no
way of telling what facts any one reader may need, a general map contains a large amount
of information. However, no one part of it is emphasized, and nothing distracts the eye too
much or calls particular attention to itself. Users approach such a map to acquire certain
information—perhaps the location of a certain town or of a street in that town.

On one level literary maps function like other maps, in that readers can glean information from them. For example, literary map users may learn what writers lived in a certain area, just as other users may learn where a certain city is by consulting a road map. However, although a pictorial map (of which a literary map is a subspecies), may be based on a general map, it has a purpose beyond the basic presentation of information. It focuses the reader's attention on some part of itself, announcing its subjects clearly and visually. It differs from a general map because it has a specific message.

Most literary maps, therefore, are not drawn to scale and contain little detailed information on topography, geology, or the locations of towns, rivers, roads, and other features of landscape. They are often simplified outlines of an area, featuring large images of authors, buildings, and geographical features associated with authors, and characters and scenes from literary works. These elements, rather than the traditional elements of a general map, command the viewer's attention. Literary maps depict ideas as much as places and present a world in which authors and books are the dominant features. For readers, the geographic knowledge can serve as a framework on which to fit the life of an author or the adventures of a book.

Another difference between a literary map and a general reference map is the relationship between viewer and object. Whereas viewers of a general map may lack knowledge of certain facts they hope to find by examining the map, viewers of literary maps enjoy the maps more if they know the subject. For example, the peruser of a *Moby Dick* or *Huckleberry Finn* map looks at it less for information about the book or its author than for the thrill of seeing representations of familiar characters and scenes from a well-known story. Residents of a certain state enjoy recognizing on a map names of authors well known in their locale. Most literary maps presuppose some knowledge on the part of the viewer, which explains why these maps are almost always associated with well-known books, authors, and traditions.

In addition to celebrating familiar works, literary maps demonstrate the importance of geography in fiction. This grounding that a sense of place brings to fiction is well described by Eudora Welty in "Place in Fiction" (1987):

> Surely once we have named [a place], we have put a kind of poetic claim on its existence; the claim works even out of sight—may work forever sight unseen. . . . Being shown how to locate, to place, any account is what does most toward making us believe it, not merely allowing us to, may the account be the facts or a lie; and that is where place in fiction comes in. Fiction is a lie. Never in its inside thoughts, always in its outside dress.

Furthermore, as the spread of identical fast-food chains and shopping malls have made the United States and much of the rest of the world more uniform, people have experienced a counterbalancing desire to celebrate those things that make one place and one group different from another. Therefore, a sense of place, of which literary maps form a part, has assumed new importance.

Celebration of place is also a form of patriotism and taking pride in one's roots. The great number of maps of U.S. states and regions featured in the Library of Congress collections reflect the pride of residents of various states in their cultural heritage, as well as the regionalism that has long been a predominant feature of American literature. Furthermore, writers sometimes become celebrities, and people's self-esteem may be enhanced when they realize they share home ground with literary stars. For example, a state that does not rank high in per capita income or quality of its educational system may boast a rich literary heritage, and a map can foster pride in that heritage among the state's school children. Moreover, because regional pride plays a major role in the creation of literary maps, the line between the literary and the historical is often amorphous: a number of the maps include historical places and figures, as well as representations of state seals, flags, flowers, birds, the state capitol building, and historic monuments.

Other motives for producing maps range from the commercial (advertising a product) to the altruistic (promoting love of reading) and the line between the two sometimes becomes thin. An author can become the principal product of a region, for example, in the case of William Shakespeare and Stratford-upon-Avon or William Wordsworth and the English Lake District. Because of their literary connections, both places have flourishing tourist industries, which have produced literary maps.

In addition to tourist boards, other producers of maps in the Library of Congress collections include library associations, publishers, civic organizations, associations of English teachers, government agencies, centennial commissions, printing equipment companies, movie producers, advertisers, and individuals who simply loved certain books and authors. A few of the maps were even produced by map-publishing companies!

Like all cultural artifacts, literary maps should be examined in relation to their context. Important things to consider are who made the maps, what were the makers' motives, in what circumstances were they created, when were they made, and for what audience were they intended. In particular, the following points should be kept in mind.

First, literary maps are not objective and neutral. Like all maps, literary maps present a highly selective view of reality, especially in terms of what is included and what left out. To be useful, maps must be selective, and every map is designed to convey a particular viewpoint. Sometimes the motive is as simple as celebrating books and writers that the mapmaker likes. It should, however, be taken as a given that literary mapmakers generally have a motive other than conveying geographic information. Because maps can be used to determine who controls both literary territory and political territory, we should examine what ulterior motives lie behind their creation.

Second, everything on a map is a matter of choice. Prospective mapmakers face a world of decisions, especially on maps such as these, most of which make no pretense to geographical accuracy. What will the subject of the map be—a state, region, or country or a favorite author or group of authors, or work? If the map is to span a large area, what time period will it cover—the entire literary history or a selected period?

For maps that cover a locality, the most difficult decision is whom to include. Because a region may have a large number of people who are in some sense authors, the mapmakers must first consider what types of authors are worthy of inclusion—fiction writers and poets only, or also biographers, essayists, naturalists, and historians. Then, how prominent must the writers be? Is recognition within the local area enough, or should the writers have achieved national distinction? Creators of literary maps can attest to the rush of candidates that any attempt to prepare a literary map brings forth. Authors of cookbooks, guidebooks, and textbooks push to get their names on the maps. Dead authors are nominated by friends, relatives, and devoted readers. Most of the maps listed in this volume have limited their authors to writers of novels, short stories, plays, poems, and other works of imaginative literature.

Decisions of whom to include depend not only on type of author but also on geographic criteria. These criteria vary from map to map, but standards used for most maps in this book include: writers born in an area who spent their lives there; writers born elsewhere who lived in an area long enough to be influenced by it and associated with it; and writers who set one or more works in a locality, even though they themselves may not have spent time there. Local pride usually leads to inclusion of authors born in an area who spent most of their lives elsewhere, such as Willa Cather, born in Virginia, but associated with Nebraska and the West.

Because American writers have been a restless lot, the same author can be claimed on a number of different maps. Missouri-born Mark Twain, for instance, spent time in Nevada, California, and New York and is listed on maps for all four states. If a map for Connecticut exists, it may note the time Twain spent in Hartford. Robert Frost, the quintessential New England poet, is claimed on a California map as a San Francisco writer because he was born there and lived there until the age of ten. Perhaps the best definition of what gives an author a claim to be on a map is provided by *Portraits of Literary Michigan*, which defines a Michigan author as "someone whose work bears the imprint of time spent in Michigan. The author, native born, adoptive, or just passing through, was affected by the varied Michigan experience."

Once content is decided, design issues must be addressed. Will the budget allow for color? How many illustrations can be used and whom or what should they show? Regardless of their intentions to be fair and objective, in making these decisions, the creators of a literary map will act on the basis of their own needs, viewpoints, and prejudices.

Third, as well as reflecting the underlying values and specific interests of their creators, literary maps reveal the tastes and values of the times and places in which they were created. By saying "these authors and these works are significant," literary maps promulgate a certain view of the literary canon, i.e., those works of literature recognized as being important enough to read, study, write about, and teach to future generations. Comparing maps from different periods gives insight into the development of that canon.

The maps in this book demonstrate how the canon of American literature has changed substantially over time. After World War I, for example, the "Schoolroom Poets"—Henry Wadsworth Longfellow, Oliver Wendell Holmes, James Russell Lowell, and John Greenleaf Whittier—began to lose their position of eminence, while Herman Melville, one of their contemporaries who had been almost forgotten, became recognized as a major writer. During the 1920s, novelists Joseph Hergesheimer and James Branch Cabell, hardly household names today, appeared on lists of great American authors along with Walt Whitman, Edgar Allan Poe, Henry James, and others who would still appear on such lists. Around that time, prominent women such as Harriet Beecher Stowe, Mary E. Wilkins Freeman, and Edith Wharton began to receive less attention than their male contemporaries Mark Twain and Stephen Crane.

Since the 1940s and 1950s, the period when many of these maps were produced, the literary canon has changed even more radically. Beginning in the 1960s, scholars who recognized the richness and diversity of American culture began to seek out and publish lost, forgotten, or suppressed literary texts that had emerged from and, in fact, illustrated that diversity. In the 1970s, scholarship began to examine the cultural implications of gender, race, and class for understanding and appreciating literature. Consequently, in the 1980s, the whole concept of a literary canon was increasingly attacked, especially on the grounds that women and minority writers were under-represented in the traditional framework. Although many critics recognized the need for some version of a canon in order to transmit valued work to future generations, they were disturbed by the tendency of the established canon to freeze responses to the texts it validated and to exclude other, less-recognized works of literary value.

In the 1990s, the teaching of literature has been undergoing fundamental changes that allow for study of diverse cultures, not a narrow group of individual authors. The canon is being expanded to include more female, African American, Asian American, Latino, and Native American voices in order to represent as fully as possible the varied cultures that make up the United States. The types of works defined as literature are also being revised to include letters, diaries, and memoirs. In addition increasing attention is being given to non-European literature, in particular to works from Latin America, Canada, Asia, and Africa. The more recent maps in the book, especially the state maps, reflect the increasing diversity of material and authors now recognized as significant.

Two Illinois maps demonstrate some of these changes in the canon. *Illinois Authors,* produced by the Illinois Association of Teachers of English in 1952, lists twenty-seven authors for the Chicago area—four are female, and one (Richard Wright) is black. The 1987 map, also entitled *Illinois Authors,* includes the same twenty-seven Chicago authors listed in 1952, but the overall number of authors featured rose dramatically to 145, of which 33 are female and at least 4 are black. And, although no black author was shown on the 1952 map, the 1987 version pictures a black female—Lorraine Hansberry.

This increasing recognition of diversity adds new dimension to a genre that has always had multiple faces. Although often reflecting academic views of the literary canon, literary maps are primarily works of popular culture. Almost-forgotten bestsellers of previous decades are well represented among these maps, for example, Stark Young's *So Red the Rose* (1934), Austin Tappan Wright's *Islandia* (1942), Archie Binns's *The Land Is Bright* (1939), and the novels of James Branch Cabell, as well as books whose popularity has survived, such as *Gone with the Wind* (1939). J .R. R. Tolkien's popularity among young people in the 1970s is reflected in a group of Middle Earth maps produced during that period. The high status once enjoyed by authors such as Joseph Hergesheimer and Sinclair Lewis, America's first Nobel Prize winner, is reflected on the maps. And such maps as the Ian Fleming map and the Raymond Chandler map celebrate authors and characters who are part of the popular rather than the highbrow tradition.

As might be expected in works of popular culture, the styles as well as the subject matter of literary maps exhibit considerable variety. Some of the map illustrators were trained and practiced as fine artists and produced exquisite examples of color and execution. Other maps are crudely drawn and look unfinished. Some maps, especially those produced from the 1930s through the 1950s, reflect the advertising and magazine illustration styles of their times. Others evoke the times in which an author wrote, for example, Regency England in the *Jane Austen Map of England*. Some are humorous, with a satirical or cartoon style, for example *Washington Writers* or *Paul Bunyan's Pictorial Map of the United States*. Some of the mapmakers poke fun at themselves, as do the makers of *A Literary Map of Canada*, which depicts the map's creators in small caricatures beside the title, each holding a pen or brush, depending on his role.

On all the maps are represented many writers—the prominent and the once-prominent, and those who may have had only a local following—and their works, whether still widely read or long forgotten. These maps show the flourishing literary traditions that have developed in the United States and other countries over the centuries.

LITERARY MAPS: A SELECTIVE HISTORY

Since ancient times mapmakers have adopted a pictorial approach to geography, using illustrations, insets, scrolls, ribbons, heraldic devices, and legendary places as a way of visualizing large spaces. Before the seventeenth century, mapmakers made extensive use of symbols, such as mythological creatures, to convey sometimes imaginary information about unfamiliar lands. As the scientific method spread and exploration and travel made the world more familiar, maps became more detailed and the style more conventional, with pictorial elements relegated to decorative borders and title cartouches.

In the nineteenth century, educators revived pictorial maps to teach not only geography but also history and literature. By the twentieth century, such pictorial maps had become popular for their decorative qualities and as expressions of civic or national pride. But, because they were often displayed on classroom walls, then discarded when they became tattered, many have become scarce. Moreover, because they were printed in limited editions, not always formally copyrighted, and distributed locally for only a short time, they may not have come into library collections. Although literary maps have existed since at least the sixteenth century, because of the ephemeral nature of such maps, most examples in the Library of Congress date from the twentieth.

Large literary maps most likely evolved from illustrations in books, many of which—for example, Sir Thomas More's *Utopia* (1516), to name an early one—contain maps that locate the book's action. The cost of paper and the cost and difficulty of printing, as well as lack of a market, may have discouraged publishers from producing poster-sized maps before the twentieth century. Whatever the reason, most of the Library's maps that predate the 1920s are loose sheets originally bound in books, for example, the 1705 *Carte du Voyage d' Enée*, which depicts the adventures of Aeneas as told in Virgil's *Aeneid*. Exceptions are the ambitious 1878 *Philological and Historical Chart*, an example of the Victorian love of classification that attempts to trace the birth, development, and progress of all world literatures in such detail as to be almost unreadable, and the visually beautiful 1908 *Stratford on Avon* map, which reflects the high status of Shakespeare in the English-speaking world and depicts his birthplace at the turn of the twentieth century, not in the playwright's own day.

The earliest map in the Library of Congress collections that is identified in its title as such is the 1899 *A Literary Map of England* by Yale University professor William Lyon Phelps. Like several of the early maps related to British literature, it is primarily a general purpose or reference map of England that shows places with literary associations, but assumes that viewers know their significance.

In the Library's collections, the first period represented by a significant number of stand-alone literary maps is the 1920s. At this date, most of the themes that continue in later maps were established. Many American-produced literary maps of this decade deal with British literature and British writers, demonstrating the importance of English literature in the American imagination, a connection that remained strong in maps produced through the 1960s. In addition, the earliest examples in the Library collections of literary maps of individual American states date from the 1920s, examples being the 1922 *Bret Harte Trail Map* and the 1927 *Literary Map of New Jersey*. Fantasy maps, represented by items depicting fairyland and Mother Goose characters also were popular.

A significant literary-map creator who began work in this decade was Paul Mayo Paine (1869–1955), head of the Syracuse Public Library from 1915 to 1942, and a newspaper book columnist and textbook writer. Although they are among the earliest examples of the genre in the Library's holdings, Paine's maps are visually among the finest in their use of color and of illustrations of authors and scenes from books. Between 1925 and 1939, Paine produced at least seven maps, most in conjunction with the R. R. Bowker Company of New York. Most of the seven concern the United States, including three entitled *The Booklovers Map of America* (1926–1939) and *The Northward Map of Truthful Tales*, which shows the northern United States and all of Canada. *The Booklovers Map of the British Isles* reflects the high status accorded English literature in Paine's time.

Considering that the word appears in the titles of four of his maps, Paine must have considered himself a booklover. As head of a large public library, he was no doubt interested in furthering literacy and love of reading. Two of his maps are explicitly for young readers: the *Map of Good Stories: Stories, Trails, Voyages, Discoveries, Explorations and Places to Read About*, a world literature map that mixes fictional and true stories of exploration and adventure; and the *Map of Adventures for Boys and Girls*, which emphasizes adventure novels of U.S. literature.

Paine's maps are very much products of his time, as if he had quickly scanned then-current book titles and listed his favorites. Consequently, many of the titles are obscure to modern readers. Moreover, he shows little familiarity with writers outside the British and American traditions: even on his world maps, he lists authors writing in English rather than writers using the native languages of the countries.

Some of Paine's work was published in the 1930s, a decade that also saw production of a large group of literary maps, with subjects as diverse as Paul Bunyan and classical mythology. At this time, the Library's earliest maps connected with individual books, for example, Stark Young's best-seller *So Red the Rose*, and individual modern authors, for example, Sinclair Lewis, appeared. The bicentennial of George Washington's birth in 1932 stimulated patriotic feeling, one result of which was the production of literary maps. The connection is made explicit in the *Map of American Literature Showing Points of Interest with Backgrounds and Facts that Influenced American Writers*. The inscription, "Bicentennial Celebration of the Birth of George Washington," appears in a prominent position, together with Washington's picture and an excerpt from his farewell address. The map also features images of and quotations from Thomas Jefferson, Daniel Webster,

John C. Calhoun, Abraham Lincoln, Theodore Roosevelt, and Woodrow Wilson, as well as a traditional group of authors of imaginative literature, most from New England. Historic sites such as Benjamin Franklin's birthplace in Philadelphia and Boston-area landmarks such as Faneuil Hall, Old North Church, and the monuments at Lexington and Concord, also appear. Moreover, the map has a large chronological chart linking English rulers from Henry VII to George V with the births of American writers through Robert Frost in 1875, an odd touch on a map celebrating the birth of the hero who liberated the United States from British rule.

The first map in the collections to challenge conspicuously an all-male pantheon of great American writers is the 1932 *A Pictorial Chart of American Literature*, compiled by Ethel Earle Wylie and illustrated by Ella Wall Van Leer (1893–1986). Anticipating modern literary trends, the map features some writers who were then contemporary (such as a young Robert Frost) and gives equal representation to America's many outstanding female writers from Anne Bradstreet to Edna St. Vincent Millay. The top border of the map pictures nineteen women and the bottom border shows nineteen men, along with their life dates and the states with which they are associated.

Information on Wylie is difficult to obtain, but her partner, Van Leer, was an artist, educator, and civic leader who received an M.A. in art and architecture from the University of California at Berkeley in 1914. Unable to gain a foothold in the male-dominated field of architecture, she turned to a career in art. She illustrated the American literature map and the similar one on British literature, both with Wylie for Rand McNally. Van Leer also painted portraits, executed murals for the Women's Athletic Club in Oakland, California, and the Men's Faculty Club at the University of California, and designed scenery and costumes for local theater groups in California, Florida, and North Carolina. She won prizes in a number of the exhibitions and art competitions in which she displayed her work. Van Leer's architectural training shows in the symmetrical and balanced design of her maps, which are executed in distinct blocklike sections. Her experience in portrait painting is reflected in the images of writers on the maps.

Despite Wylie and Van Leer's attempt to gain recognition for contemporary and female writers, maps from the 1940s tended to feature traditional subjects and the standard canon. Overviews of British and American literature continued to appear, along with some of the Library's earliest maps celebrating entire regions, such as the South, Southwest, and New England. As might be expected given America's participation in

World War II, some literary maps became an extension of the war effort. An example is the 1944 *Adventures of Mark Twain*, which celebrates Twain's patriotism (and ignores his antiwar writings) and urges viewers to buy war bonds. In 1942 Gladys North and Sterling North (he was the Literary Editor of the *Chicago Daily News* and the *New York Post*) produced a map entitled *Being a Literary Map of These United States Depicting a Renaissance no less Astonishing than that of Periclean Athens or Elizabethan London*. "Dedicated to those who have created an America Worth Defending," the map contains a long patriotic inscription asserting that America's authors have communicated love of country and defended democracy through their writings. The Norths claim that "if this map is slanted toward the democratic American dream it should be remembered that such is the slant of literate America," and dedicate the map to "those who have dedicated their lives to this defense either with pen or sword."

One reflection of the prosperity, optimism, and pride in country that flourished in the 1950s was a boom in literary mapmaking. In the 1950s, the United States emerged as a superpower and American popular culture began to have worldwide influence. The long-standing sense of American literature's inferiority when compared to European literature disappeared. Moreover, as the baby-boomer generation entered school, textbook publishing flourished, and publishers produced maps to be used in classrooms along with their books. The number of English teachers increased, adding members and financial resources that enabled their associations to produce literary maps. During this time, many state maps and maps connected with individual works, such as plays by Shakespeare and epics by Homer and Virgil, appeared.

A prolific literary-map producer who began in the 1940s but reached his peak in the 1950s and 1960s was Henry John Firley (1900–1973), head of the English Department at Glenbard West High School in Glen Ellyn, Illinois, and an author, poet, and member of the National Council of Teachers of English. Working with the Denoyer-Geppert Company of Chicago, an educational publisher, Firley compiled colorful and highly detailed maps. Intended for classroom use, these maps were offered in a variety of formats, including framed, mounted for hanging on a wall, or installed on a spring roller, like a window shade. Although they now are somewhat dated by their reliance on a traditional literary canon, some of Firley's maps are still being distributed in the 1990s.

Like Paul Paine's maps, Firley's covered a variety of subjects. Not surprisingly for its time, Firley's first map, the 1940 *Literary-Pictorial British Isles*, featured British literature.

For his next map, the 1942 *Literary-Pictorial New England*, Firley turned to the oldest and most traditionally influential literary region of the United States. These two projects are essentially general reference maps with literary places marked but not explained. Small insets provide some specifically literary information, but on the whole the viewer is expected to know the literary associations of the places and to recognize the images representing them.

In his post-World War II maps, however, Firley fully exploited the possibilities of the pictorial map format, using colorful illustrations, insets, scrolls, ribbons, lists, and other devices to organize visually vast amounts of information. In *A Glossateer of World Literature* (1961), a booklet to accompany some of the maps, he describes them as "a literary type—with paragraphs of color, chapters of space, and outline of symbol—providing a readable guide for the travel sketch, the historical narrative, the national epic, the colorful legend, the biographical essay, and the human drama." Firley outlines ways in which teachers could use the maps to further understanding of literature; among methods he suggests are teaching about symbolism from the imagery on the map, establishing a feeling of sympathy for the literature of a particular locale, revealing the effect of the environment upon the individual, and projecting an author's meaning back into the environment in which he or she lived. As might be expected from a published poet, Firley waxed lyrical about the literary map as: "a miraculous design of the world's contributions to the humanities, woven with the threads of actual and fabled lives. . . . A myriad of dramas within a drama, presenting a world in protean forms with mountains growing legend, prairie grass whispering an epic, the sea reciting a saga."

Intended for classroom use, Firley's maps were shaped by the standard high school curriculum of the 1950s and 1960s. Titles include the 1952 *Pictorial Map Depicting the Literary Development of the United States* and the 1965 *Pictorial Map of Colonial-Revolutionary American Literature* for American literature classes, and the 1959 *Pictorial Map of Mediterranean Mythology and Classical Literature*, for English and Latin classes.

In his 1955 *A Panorama of World Literature*, Firley reached beyond Britain and the United States to tackle world literature in one of the most ambitious maps reproduced in this book. Firley's magnum opus deals with selected literature of the United States, Europe, the Middle East, and Asia available in English and shows authors from ancient times to the twentieth century. Insets show the British Isles; Iceland; China and Japan; the cradle of religions; the history of the alphabet; Nobel Prize winners; the Indian subcontinent; famous voyages and sea stories; and national epics. Other insets list authors born in New York City, London, and Paris.

Firley was attuned to the effect of the environment on literary history, and in the *Glossateer* he explained the ways in which he saw literary maps as effective aids for teaching language arts:

> From the literary maps comes an extra stimulus which lends a sense of reality to the fictional portrayal of place and dimension, distance, and time. This seeming closeness to reality is felt by the reader as he visualizes a narrative with the aid of a map; for the reader, the maps hold a power beyond mere abstract symbolism. The imaginative power of the author can better be illustrated if the flame of his experience is reflected by the background of graphic concepts.

At roughly the same time as Firley's maps were being published, the Harris-Seybold (later Harris Intertype) Company of Cleveland, Ohio, was producing a significant group of pictorial maps based on British and American classics. Each July from 1953 through 1964, the company printed a calendar to advertise and promote the capabilities of the lithographic printing equipment it sold. In addition to almost 20,000 graphic arts firms, the maps were distributed to schools and libraries.

Harris-Seybold used its high-tech printing equipment in a display of old-fashioned romance and adventure and an evocation of nostalgia. Insights into the thinking behind the maps appear in a leaflet accompanying the *Ivanhoe* map, which states that Harris-Seybold hoped the map would "give you pleasure today by reminding you of the pleasure of yesteryear." The text recalls the excitement of childhood reading: "Remember when you first read it? How you rode, fought and bled with Ivanhoe and the Black Knight? . . . You ate it up . . . you and every other red-blooded boy in the English-speaking world. Artist Everett Henry's picture-map brings it all back." The text further suggests that the recipient might enjoy rereading the book.

As the *Ivanhoe* leaflet makes explicit, the books featured were popular with the "red-blooded boys" of the 1920s, 1930s, and 1940s, who by the 1950s were running businesses. Classics that traditionally were preferred by girls (who presumably were not buying printing equipment in the 1950s)—for example, *Little Women*, *Pride and Prejudice*, and *Jane Eyre*—did not appear as map subjects.

Harris-Seybold's pride in these maps is shown in an article in *Craftsman*, the company newsletter, of August 1955: "In less than two years, the fascinating "Map-of-A Book" Calendar subjects . . . have become famous in the graphics arts industry. The painting for *Robin Hood*, depicting tales of Sherwood Forest, bids to enlarge this fame as it recreates a land of legend in colorful detail. Through the eyes of Everett Henry, distinguished illustrator and cartographer, who paints original canvasses on special assignment from Harris-Seybold, we can see again the English shires where Sherwood Forest grew, and glimpse some of the adventures of Robin Hood and his band."

The company spared no expense on the maps, either for printing or for artwork. Nine of the twelve maps are by E. Everett Henry (1893–1961), a well-known, top-ranking New York commercial artist. During the 1930s and 1940s, Henry's advertisements for clients that included Chase and Sanborn coffee, U.S. steel, and Dole pineapple appeared in popular magazines such as the *Saturday Evening Post* and *Life*. Henry also was a fine artist who had had a thorough academic training at the School of Fine and Applied Art, New York; New York University; and Columbia University. He taught at the School of Fine and Applied Art, and one of his works is in the permanent collection of the Whitney Museum. His book illustrations appeared in the Limited Editions Club's 1934 *Frankenstein*.

Henry was particularly known for mural paintings, which he produced for club cars of the Pennsylvania Railroad and for buildings at the New York World's Fair of 1939–1940. One source says that he was noted for his "mural maps" and his maps of estates. Before his Harris-Seybold commissions, he had previously produced literary maps, one of which, *Our United States*, was reproduced in the *New York Herald Tribune* book section on March 5, 1933.

Henry's mural-painting experience is apparent in the Harris maps, which are like small murals, with a story line clearly depicting the best-known episodes from a particular book. Epic in sweep, they demonstrate a highly developed decorative sense and a mastery of the techniques of unifying diverse elements into one design. Henry's style is realistic and has a three-dimensional quality. His skillful manipulation of light values is especially apparent in the *Moby Dick* map.

Henry's style suits his subjects well. The maps feature lively color illustrations of episodes from romantic and adventure novels: *The Adventures of Tom Sawyer* (1953), *Treasure Island* (1954), *The Adventures of Robin Hood and His Merry Men* (1955), *Moby Dick* (1956), *A Tale of Two Cities* (1957), *Ivanhoe* (1958), *The Adventures of Huckleberry Finn* (1959), *The Virginian* (1960), and *The Red Badge of Courage* (1961).

Following Henry's death in 1961, Paul Riba produced *The Call of the Wild* (1962), and Ken Riley *The Last of the Mohicans* (1963) and *Robinson Crusoe* (1964) for Harris in a style modeled on Henry's. However, Henry's maps have an originality and vigor lacking in the maps by these later artists. By the mid 1960s, production costs became prohibitive, and the company stopped producing the maps.

The literary map that attracted the most public attention in its own time was *William Gropper's America: Its Folklore*, the case of which demonstrates how literary maps can be used for political purposes of various kinds. Born in poverty in New York City, William Gropper (1897–1977) used art to ennoble the poor, expose social injustice, and satirize political opportunism. He worked for mainstream newspapers and magazines and also contributed to radical journals such as the *Masses* and visited the Soviet Union.

Soon after World War II, Gropper's map was created for distribution abroad by U.S. government agencies as a celebration of American culture. In 1953 the map attracted the attention of Senator Joseph McCarthy. McCarthy found little that was objectionable about the map itself, but he denounced Gropper's art in general as communist-directed, anti-American propaganda and asserted that the U.S. government should not promote his work. After he was attacked by McCarthy, Gropper's career suffered for a number of years.

A noted painter, Gropper, like Everett Henry, had created murals, including several in the Department of Interior building in Washington, D.C., that were installed in 1939. His map reflects that background, as well as his career as a cartoonist and caricaturist. As might be expected in the work of an accomplished graphic artist, drawing is the backbone of Gropper's folklore map. The map is crowded with energetic, colorful figures in motion—Paul Bunyan wielding his axe, John Henry raising his hammer over his head, and a Salem witch flying on a broom. In depicting folk heroes, Gropper celebrates the shaping of the American nation from different ethnic strains, the taming of the wilderness, and the settlement of the land that are part of the national mythology.

Similar themes are celebrated in the work of another important map illustrator of the 1950s and early 1960s—James Lewicki (1917–1980), who produced *A Storyteller's Map of American Myths*. The map was the culmination of a five-part series on "Folklore in America," published in *Life* issues of August 31 and November 2, 1959, and January 25, April 11, and August 22, 1960. The idea for the project, including the map and other artwork for the series, came from the artist. Assisted by his wife Lillian (b. 1914) as researcher and artist and his children as models, Lewicki spent five years working on the project, later republished as *The Life Treasury of American Folklore* (1961). A frequent contributor of illustrations to *Life* and other magazines, he was a faculty member of the

School of the Arts at C. W. Post Center of Long Island University. He also produced a series of illustrations for a limited edition of Sir James Frazer's *The Golden Bough.*

Lewicki created approximately one hundred characters from American folklore, which he portrayed as robust figures in rich and bright colors. Some stories, such as Rip Van Winkle, are told in their entirety, with the various incidents illustrated.

The Lewickis spent hours of research on each character in order to get the details right, often working from morning to night for months at a time. In 1971, Lewicki described the experience in the magazine *North Light* : "My mind and body ached, but I was sustained by the thought that I was working on my own idea, on the single largest illustration project ever commissioned by one of the largest magazines in the world. At the end of three years I had finished, I was exhausted but exhilarated at the same time— *I had done it.*" Lewicki's images, like Gropper's, are a vivid presentation of the common American mythology of the last several centuries.

The Library of Congress collection contains few maps from the late 1960s and 1970s. Rising costs and the social turmoil of the time may have caused fewer literary maps to be produced than in the preceding decades. Although the bicentennial of American independence in 1976 might have been expected to inspire a patriotic burst of literary mapmaking to equal that around the George Washington birth bicentennial, the Library's collections show little evidence of it. Although a few fine state maps appeared, the Library's most significant map of 1976 was produced by the District of Columbia Council of Teachers of English. *Black Writers for Young America* resulted from the growing recognition of the contributions to literature of nonwhite writers. Although Claude McKay, James Weldon Johnson, Booker T. Washington, Paul Laurence Dunbar, and W. E. B. Dubois had appeared on the 1933 *Readers' Picto-Map of the United States* as well as others produced before the 1970s, no previous map in the Library's collections had made African American writers its focus. Other significant maps of the 1970s and 1980s came from outside the United States. For example, the former Soviet Union's Glavnoe upravlenie geodezii i kartografii (Main Administration for Geodesy and Cartography) produced a large group of literary maps. This government agency mapped the literary sites of Leningrad and Moscow, as well places associated with Leo Tolstoy, Mikhail Lermontov, Alexander Pushkin, and other noted pre-Soviet authors. Unlike most literary maps, these are cartographically detailed enough to be used to locate actual places. The maps are illustrated with photographs of authors, their homes, and sites associated with them, as well as with other museums and monuments. Updated every few years, the maps contain a wealth of information for readers of Russian and demonstrate the former Soviet Union's support for the nation's cultural history. The maps also demonstrate the connection of literary culture to patriotism and provide an example of the way in which literature and culture can be used for propaganda purposes. Just as the United States produced a large number of literary maps when at the height of its power in the 1950s and 1960s, the Soviet Union produced them during its heyday as a superpower.

A number of British firms also produced literary maps in the 1980s, with subjects such as William Wordsworth, Robert Burns, other Scottish poets, and literary London. In the same decade in the United States, many states produced new maps, and a map of Appalachia appeared, reflecting increasing interest in regions.

The decade's most exciting American maps came from the Aaron Blake Company of Los Angeles. From the mid to the late 1980s, the company published twelve literary maps related to favorite books and authors of their producers, the husband-and-wife team of Molly Maguire and Aaron Silverman. The couple began with an interest in Raymond Chandler. Driving around Los Angeles looking for sites mentioned in his work, they found that many still existed, little changed from when Chandler described them. The result was *The Raymond Chandler Mystery Map of Los Angeles* (1986), which, unlike many literary maps, could be used to tour sites mentioned in the author's works. With Silverman as her business partner, Maguire, who had received undergraduate degrees in American and English literature and had done graduate work in video art and design, created a series of maps relating to important literary places and well-known authors. Each map is colorful and lively, and its style reflects the spirit of the original works; the Chandler map, for example, is in the style of a pulp-novel cover of the 1940s.

Like the Harris-Seybold maps, the Blake Company's maps cover a wide range of authors and subjects. In addition to the Chandler map, titles include *The Ernest Hemingway Adventure Map of the World* (1986), *The John Steinbeck Map of America* (1986), *The Literary Map of Los Angeles* (1987), *The Beat Generation Map of America* (1987), *The Jane Austen Map of England* (1987), *The Sherlock Holmes Mystery Map* (1987), *The Ian Fleming Thriller Map* (1987), *The Literary Map of Paris* (1988), *The Literary Map of Latin America* (1988), *The Literary Map of the American South* (1988) , and *The Literary Map of N*[ew] *Y*[ork] (1988). Having found the maps unprofitable, the company stopped producing them.

In the 1990s, the Library has received several maps from newly democratic Eastern European countries, such as the *Magyar irodalomtörténeti térkép* (Map of Hungarian Literary History) and *Ein Reiseführer durch Franz Kafkas Prag* (Guide to Franz Kafka's Prague). Demonstrating yet again the close connection between literature and patriotism, these maps indicate an attempt to reclaim political power by asserting literary power.

In the 1990s in the United States, *Language of the Land*, the Library of Congress exhibition that inspired this book, has encouraged a revival of literary mapmaking. Originally opened at the Library of Congress in 1993, this exhibit has traveled to more than twenty sites around the United States, including sixteen state Centers for the Book. As part of their programming during the exhibition run, a number of the state Centers for the Book produced literary maps. Those maps are included in this book, and others are in production. One can only hope that this interest in literary mapmaking will continue, and that some of the states and regions that are not yet represented will produce maps.

The lack of maps for certain areas may seem puzzling to readers of this book although, in preparation for the exhibit and book, unsuccessful attempts were made to locate maps for missing American states. Literary maps not represented in the Library of Congress collections undoubtedly exist. However, literary maps were not found for some surprising places, including most of the New England states, which have some of the oldest literary connections in the country, and the national capital of Washington, D.C. (A project to remedy this oversight is in progress.) In addition to these regional maps, perhaps someone will also produce maps for authors whose works seem to cry out for a one, such as Anthony Trollope and William Faulkner. (These authors have been treated in small, black-and-white maps in books, one drawn by Faulkner himself, but do not seem to have been represented in a large, color map.)

Predicting the future is hazardous, but perhaps eventually literary maps will exist in electronic form, with viewers able to click on an icon representing a region, author, or book and call up a detailed map, photographs, biographical information, bibliographies, and other information. Whatever form literary maps may take in the future, they will still have the power that Tom Sawyer attributes to places mentioned in books—making concrete the visualization of characters and locations that is one of the great pleasures of reading.

Martha Hopkins
Exhibit Director
Interpretive Programs Office

World Literature

"Journey over all the universe in a map, without the expense and fatigue of travelling, without suffering the inconveniences of heat, cold, hunger, and thirst."   **Miguel Cervantes**

Map of Adventures for Boys and Girls: Stories, Trails, Voyages, Discoveries, Explorations and Places to Read About

PAUL M. PAINE
Compiler

New York: R.R. Bowker Company, 1925
47 x 67 cm
Color
G3201 .E65 1925 .P3

This map of the world mixes fiction and true stories of exploration and adventure. On the various continents are printed the titles of books and the locations of places associated with them. Dotted lines trace historic journeys such as those of Marco Polo (1254–1354), Christopher Columbus (c. 1451–1506), and Ferdinand de Magellan (c. 1480–1521), as well as fictional journeys, for example, the voyage of the *Pequod* in *Moby Dick* (1851) by Herman Melville. Insets on the bottom corners list important literary places and characters as well as historical characters in the British Isles and in the thirteen original U.S. states. Compiler Paul M. Paine (1869–1955), who gathered the information on the map, was head of the Syracuse Public Library from 1915–1942, a newspaper book columnist, textbook writer, and creator of a number of other literary and historical maps.

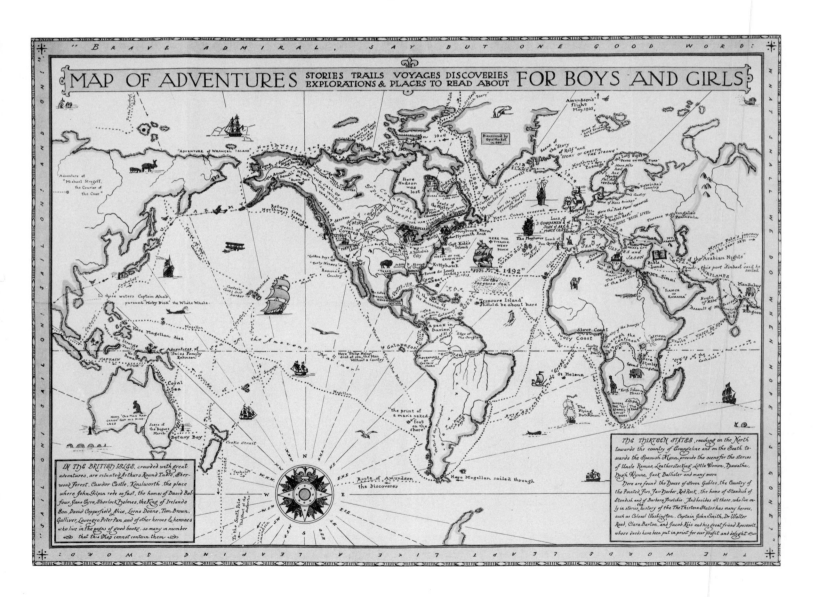

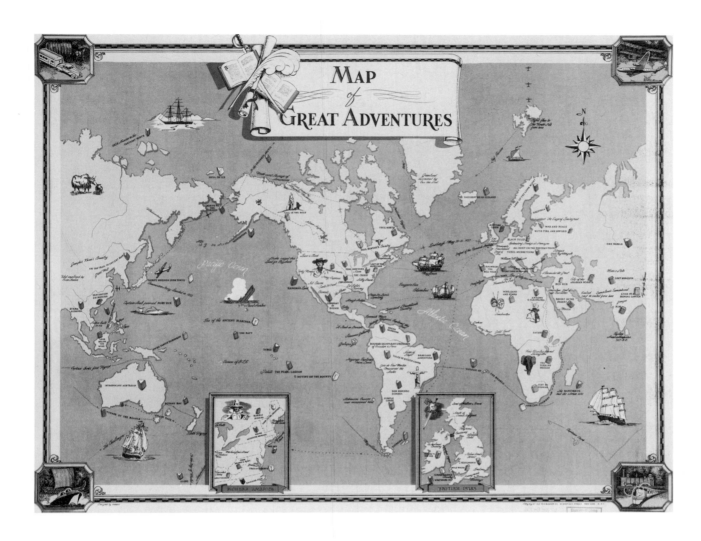

Map of Great Adventures

F. Haase
Designer

New York: R.R. Bowker, 1946
43 x 60 cm
Color
G3201 .E65 1946 .H3

This world map lists selected titles of works that describe adventures—historical and fictional. Historical adventures include the 1831–1836 voyage of Charles Darwin (1809–1882) on the *Beagle*, the flights over the North and South Poles of Admiral Richard E. Byrd (1888–1957), the 1870–1871 search of Sir Henry Morgan Stanley (1841–1904) for Dr. David Livingstone (1813–1873), and the 1927 transatlantic flight of Charles Lindbergh (1902–1974). Fictional adventures include *Moby Dick* (1851) by Herman Melville, *Robinson Crusoe* (1719) by Daniel Defoe, and *Swiss Family Robinson* (1812–1813) by Johann David Wyss. A "Pioneer America" inset lists titles such as *Drums Along the Mohawk* (1936) by Walter Edmonds (1903–1998), *John Brown's Body* (1928) by Stephen Vincent Benét (1898–1943), and *Rabble in Arms* (1933) by Kenneth Roberts (1885–1957). A "British Isles" inset locates the settings of *Kenilworth* (1821) by Sir Walter Scott, *Riders to the Sea* (1904) by J. M. Synge, and Robin Hood's Sherwood Forest, among others. Illustrations in each corner contrast modes of travel, past and present, including a covered wagon and a car and trailer, a Viking ship and a modern ship, an early train and a diesel locomotive, and a biplane and a modern plane.

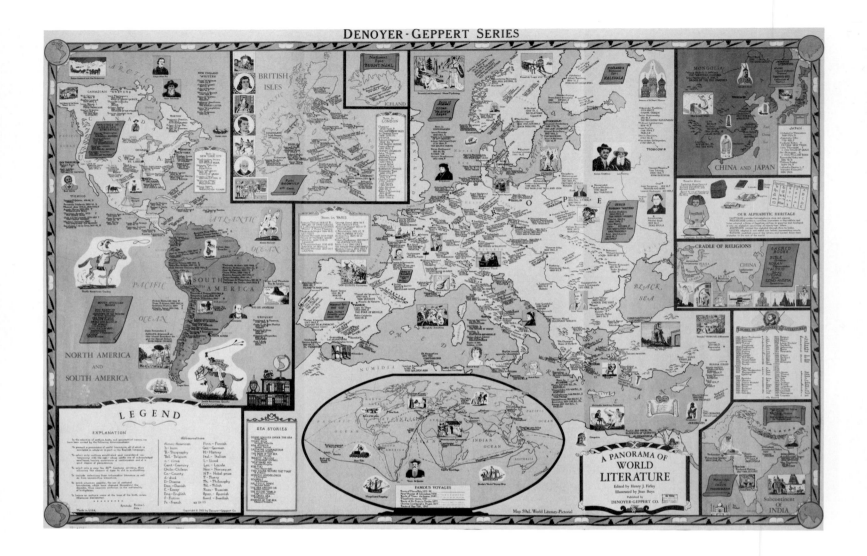

A Panorama of World Literature

HENRY J. FIRLEY
Editor

JEAN BOYS
Illustrator

Chicago: Denoyer-Geppert Company, 1955
95 x 153 cm
Color
G3201 .E65 1955 .B6

This large map shows the world, excluding sub-Saharan Africa. The map identifies the birthplaces of selected authors, along with birth and death dates, and the literary genre for which the author is best known. The authors, some of whom are pictured, lived from ancient times to the twentieth century, and authors whose works are available in English are highlighted. Insets show the British Isles; Iceland; China and Japan; the cradle of religions; the history of the alphabet; Nobel Prize winners; the subcontinent of India; famous voyages and sea stories; and national epics. Other insets list authors born in New York City, London, and Paris. Further information on the map is contained in Henry J. Firley, *A Glossatteer of World Literature* (PN43 .F5), a manual developed to go with this and two other maps in the Denoyer-Geppert Series, *A Pictorial Map of Mediterranean Mythology and Classical Literature* (G6531 .E6 1959 .F5) and *A Pictorial Map Depicting the Literary Development of the United States* (G3701 .E65 1952 .D4).

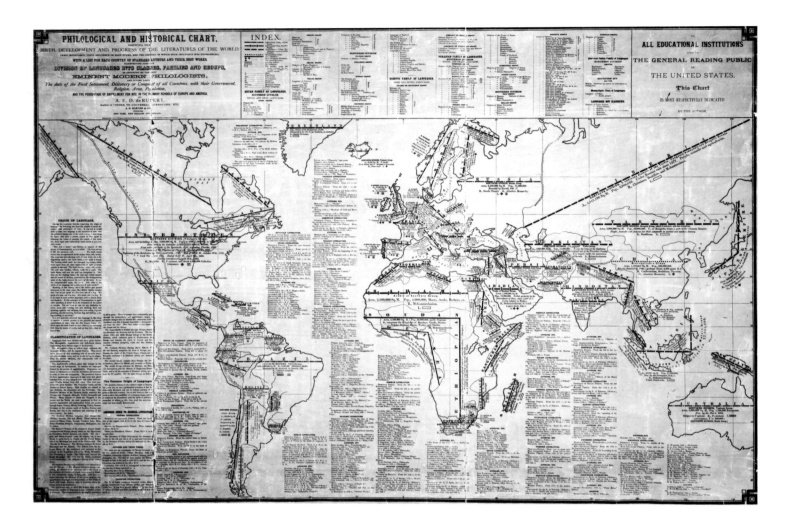

Philological and Historical Chart, Birth, Development, and Progress of the Literatures of the World. . . .

A. E. D. RUPERT
Compiler

New York: A.S. Barnes & Co., 1878
66 x 123 cm
Black and white
G3201 .E65 1878 .D4

T he complete title of this map is *Philological and Historical Chart, Birth, Development, and Progress of the Literatures of the World, Their Importance, Their Influence on Each Other, and the Century in Which Such Influence Was Experienced: With a List for Each Country of Standard Authors and Their Best Works, Illustrating Also the Division of Languages into Classes, Families, and Groups, as Arranged by the Most Eminent Modern Philologists, and Giving, Lastly, the Date of the First Settlement, Discovery or Conquest of all Countries, with Their Government, Religion, Area, Population, and the Percentage of Enrollment for 1872, in the Primary Schools of Europe and America.* The title gives a sense of the level of detail and classification embodied in this work by A .E. D. Rupert, who is identified as the author of *Index to Universal Literature.* The map shows an outline of the world, with markings showing the language group, population, religion, and other statistical information for the different areas. Indexes around the borders give the periods of literature and main influences and the most important authors and their works for major Western, Middle Eastern, and Asian languages. The chart is respectfully dedicated to "All Educational Institutions and the General Reading Public of the United States."

The World in Storybooks

Mary Gould Davis
Editor

Amy Jones
Cartographer

New York: R.R. Bowker, 1946
45 x 62 cm
Color
G3201 .E65 1946 .J6

Edited by Mary Gould Davis, winner of the 1933 Newberry Medal, *The World in Storybooks* depicts fictional characters for each continent. A banner across the top lists stories associated with each of the regions, although the stories may not have been written by authors from those places. For North America, books such as *The Adventures of Huckleberry Finn* (1884) by Mark Twain and *The Little House in the Big Woods* (1932) by Laura Ingalls Wilder are listed. Europe is represented by "The Little Mermaid," by Hans Christian Andersen, *Hans Brinker* (1865) by Mary Mapes Dodge, and the *Fables* of Aesop, among others. Illustrations at the bottom portray scenes from *The Wonderful Adventures of Nils* (1907) by Selma Lagerlöf, *Heidi* (1880) by Johanna Spyri, "The Elephant's Child" from *Just So Stories* (1902) by Rudyard Kipling, *The Adventures of Tom Sawyer* (1876) by Mark Twain, *Alice in Wonderland* (1865) by Lewis Carroll, *Pinocchio* (1883) by Carlo Lorenzini, and *The Legend of the Palm Tree* (1940) by Margarida Estrela Bandeira Duarte. The top left corner shows Santa Claus and his reindeer, and the upper right portrays Aladdin on a flying carpet.

Individual Regions and Countries

"Every continent has its own great spirit of place. . . . Different places on the face of the earth have different vital effluence, different vibration, different chemical exhalation, different polarity with different stars: call it what you like. But the spirit of place is a great reality."

D. H. Lawrence
Studies in Classic American Literature, 1923

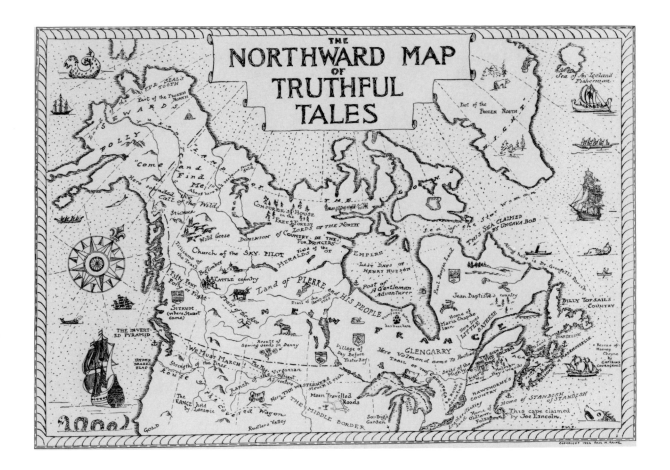

FAR NORTH

The Northward Map of Truthful Tales

PAUL M. PAINE
Compiler

[Syracuse?]: Paul M. Paine, 1926
27 x 39 cm
Black and white
G3401 .E65 1926 .P3

Drawn in a whimsical style reminiscent of old maps, with sailing ships and sea monsters around the borders, *The Northward Map of Truthful Tales* shows the northernmost area of the United States and all of Canada, Iceland, and Greenland. National borders and state and province borders are marked by dotted lines, but not labeled. Literary places identified in the United States include "Leatherstocking Land," the setting of the Natty Bumppo stories of James Fenimore Cooper; the region associated with Nathaniel Hawthorne; the Middle Border, site of *Main Travelled Roads* (1891) by Hamlin Garland; the Wyoming ranch where *The Virginian* (1902) by Owen Wister is set; and the location of *The Call of the Wild* (1903) by Jack London (1876–1916). The focus of the map is on Canada. In Canada, marked sites are associated with Gilbert Parker's *Pierre and His People* (1892) and *When Valmond Came to Pontiac* (1895); Stewart Edward White's *Conjuror's House* (1903); Dillon Wallace's *Ungava Bob* (1907); and Bertrand Sinclair's *Big Timber* (1916). Sites identified with historic people such as Henry Hudson, and historic sites such as covered wagon routes and the parallel of "fifty four forty or fight" are also marked. Paul M. Paine (1869–1955), head of the Syracuse Public Library from 1915–1942, was a newspaper book columnist, textbook writer, and creator of a number of literary and historical maps.

LATIN AMERICA

The Literary Map of Latin America

MOLLY MAGUIRE
Designer

MIKE CRESSY
Illustrator

Los Angeles: Aaron Blake, 1988
68 x 51 cm
Color *(See color section.)*
G3292 .L3 .E65 1988 .A2

Courtesy of Molly Maguire and Aaron Silverman

The *Literary Map of Latin America* features Latin-American novelists and poets, many of them Nobel-prize winners, who have dramatized political, social, and emotional struggles using the extreme geography of the region as inspiration. It offers an historical overview of the literature of each country, significant writers, and the important locales in their lives and works. The map identifies more than ninety sites of birthplaces, locales of works, homes, and other hangouts of Latin American writers. Numbers on the map are indexed to an explanatory key. The colorful map is drawn in the shape of a parrot, with Central America as a wing and Cuba as the head. Writers whose works are available in English translations are emphasized. At bottom left is a scene of soldiers, an Indian woman and child, and the Andes mountains with Machu Picchu. Research and design for the map were performed by Molly Maguire, who produced a series of literary maps in the 1980s.

MEDITERRANEAN WORLD

A Literary-Historical Map of the Mediterranean World

Mabel A. Bessey and
Dora Tamler
Compilers

The Scholastic, Vol. 20, No. 5, April 2, 1932,
     pp. 22–24
29 x 42 cm
Black and white
G5672 .M4E65 1932 .T3

A Literary-Historical Map of the Mediterranean World shows the portions of Europe, Asia, and Africa that border the Mediterranean Sea, an area where many of the oldest works in Western literature were written. On the map sixty-four literary and historical sites are located for Spain, France, Italy, Greece, Africa, Russia, the Balkans, and Asia Minor. Many of the places are associated with English-language authors. Those given for Spain relate to the epic poem *El Cid*, Miguel Cervantes's *Don Quixote de la Mancha*, and Georges Bizet's opera *Carmen*; for France, Edmond Rostand's play *Cyrano de Bergerac*, and Alexander Dumas's novel *The Count of Monte Cristo*; for Italy, William Shakespeare's plays *The Merchant of Venice* and *Othello* and poems by Robert Browning; for Greece, Homer's *Odyssey* and poems by Lord Byron; for Asia Minor and Africa, Homer's *Iliad* and *Odyssey,* and the *Arabian Nights*. Places on the map are keyed by number to a list, which gives titles and authors and sometimes quotations from works.

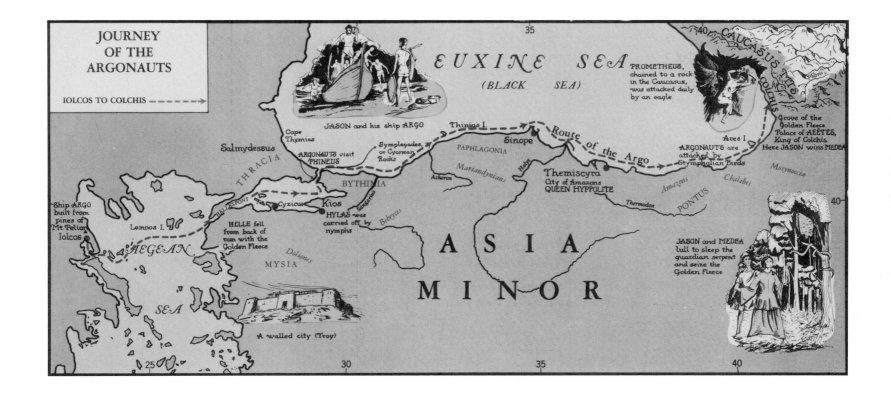

The map shows labels including:

JOURNEY OF THE ARGONAUTS

IOLCOS TO COLCHIS ------>

EUXINE SEA (BLACK SEA)

JASON and his ship ARGO

PROMETHEUS, chained to a rock in the Caucasus, was attacked daily by an eagle

Grove of the Golden Fleece. Palace of AEËTES, King of Colchis. Here JASON wins MEDEA

CAUCASUS TIS — COLCHIS

Salmydessus

Cape Thymias

ARGONAUTS visit PHINEUS

THRACIA

Symplegades, or Cyanean Rocks

PAPHLAGONIA

Thinias I.

Sinope

Route of the Argo

ARGONAUTS are attacked by Stymphalian Birds

Ares I.

Mosynoecia

BYTHINIA

Acheron

Mariandynians

Halys

Themiscyra City of Amazons QUEEN HYPPOLITE

Amazons

Chalybes

Ship ARGO built from pines of Mt. Pelion Iolcos

Lemnos I.

HELLESPONT

Cyzicus

Kios

HYLAS was carried off by nymphs

Bebryces

Sangarius

Thermodon

PONTUS

JASON and MEDEA lull to sleep the guardian serpent and seize the Golden Fleece

HELLE fell from back of ram with the Golden Fleece

Doliones

MYSIA

ASIA MINOR

AEGEAN SEA

A walled city (Troy)

A Pictorial Map of Mediterranean Mythology and Classical Literature

Henry J. Firley
Editor

Chicago: Denoyer-Geppert Company, 1959
109 x 160 cm
Color
G6531 .E6 1959 .F5

A Pictorial Map of Mediterranean Mythology and Classical Literature relates classical and mythological literature to the geography of the Mediterranean region. It includes drawings of ancient legends, myths, and tales, including illustrations of the flight of Icarus, Pegasus the flying horse, and Pandora opening the box. Located on the maps are likenesses of deities, Trojan War heroes, and historical personalities such as Alexander the Great (356–323 BC), Hannibal (247–182(?) BC), and Julius Caesar (100–44 BC). Busts of authors Homer and Virgil are shown with busts of the main characters of their most famous epics—Odysseus and Aeneas. A time line highlights Greek and Roman authors. Insets feature Caesar's Gallic Wars, Homer's world, ancient Athens, imperial Rome, and the voyage of Jason and the Argonauts (shown). The map gives special emphasis to the Trojan War; the journey of Aeneas, recounted in the *Aeneid* (30–19 BC) by Virgil; and the wanderings of Odysseus, detailed in the *Odyssey* by Homer. Further information on the map is contained in Henry J. Firley, *A Glossatteer of World Literature* (PN43 .F5), a manual developed to go with this and two other maps in the Denoyer-Geppert Series, *A Panorama of World Literature* (G3201 .E65 1955 .B6) and *A Pictorial Map Depicting the Literary Development of the United States* (G3701 .E65 1952 .D4).

AUSTRALIA

The Writers' State: A Literary Map of Victoria

RON BROOKS
Designer

[Melbourne]: Victoria 150 Literature
    Committee, 1981
59 x 89 cm
Color
G8991 .E65 1984 .B7

Compiled by members of the Association for the Study of Australian Literature, *The Writers' State: A Literary Map of Victoria* records literary places in the Australian state of Victoria and its capital city, Melbourne. On the left side are images of thirteen writers, including novelist and critic Vance Palmer, critic Nettie Palmer, poet John Shaw Neilson, and novelists Katherine Susannah Pritchard, Frank Davison, and George Johnston. Also shown are book jackets and magazine covers. An inset in the upper right corner identifies literary sites in Melbourne. Scattered over the map are names and titles of authors associated with various places. A note credits *The Oxford Literary Guide to Australia* (PR9607 .O94 1987) as the source for information on the map.

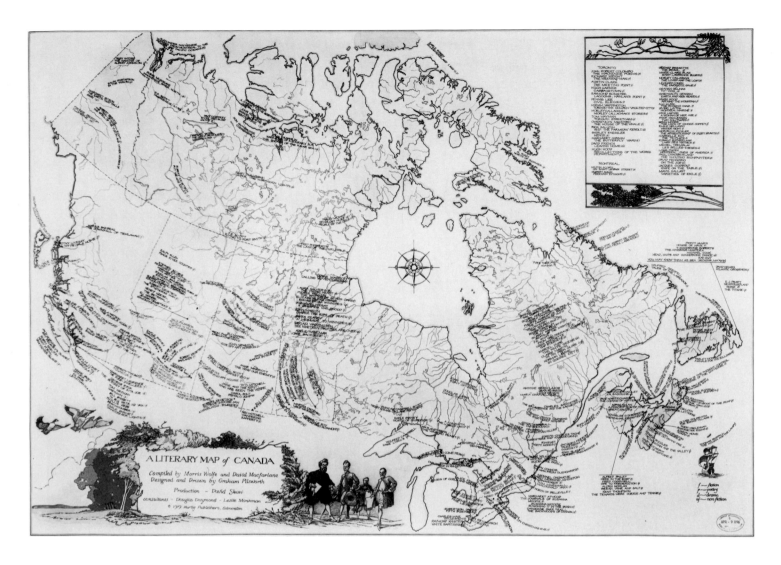

CANADA

A Literary Map of Canada

MORRIS WOLFE AND DAVID MACFARLANE
Compilers

GRAHAM PILSWORTH
Designer and Illustrator

DAVID SHAW
Production Manager

Edmonton, Alberta: Hurtig Publishers, 1979
65 x 94 cm
Color
G3401 .E65 1979 .W6

Courtesy of Hurtig Communications Ltd.

A Literary Map of Canada shows an outline of the country's provinces on which are shown authors and titles of works set in them. Writers from Toronto and Montreal are listed in a separate box. Letters in parentheses following the titles indicate whether the book is fiction, poetry, drama, or nonfiction. Although some Montreal titles are in French, the map focuses on English-language books or those that have been translated into English. Among those mentioned are Louis Hémon's *Maria Chapdelaine* (1916), Robertson Davies's *Fifth Business* (1970), Alice Munro's *Lives of Girls and Women* (1971), and Michel Tremblay's *Les Belles-Soeurs* (1972). The four men to the right of the title are the map's creators *(l-r)*: Morris Wolfe, David Macfarlane, Graham Pilsworth, and David Shaw, each holding a pen or brush, depending on his role.

Writer's Map of Ontario

John Robert Colombo
Compiler

David Shaw
Illustrator

Toronto: Colombo and Company, 1992
76 x 108 cm
Color
G3461 .E65 1992 .C6

Courtesy of John Robert Colombo

Produced with the assistance of the Ontario Heritage Foundation, the *Writer's Map of Ontario* is a guide to 141 sites of literary interest in the Province of Ontario. One of the largest provinces of Canada, Ontario includes two important cities: Ottawa, the nation's capital, and Toronto, the country's most populous city and the center for English-language culture and communications. On the map, references are given to literary writers of general interest whose works are in print and who are included in Canadian school curricula. Among them are Robertson Davies, born in Thamesville, and Alice Munro, born at Wingham. The front of the map features an outline of the province, with numbers keyed to place names in the margins. Extensive text explains the literary significance of each place. On the verso are texts dealing with subjects such as the Franco-Ontario voice, contemporary native writers, Ontario films, literary place names, books about the province, small presses, and quotations about Ontario. The map verso features advertisements from the bookstores, publishers, and other organizations that sponsored the map.

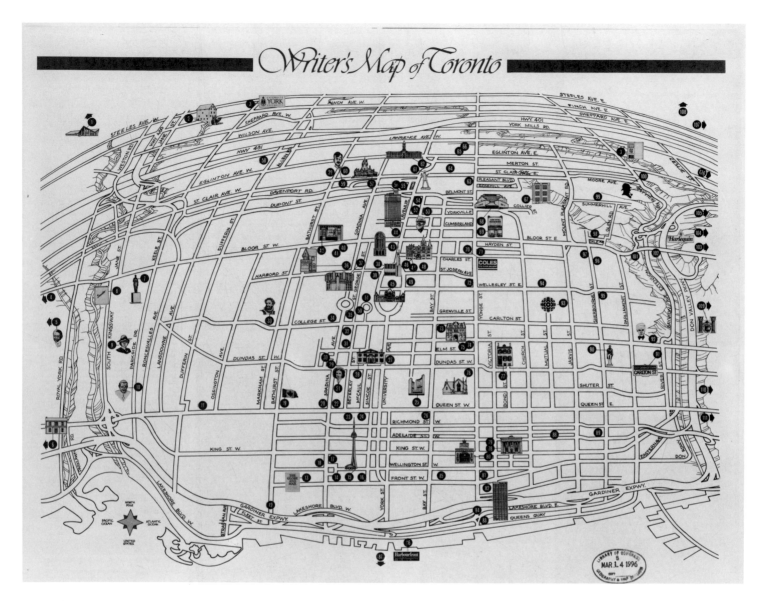

Writer's Map of Toronto

John Robert Colombo
Compiler

Gerard Williams
Illustrator

Toronto: Colombo and Company, 1991
63 x 97 cm
Color
G3464 .T7E65 1991 .C6

Courtesy of John Robert Colombo

Language of the Land

The *Writer's Map of Toronto* is a guide to 111 sites of literary interest in the area of Toronto, Canada's most populous city and the center for English-language culture and communications. The front of the map features a street map of the city, with numbers keyed to places in the margins. Extensive text explains the literary significance of each place. Those described include authors' homes, bookstores, publishers' offices, libraries, hotels where noted authors stayed, and places associated with fictional characters. Featured authors who have lived in the city and set works there include Robertson Davies, author of the *Deptford Trilogy* (1970s) and the *Cornish Trilogy* (1980s) and Margaret Atwood, author of *Lady Oracle* (1976) and *The Cat's Eye* (1988). On the verso are texts dealing with subjects such as books about Toronto, works set there, films shot in the city, book awards, the city as a publishing center, and its library system. The map also features advertisements from the bookstores, publishers, and other organizations that sponsored the map.

33

La France régionale et ses écrivains

Copyright 1932, Audi-Péchin ©aF   5176

EUROPE
France

La France régionale et ses écrivains
(Regions of France and Their Writers)

[France]: Audi-Péchin, 1932
In French
33 x 28 cm
Color
G5831 .E65 1932 .A9

*L*a France régionale et ses écrivains locates authors by the French province with which they are associated. Writers in the French-speaking part of Belgium are also included. A key around the borders alphabetically lists the provinces, with the names of authors, their principal works, and the dates of the works. Life dates and place of birth are given for some authors. Among the authors featured are Honoré de Balzac, Prosper Mérimée, George Sand, Gustave Flaubert, Guy de Maupassant, Alphonse Daudet, and Emile Zola.

The Literary Map of Paris

MOLLY MAGUIRE
Designer

LINDA AYRISS
Illustrator

Los Angeles: Aaron Blake Publishers, 1988
49 x 66 cm
Color
G5834 .P3E65 1988 .A2

Courtesy of Molly Maguire and Aaron Silverman

*T*he *Literary Map of Paris* offers an overview of Parisian literary life from the time of Michel de Montaigne (1533–1592) to the 1980s. Numbers on the map are keyed to two indexes. One index lists sites associated with well-known French novelists, poets, philosophers, and essayists. Another separately lists places frequented by famous expatriate writers. Literary salons, cafes, and cemeteries with literary connections and well-known buildings such as the Eiffel Tower and the Arc de Triomphe are also identified on the map. At the bottom is a scene in the well-known literary café Aux Deux Magots, with images of Gertrude Stein and Oscar Wilde, two of its many famous patrons, in the foreground. Pictured around the edge of the map are French authors Simone de Beauvoir, Honoré de Balzac, Jean Cocteau, Jules Verne, René Descartes, André Malraux, Colette, Guillaume Apollinaire, Victor Hugo, Alexander Dumas, Marcel Proust, and Jean-Paul Sartre. Research and design for the map were performed by Molly Maguire, who produced a series of literary maps in the 1980s.

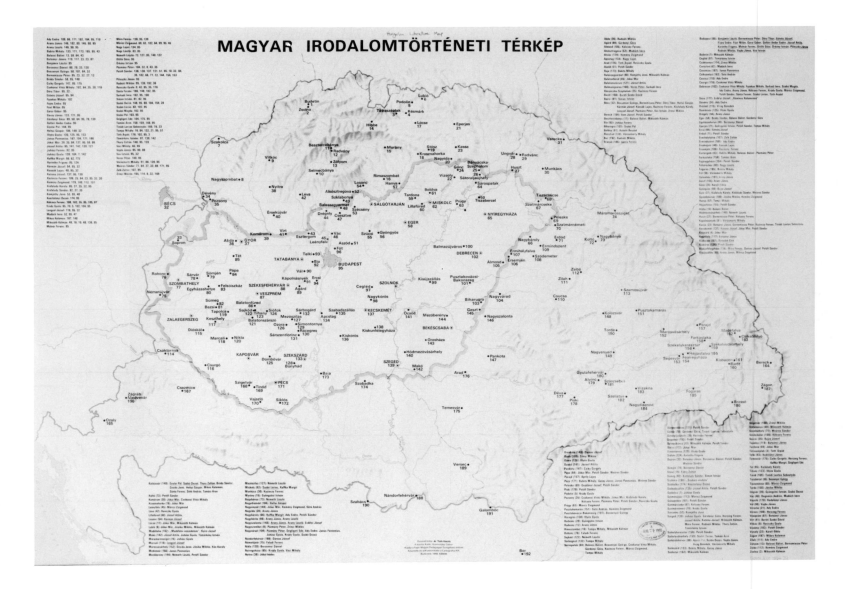

MAGYAR IRODALOMTÖRTÉNETI TÉRKÉP

Hungary

Magyar irodalomtörténeti térkép
(Map of Hungarian Literary History)

KÁROLY TÓTH
Compiler

Székesfehérvár, Hungary, Fejér Megyei
    Pedagógiai Szolgáltató Intézet, 1994
In Hungarian
68 x 99 cm
Color
G6501 .E65 1994 .T6

Courtesy of Fejér Megyei Pedagógiai Szolgáltató Intézet

Published by the Pedagogical Service Institute of the County of Fejér, *Magyar iro-dalomtörténeti térkép* is a literary map of the modern Republic of Hungary and surrounding areas that form "Historical Hungary," territory that was at one time within the country's borders. At the top is an alphabetical list of more than eighty major authors. A larger place-name list identifies authors associated with a locale, with their names underlined if they were born there. Numbers on the map correspond to the places. Major authors listed include Janus Pannonius, a fifteenth-century humanist poet; Sándor Petőfi, a nineteenth-century writer considered the greatest Hungarian poet; Endre Ady, an early twentieth-century poet; Magda Szabó and Margit Kaffka, twentieth-century novelists; and Ferenc Molnár, a twentieth-century dramatist.

Ireland

Story Map of Ireland

Chicago: Colortext Publications, 1935
43 x 34 cm
Color
Ethel M. Fair Collection 187

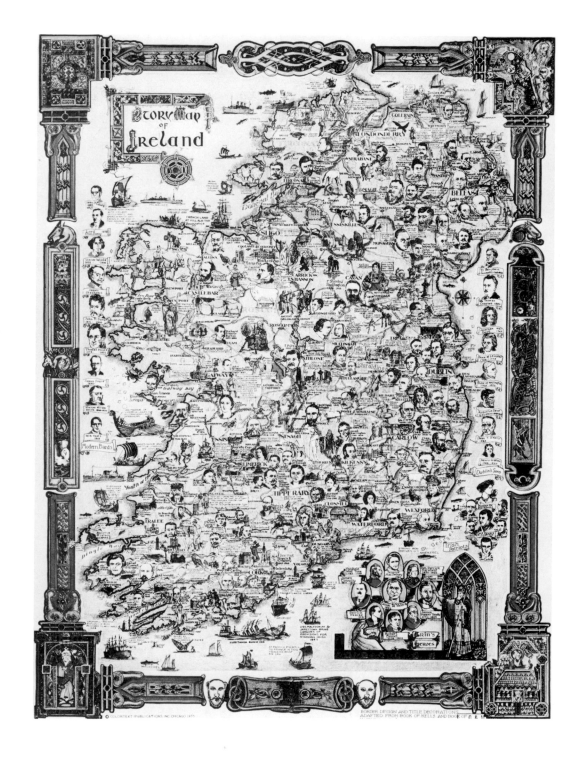

The *Story Map of Ireland* combines figures from Irish literature and history. On a map of the country, including northern Ireland, images of people are placed near places associated with them or their work. Along the left side is an illustrated list of "Modern Bards"—Sean O'Casey, Edward, Lord Dunsany, Oscar Wilde, James Stephens, John M. Synge, Thomas Moore, James Joyce, Michael William Balfe, and W. B. Yeats. Images of other writers, such as Jonathan Swift, Oliver Goldsmith, and George Bernard Shaw, are featured on the body of the map, as are titles of some literary works. The borders of the map and title decorations are adapted from two illuminated Celtic manuscripts produced in Ireland, *The Book of Kells* (6th c.) and the *Book of MacDurnan* (10th c.).

SOVIET UNION
Central Russia

Literaturnye mesta TSentral'noi Rossii (k iugu ot Moskvy), turistskaia skhema
(Literary Places of Central Russia to the South of Moscow, A Tourist Map)

V. S. Titkova
Editor

Moscow: Glavnoe upravlenie geodezii i
    kartografii, 1981
In Russian
96 x 27 cm
Color
G7061 .E65 1981 .S6

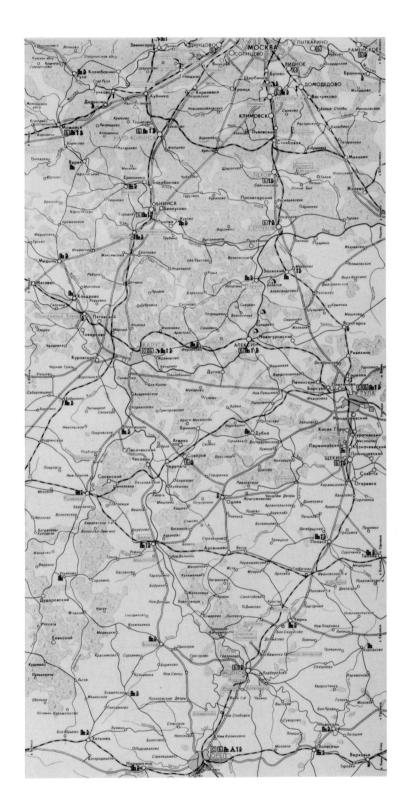

*L*iteraturnye mesta TSentral'noi Rossii gives information on literary sites in the area of central Russia between Moscow on the north, Orel on the south, Tula in the east, and the Kaluga area in the west. Places with literary connections are highlighted on the map, and a key gives the names of places and what happened there. Authors connected to the region include I. A. Bunin, Anton Chekhov, Afanasii Fet, Nikolai Gogol, Mikhail Lermontov, Nikolai Leskov, Nikolai Nekrasov, Alexander Pushkin, Leo Tolstoy, Feodor Tiutchev, and Ivan Turgenev. Chekhov's home, Melikhova; the monument to Chekhov; an oak tree associated with Turgenev; and Tolstoy's home, Yasnaya Polyana, are illustrated. This map is a revision of the 1977 *Literaturnye mesta TSentral'noi Rossii, turistskaia skhema* (Literary Places of Central Russia, A Tourist Map) (G7061 .E65 1977 .R8).

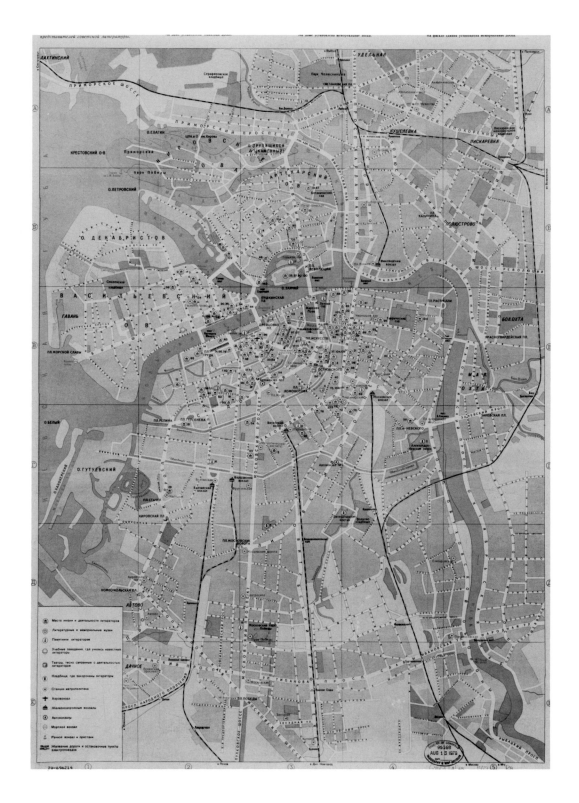

Leningrad

Literaturnye mesta Leningrada, turistskaia skhema
(Literary Places of Leningrad, A Tourist Map)

G. A. Skachkova,
Editor

Moscow: Glavnoe upravlenie geodezii i
  kartografii, 1979
In Russian
65 x 46 cm
Color
G7004 .L4E65 1979 .R8

*L*iteraturnye mesta Leningrada, turistskaia skhema gives information on
literary sites in Leningrad (now St. Petersburg) connected with 127 authors.
The city has one of the richest literary
traditions in Russia, and writers who
have lived and worked in the city include
A. S. Griboedov, Alexander Pushkin,
Mikhail Lermontov, Nikolai Gogol,
Nikolai Nekrasov, Feodor Dostoyevksy,
and Maxim Gorky. The cover pictures a
statue of Pushkin on Arts Square. Other
color photographs show the desk at
which Dostoyevsky worked, the exterior
of Pushkin's apartment, and the famous
Dom Knigi bookstore. Symbols on the
map are keyed to places where authors
lived and worked, museums, memorials
to authors, monuments to authors, educational institutions where they studied,
theaters with connections to authors,
and grave sites. A list of names of authors gives their life dates and other information about their lives and works.
A slightly revised map was issued in
1983 (G7004 .L4E65 1983 .S6).

Literaturnye pamiatnye mesta Leningrada, turistskaia skhema
(Literary Memorials of Leningrad, A Tourist Map)

Moscow: Glavnoe upravlenie geodezii i
    kartografii, 1983
In Russian
81 x 48 cm
Color
G7004. L4E65 1983.S6

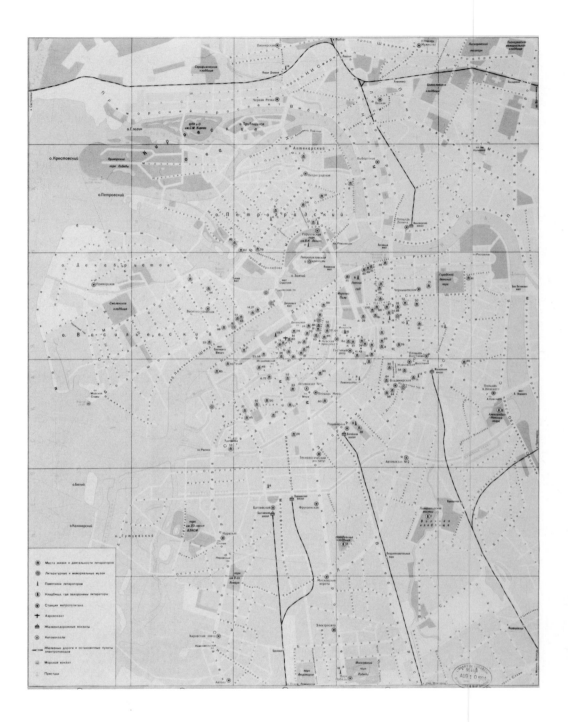

L iteraturnye pamiatnye mesta Leningrada, turistskaia skhema, locates literary sites in Leningrad (now St. Petersburg), a city that has one of the richest literary traditions in Russia. Among the writers who lived and worked in the city are Alexander Pushkin, Mikhail Lermontov, A. S. Griboedov, Nikolai Gogol, Nikolai Nekrasov, Feodor Dostoyevksy, and Maxim Gorky. Color photographs show an aerial view of the city, the desk at which Dostoyevsky wrote, and the Fontanka Canal, which has numerous literary associations. Symbols on the map are keyed to places where authors lived and worked, museums, memorials to authors, monuments to authors, educational institutions where they studied, theaters with connections to authors, and grave sites. A list of names of authors gives their life dates and other information about their lives and works. The key also gives cross references to other parts of the key that contain additional references to a particular author. A revised version, *Literaturnye pamiatnye mesta, turistskaia skhema, Leningrad* (Literary Memorial Places, A Tourist Map, Leningrad, G7004 .L4E65 1987 .S6), was issued in 1987.

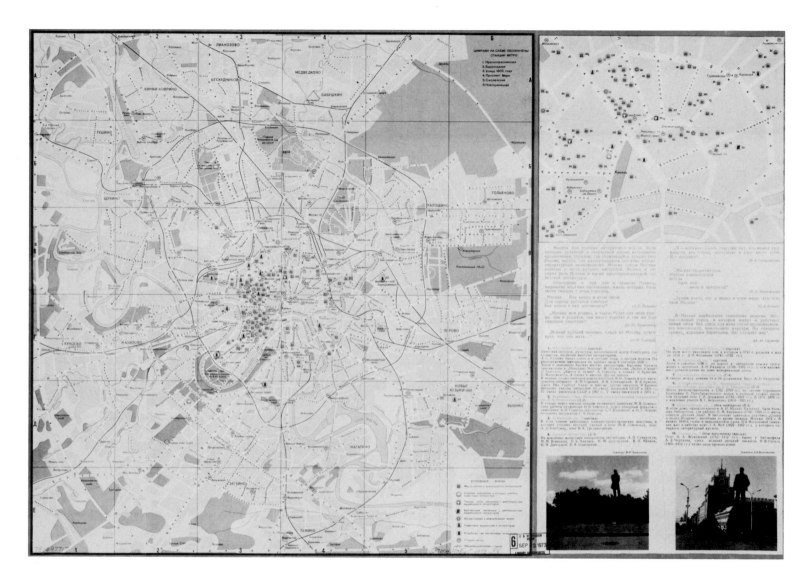

Moscow

Literaturnaia Moskva, turistskaia skhema
(Literary Moscow, A Tourist Map)

V.S. Titkova
Editor

Moscow: Glavnoe upravlenie geodezii i
    kartografii, 1973
In Russian
47 x 45 cm
Color
G7004 .M7E65 1973 .R8

*L*iteraturnaia Moskva gives information on literary sites in Moscow inside the ring road that surrounds the city. An inset map shows the central area of Moscow around the Kremlin in detail. The map features quotations celebrating Moscow from the works of poets Alexander Pushkin, Mikhail Lermontov, Vladimir Mayakovsky, and Sergei Esenin and novelist Leo Tolstoy. The Pushkin Museum, and statues of novelist Nikolai Gogol, Lermontov, and Mayakovsky are illustrated in color photographs. Text gives names of places and streets, with their literary associations. A numbered key identifies places where authors lived and worked, museums, memorials to authors, monuments to authors, educational institutions where they studied, libraries related to authors' activities, theaters with connections to authors, and grave sites.

Literaturnaia Moskva, turistskaia skhema
(Literary Moscow, A Tourist Map)

V. S. Titkova and I. E. Valueva
Editors

Moscow: Glavnoe upravlenie geodezii i
    kartografii, 1977
In Russian
59 x 47 cm
Color
G7004 .M7E65 1977 .R8

*L*iteraturnaia Moskva gives information on literary sites in Moscow inside the ring road that surrounds the
city. Text on the map celebrates Moscow
as the spiritual and creative center of
Russia, where all the best minds congre-
gated, and points out the many streets
named for writers. A key details the literary associations of the Kremlin and Red
Square, then lists individual authors
with information about their lives and
work. Illustrations shows statues of
dramatist A. S. Griboedov, poets Alexander Pushkin and Mikhail Lermontov,
and fiction writers Nikolai Gogol and
Leo Tolstoy, all of whom lived and
worked in Moscow. An inset map shows
the central area of Moscow around the
Kremlin in detail. A numbered key identifies places where authors lived and
worked, museums, memorials to authors, monuments to authors, educational institutions where they studied, libraries related to authors' activities,
theaters with connections to authors,
and grave sites. The map is a revision of
a 1973 map (G7004 .M7E65 1973 .R8).

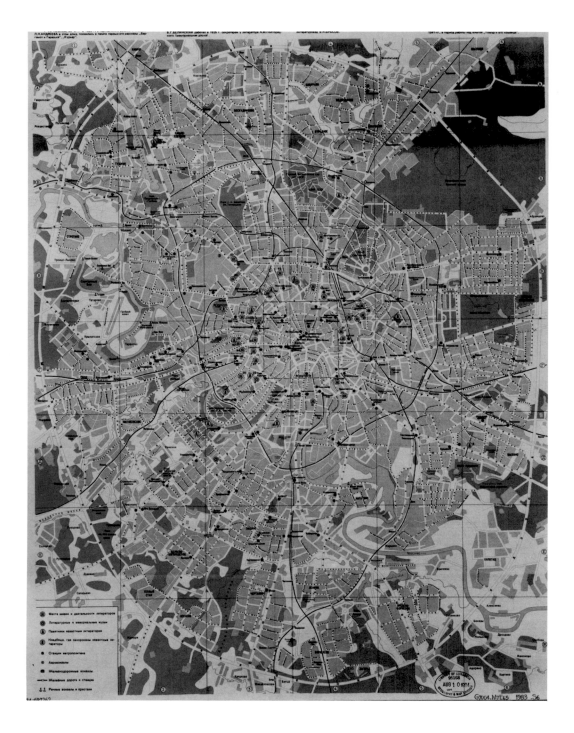

Moskva, literaturnye mesta, turistskaia skhema
(Moscow, Literary Places, A Tourist Map)

Moscow: Glavnoe upravlenie
geodezii i kartografii, 1983
In Russian
60 x 47 cm
Color
G7004 .M7E65 1983 .S6

*M*oskva, literaturnye mesta identifies literary sites in Moscow and surrounding areas. An inset map shows the central area of Moscow around the Kremlin in detail. A key details the literary associations of the Kremlin and Red Square, then lists individual authors under various categories, with information about their lives and work. One section includes information about foreign writers, such as H. G. Wells and John Reed, who visited Moscow. One category deals with major writers' museums, such as the homes of poet Alexander Pushkin (1799–1837), journalist and novelist Alexander Hertzen (1812–1870), novelists Feodor Dostoyevksy (1821–1881) and Leo Tolstoy (1828–1910), fiction writer and dramatist Anton Chekhov (1860–1904), futurist poet Vladimir Mayakovsky (1893–1930), and fiction writer Maxim Gorky (1868–1936). The sites of the Literary Museum and twenty-five monuments to writers are also identified. A numbered key identifies places where authors lived and worked, museums, memorials to authors, monuments to authors, educational institutions where they studied, libraries related to authors' activities, theaters with connections to authors, and grave sites.

Tbilisi

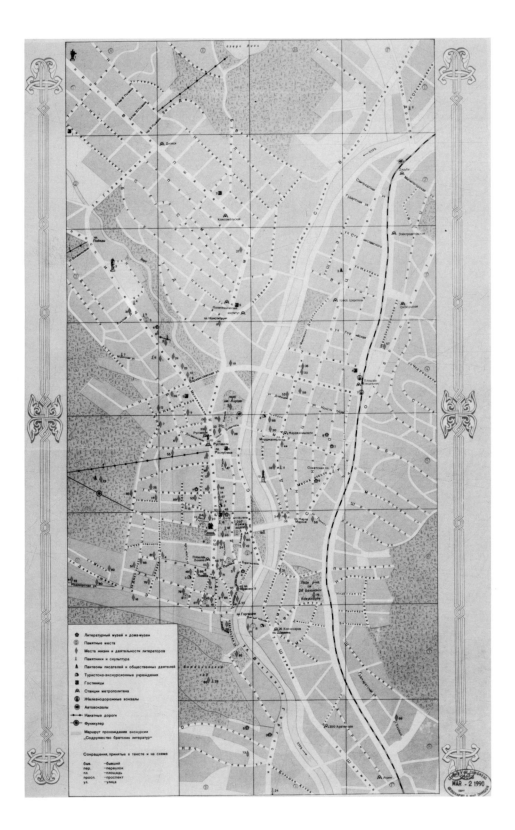

Literaturnye mesta Tbilisi, turistskaia skhema
(Literary Places of Tbilisi, A Tourist Map)

Moscow: Glavnoe upravlenie geodezii i
    kartografii, 1989
In Russian
57 x 28 cm
Color
G7004. T32E65 1988 .S6

*L*iteraturnye mesta Tbilisi gives information on literary sites in Tbilisi, the
ancient capital of Georgia. The main city
and cultural center of the Transcaucasus
region, Tbilisi has long attracted Russian
writers and writers of other nationalities.
Among the Russian authors who visited
the city and are noted on the map are
Alexander Pushkin, Mikhail Lermontov,
Leo Tolstoy, Anton Chekhov, Maxim
Gorky, Aleksei Tolstoy, Sergei Esenin,
and Boris Pasternak. A separate section
on the map lists Georgian writers and
another section lists foreign writers, such
as Alexander Dumas, who visited Tbilisi.
The map cover features a statue of characters from the novel *Granny, Iliko, Illar-
ion, and I* (1960) by Georgian Nodar V.
Dumbadze, who is buried in Tbilisi. The
novel, which has a strong autobiographical element, tells about the wartime
childhood of an orphaned Georgian boy
and his studies at Tbilisi University.
Other photographs show statues of
major Georgian poets Shota Rustaveli
and N. M. Baratushvili and playwright
A. S. Griboedov. A numbered key identifies places where authors lived and
worked, literary museums, memorials to
authors, and sculptures.

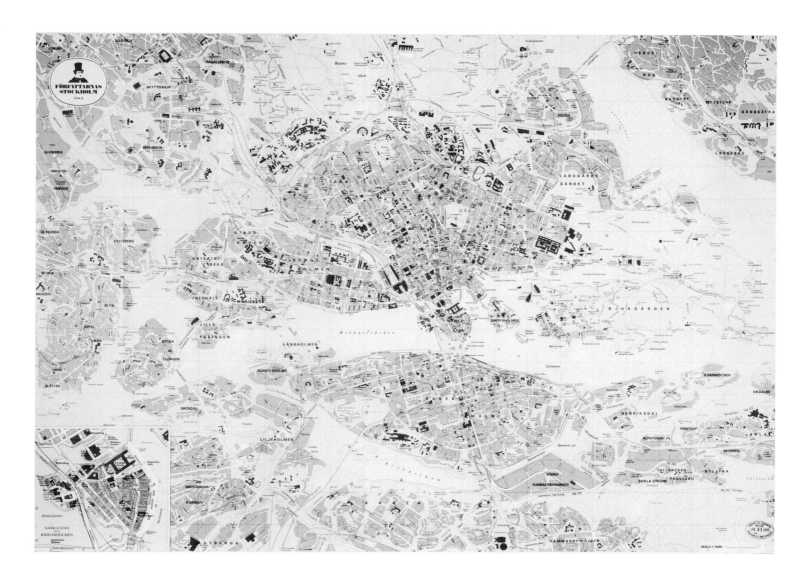

SWEDEN

**Författarnas Stockholm: karta
and guide**
(The Writers' Stockholm: A Map and Guide)

Thorlief Hellborn
Compiler

Stockholm: Norstedts, ca. 1990
In Swedish
66 x 44 cm
Color
G6954 .S7E65 1990 .G5

The map shows gathering places, such as pubs, restaurants, wine cellars, and cafes, where writers worked or socialized. It also indicates where writers were born, lived, and were buried. Places associated with their works are also located. Among the featured authors are Selma Lagerlöf, who wrote *The Wonderful Adventures of Nils* (1907); Astrid Lindgren, who wrote *Pippi Longstocking* (1944); Vilhelm Moberg, who depicted the travails of Swedes who emigrated to the United States; Maj Sjöwall and Per Wahlöö, who coauthored the Martin Beck mystery series; dramatist August Strindberg; and eighteenth-century balladeer Carl Michael Bellman. The map is accompanied by a fifty-three-page booklet that contains biographical sketches of the authors and discussions of their work. The last pages of the booklet contain a key linked to numbers on the map.

Britain

"Britain's a world by itself."   **William Shakespeare**
Cymbeline

The Booklovers' Map of the British Isles

PAUL M. PAINE
Compiler

New York: R.R. Bowker, 1927
66 x 49 cm
Color
G5741 .E65 1927 .P3

A motto around the border of this map showing Great Britain and Ireland reads "How Small the Map of Britain Is on Paper and Yet How Packed with Fancies." On the map itself are marked such important actual literary sites as the home of Henry James (1843–1916) at Rye; the field of daffodils described by William Wordsworth in "I Wandered Lonely As a Cloud"; fictional places such as Wessex, the setting for the novels of Thomas Hardy (1840–1928); and Barchester, the setting for several novels of Anthony Trollope (1815–1882). Inset maps show the literary capitals of London and Edinburgh. Sites featured in London include the homes of Thomas Carlyle (1795–1881) and Charles Lamb (1775–1834), and the site of Shakespeare's Globe Theatre. In Edinburgh, the home of Robert Burns (1759–1796), the monument to Sir Walter Scott (1771–1832) and the home of James Boswell (1740–1795) are marked. Also shown are selected literary sites in the Channel Islands and on the north coast of France. The map is accompanied by a separate key that identifies the authors and books associated with the various marked sites. Paul M. Paine (1869–1955), head of the Syracuse Public Library from 1915–1942, was a newspaper book columnist, textbook writer, and creator of a number of literary and historical maps.

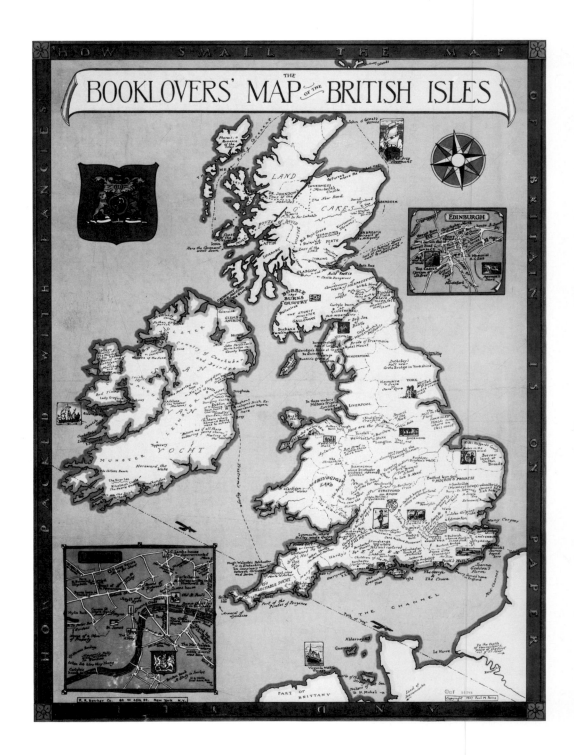

Language of the Land

The Booklovers Map of the British Isles

DOLLI TINGLE
Compiler

New York: R.R. Bowker, 1946
63 x 47 cm
Color
G5741 .E65 1946 .T5

A simpler version of the 1927 map by the same company, this Booklovers Map marks off areas of Britain such as "Bobbie Burns Country," the Scottish homeland of poet Robert Burns (1759–1796); "Bronte Country," the Yorkshire home of novelists Charlotte (1816–1855); Emily (1818–1848), and Anne Brontë (1820–1849); "Hardy Country," the Wessex of the novels of Thomas Hardy (1840–1928); and "King Arthur's Country." Titles of famous works are placed at the locations where they took place. Homes of writers such as Lord Byron, James Boswell, and Sir Walter Scott are also indicated. Glamis Castle and Birnam Wood, places mentioned in *Macbeth* by William Shakespeare, are identified. Quotes from the poems by Robert Browning and Thomas Moore are given in the margins. An inset map marks famous London sites associated with Shakespeare, the *Canterbury Tales* (ca. 1387–1400) by Geoffrey Chaucer, *Vanity Fair* (1848) by William Thackeray, and *The Strange Case of Dr. Jekyll and Mr. Hyde* (1886) by Robert Louis Stevenson.

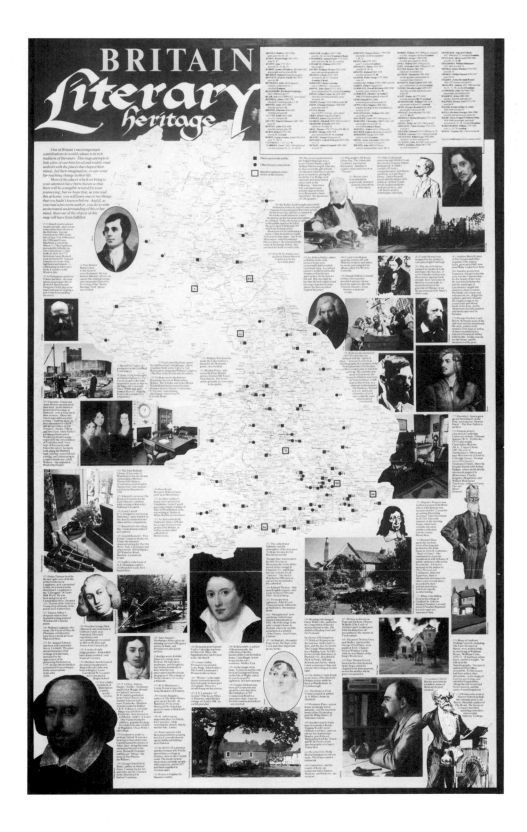

Britain: Literary Heritage

Leena Shaw and Catherine Peel
Editors

Tony Fandino and Derrick McRobert
Designers

London: British Tourist Authority, 1983
68 x 42 cm
Color
G5741 .E65 1983 .B7

Designed for tourists, this map features writers of imaginative literature who are still widely read and appreciated and who spent most of their lives in Britain. At the top of the map is a listing of such authors from Matthew Arnold to Virginia Woolf. Images of authors taken from paintings in Britain's National Portrait Gallery are shown on the map, along with places associated with the authors. Those places open to the public are specially marked. Numbers on the map refer to text around the margin, which explains the significance of the sites. Numbers within squares refer to the verso of the map, where the selected areas are given special treatment. Those areas include The Lake District, home of William Wordsworth and Beatrix Potter; The "Land of Burns," where the home of Robert Burns can be visited at Alloway; "Scott's Country," where tourists can visit Abbotsford, home of Sir Walter Scott; "Shakespeare Country," featuring scenes of Stratford-upon-Avon; "Literary London," home of many authors; "Hardy's Wessex," setting for the novels of Thomas Hardy; and Kent, associated with the *Canterbury Tales* by Geoffrey Chaucer, Canterbury native Christopher Marlowe, and Charles Dickens, who lived in Rochester.

A Literary Map of the British Isles

Karl J. Holzknecht
Compiler

New York: Oxford University Press, 1934
32 x 25 cm
Color
G5741 .E65 1934 .H6

This map is a general map of the British Isles with a key on the reverse that provides the literary significance of places such as authors' birthplaces and residences. The key lists book titles as well as place and author names in alphabetical order and furnishes the map coordinates for the places. Red capital letters mark areas of the British Isles associated with especially noted writers, such as Thomas Hardy, William Shakespeare, Jane Austen, Edmund Spenser, Walter Scott, and Robert Burns. A few selected book titles are also noted on the map.

***A Literary Map of the British Isles:
To Accompany English Literature
in the Ginn Literature Series***

Boston: Ginn and Company, 1964
62 x 50 cm
Color
G5741 .E65 1964 .G5

Although this map shows localities and regions mentioned in some works of English literature, for the most part, it is a general map of England locating major cities. The Lake District, home of William Wordsworth and Beatrix Potter, and the areas associated with the Brontë sisters and Thomas Hardy are specially identified. Birnam Wood and Dunsinane, Scottish places associated with William Shakespeare's *Macbeth*, are also marked. A "Central London" inset shows homes of Charles Dickens and Samuel Johnson and tourist sites.

Language of the Land

A Literary Map of England

WILLIAM LYON PHELPS
Preparer

Boston: Ginn & Company, ca. 1899
33 x 28 cm
Color
G5751 .E65 1899 .P4

A Literary Map of England is primarily a cartographically accurate representation of England, Wales, and southern Scotland. English and Welsh counties are distinguished by different colors. The map shows literary places, for example, Abbotsford, Scotland, home of Sir Walter Scott; Steventon, Hampshire, Jane Austen's home; and Tintern Abbey, Monmouthshire, setting of a poem by William Wordsworth, but does not explain their significance. Viewers must supply their own literary associations for the places listed.

The Macmillan Literary Map of the
British Isles: To Accompany the
Macmillan Pocket Classics, the
Modern Readers' Series, and the
Works of Many Contemporary
British Authors

MARTIN GAMBLE
Illustrator

New York: Macmillan Company, 1927
90 x 58 cm
Color
G5741 .E65 1927 .G3

*T*he *Macmillan Literary Map of the
British Isles* is a general reference map,
with literary places from Abbotsford (the
home of Sir Walter Scott) to Youghal, Ireland (childhood home of dramatist
William Congreve), located on a key. Selected cathedrals and castles are pictured,
as are Haworth, the home of the Brontë
sisters; the birthplace of Alfred Tennyson;
the route of the pilgrims in *The Canterbury Tales* by Geoffrey Chaucer
(1345?–1400); and Birnam Wood, mentioned in *Macbeth* by William Shakespeare. Inset maps show the Lake District
and London. The map of London shows
literary landmarks, for example, Shakespeare's Globe Theatre and the Tabard Inn
from Chaucer's *The Canterbury Tales*,
from the fourteenth to the nineteenth centuries. The areas of the country associated
with Robert Burns, William Wordsworth,
George Eliot, Thomas Hardy, Charles
Kingsley, Eden Phillpotts, and the novel
Lorna Doone (1869) by Richard Blackmore
are marked. In Ireland the territory associated with William Butler Yeats, J. M.
Synge, and the legendary bard Ossian (3rd
century AD) are located. The map was
reissued in 1928.

A Pictorial Chart of English Literature

ETHEL EARLE WYLIE
Compiler

ELLA WALL VAN LEER
Illustrator

[Chicago?]: Rand McNally, 1929
78 x 59 cm
Color *(See color section.)*
G5741 .E65 1929 .W9

A Pictorial Chart of English Literature is a companion to the *Pictorial Chart of American Literature* (G3701 .E65 1932 .W9) by the same compiler and illustrator. The map shows England, Wales, Scotland as far north as Loch Lomond, and a small part of western Ireland. The names of important literary places are on sign posts, and the names of authors identified with them are beneath. Selected authors are pictured—among them William Shakespeare, John Milton, Joseph Addison, William Wordsworth, Samuel Taylor Coleridge, Robert Southey, Jane Austen, Charles Dickens, Alfred Tennyson, and Robert Burns. The sides of the map feature scenes from English history and quotations from *Beowulf* (8th c.), the *Anglo-Saxon Chronicle* (911), Layamon, Geoffrey Chaucer, Thomas Malory, Edmund Spenser, Francis Bacon, John Milton, Jonathan Swift, Joseph Addison, Thomas Carlyle, and Edward Bulwer-Lytton.

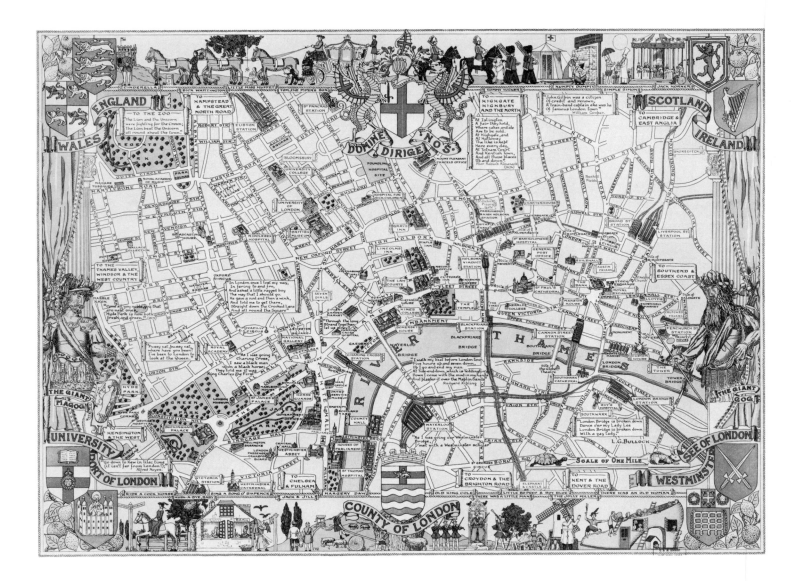

LONDON

Children's Map of London

Edinburgh: John Bartholomew and Son, n.d.
56 x 77 cm
Color
Ethel M. Fair Collection 336

The *Children's Map of London* shows twentieth-century London, with landmarks such as Buckingham Place, Hyde Park, and the Tower indicated. Insets contain lines from nursery rhymes as well as poems that mention London by William Cowper, Rudyard Kipling, and Alfred Noyes. The map's corners contain the arms of England, Wales, Scotland, Ireland, the University of London, and the See of London. Gog and Magog, giant effigies in the London Guildhall, are shown in the left and right borders. Around the top and bottom borders are illustrations of Cinderella, Dick Whittington, Miss Muffet, Tommy Tucker, Humpty Dumpty, Simple Simon, Jack Horner, Jack and Jill, Margery Daw, Old King Cole, Little Bo Peep, The Old Woman in the Shoe, and other fairy-tale nursery-rhyme characters. A note says that royalties from the map were to be given to London's Hospital for Sick Children.

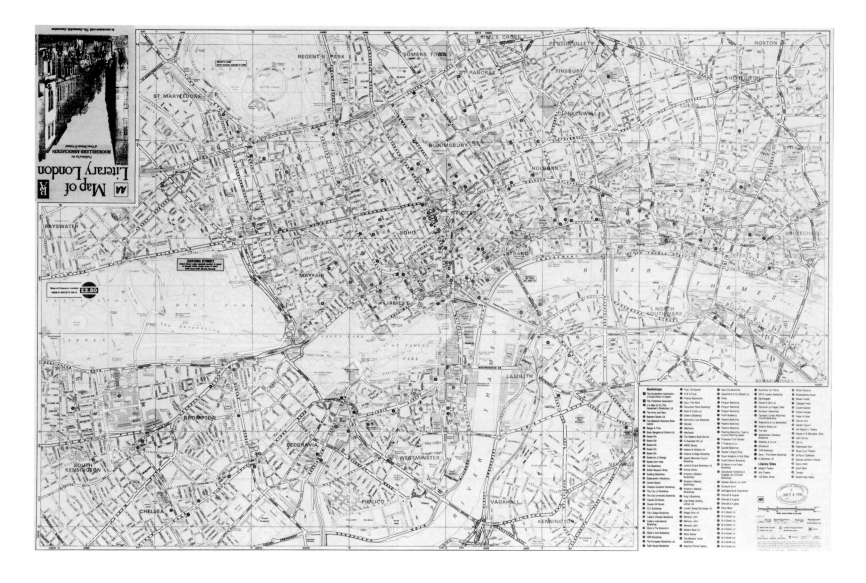

Map of Literary London

Basingstoke, Hampshire:
   Automobile Association, 1988
60 x 90 cm
Color
G5754 .L7Q46 1988 .A9

Published by the Booksellers Association of Great Britain and Ireland in Association with the Automobile Association of Great Britain, the *Map of Literary London* is an updated version of a 1968 map. Essentially a road map of Central London, it locates more than one hundred bookshops, as well as major buildings. Literary sites identified are primarily theaters and hotels. Baker Street, home of Sherlock Holmes in the stories by Arthur Conan Doyle; a home of Charles Dickens; and the home of Samuel Johnson are marked. On the verso are advertisements for London bookstores.

United States

"A good work of fiction is a better guide to a region than a bad work of fact."

Lawrence Clark Powell
Heart of the Southwest

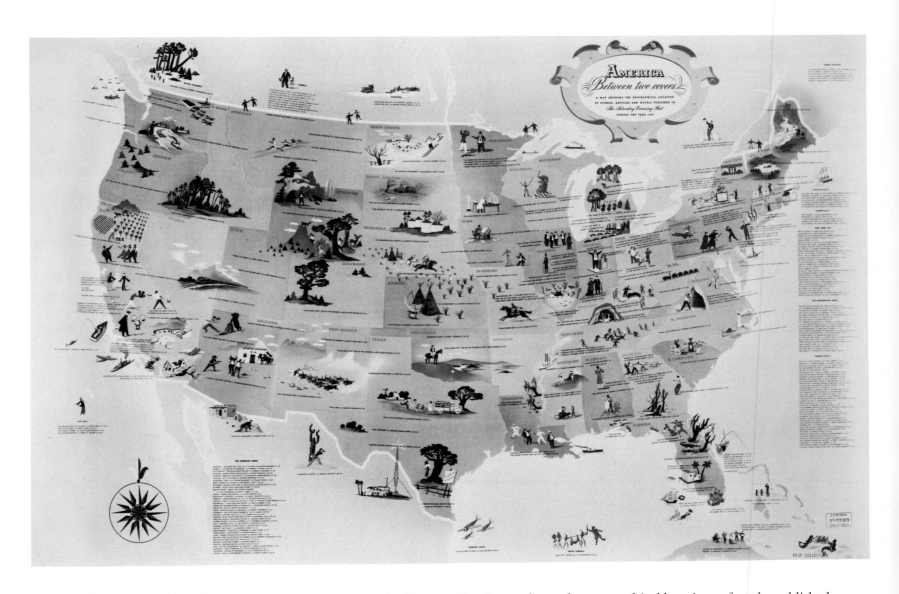

America Between Two Covers

[Philadelphia?]: *The Saturday Evening
  Post,* ca. 1941
68 x 107 cm
Color
Ethel M. Fair Collection 628

*A*merica Between Two Covers shows the geographical locations of works published
in *The Saturday Evening Post* in 1940. The map shows the forty-eight contiguous
states, plus parts of Canada and Mexico, the Bahamas, and Cuba. Titles, authors, and
dates of publication are located in the region with which the works are related, along
with illustrations. Writing pertaining to areas outside the boundaries of the map, such
as the "Far East" and the "North Atlantic," is listed under these headings in the margins.
The categories "Massachusetts," "Connecticut," "New York City," "The Washington
Scene," "The American Scene," and "World War II" are represented by so many articles
that each is also listed separately. Well-known authors who wrote for the *Saturday
Evening Post* in 1940 include W. Somerset Maugham, MacKinlay Kantor, Marjorie Kinnan Rawlings, and Pearl Buck.

American Literature

Logan, Iowa: Perfection Form Company, 1967
102 x 143 cm
Color
G3701 .E65 1967 .P4

Reprinted courtesy of Perfection Learning Corporation, Logan, Iowa

American Literature, a comprehensive guide to the literature of the forty-eight contiguous states and Alaska, identifies prominent authors and works from every state, with a brief biographical sketch or a brief summary of a major work for every author. In addition to the outline map of the United States, there are insert maps of the East Coast as far south as North Carolina, New York City, the Boston area, and the state of Massachusetts. Another insert entitled "Main Currents in American Literature" divides the literary history of the United States into four periods: the Colonial Period (1607–1765), the Revolutionary Period (1765–1800), the Romantic Period (1800–1865), and the Triumph of Realism (1865–Present). The map is illustrated with scenes from well-known literary works such as Jack London's *The Call of the Wild* (1903), Mark Twain's *The Adventures of Huckleberry Finn* (1884), and Washington Irving's "Rip Van Winkle" (1819). The main quotation on the map comes from William Faulkner's Nobel Prize Acceptance Speech of 1950; other quotes describe the distinct characteristics of New England, the South, the Midwest, and the West.

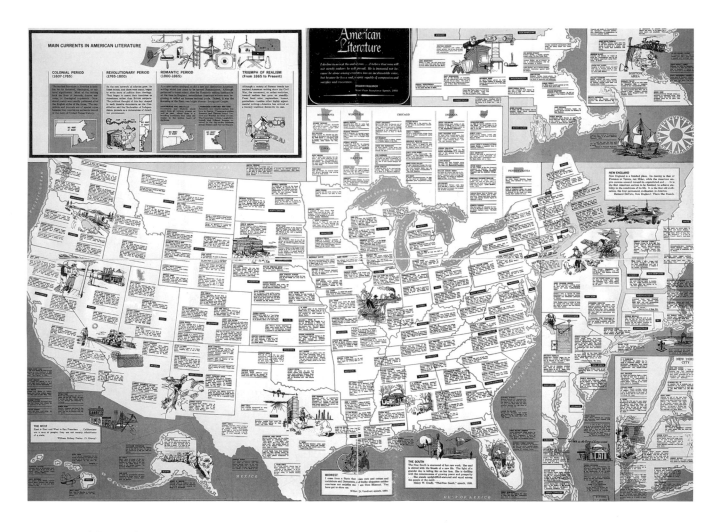

The Beat Generation Map of America

Molly Maguire
Designer

Stan Grant
Illustrator

Los Angeles: Aaron Blake, 1987
52 x 59 cm
Color
G3701 .E65 1987 .A2

Courtesy of Molly Maguire and Aaron Silverman

Designed as a scene in a jazz club, the *Beat Generation Map of America* pictures a quartet composed of jazz greats Charlie "Bird" Parker (1920–1955), Shelly Manne (1920–1984), Miles Davis (1926–1991), and Thelonius Monk (1917–1982) performing while writer Jack Kerouac (1922–1969) recites before an audience of well-known "beat generation" authors. The map features personalities, books, important events, and locales connected with the antiestablishment beat movement of the late 1940s and 1950s. Inset maps identify homes and hangouts in New York City, San Francisco, Berkeley, and Los Angeles of authors such as Kerouac, Lawrence Ferlinghetti, William Burroughs, and Denise Levertov. Research and design for the map were performed by Molly Maguire, who produced a series of literary maps in the 1980s.

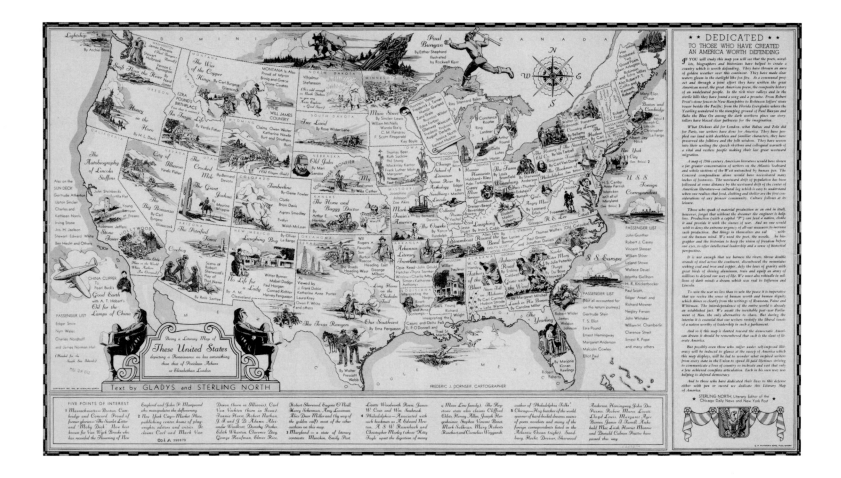

Being a Literary Map of These United States Depicting a Renaissance No Less Astonishing Than That of Periclean Athens or Elizabethan London

GLADYS AND STERLING NORTH
Editors

FREDERIC DORNSEIF
Cartographer

New York: G.P. Putnam's Sons, 1942
44 x 75 cm
Color
G3701 .E65 1942 .N6

"Dedicated to Those Who Have Created an America Worth Defending," this map produced during World War II exudes patriotic fervor. Its title evokes two periods of high culture, Periclean Athens and Elizabethan London, as proper points of comparison for the literature of the United States. A shield at the bottom displays an American eagle, flanked by red and white striped bunting. A text by Sterling North (1906–1974), author and Literary Editor of the *Chicago Daily News* and *New York Post,* and his wife Gladys, equates defense of literature with the defense of democracy itself. Names and images of authors and titles and scenes from books are provided for each state. At the bottom of the map is a list of famous literary areas—Massachusetts, New York City, Maryland, Philadelphia, and Chicago—with information on authors who lived in each place. Expatriate authors and foreign correspondents are listed in the two oceans, depending on whether they left for Europe or the South Seas.

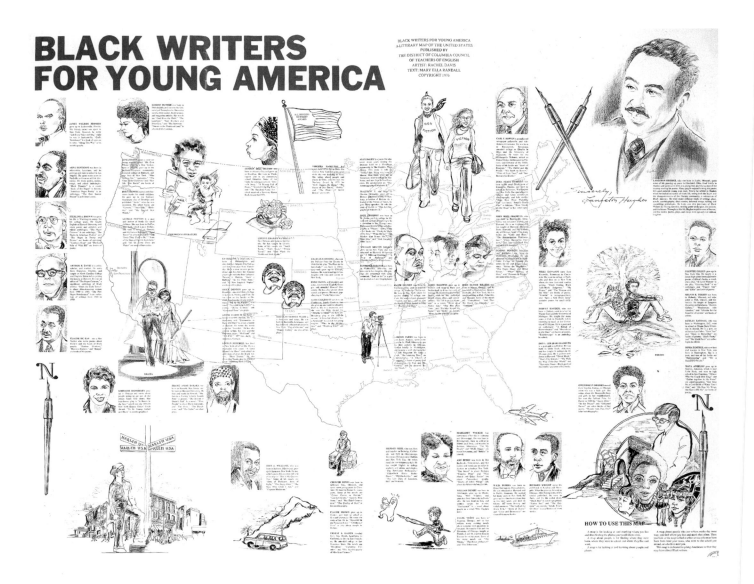

Black Writers for Young America

Rachel Davis
Illustrator

Washington, D.C.: District of Columbia
    Council of Teachers of English, 1976
86 x 11 cm
Color *(See color section.)*
G3701 .E65 1976 .D5

Produced by the District of Columbia Council of Teachers of English for the United States Bicentennial in 1976, *Black Writers for Young America* features portraits and short biographical sketches of approximately sixty significant African American authors. At the upper right is a larger sketch of Langston Hughes, with his signature. In the background is an outline of the United States on which key places associated with black authors are noted. Eatonville, Florida, associated with Zora Neale Hurston, and New York's Harlem, site of the Harlem Renaissance, an important literary movement of the 1920s, are among those marked.

Booklovers Map of America: A Chart of Certain Landmarks of Literary Geography

PAUL M. PAINE
Compiler

New York: R.R. Bowker, 1926
55 x 77 cm
Color
G3701 .E65 1926 .P3

Against an outline map of the forty-eight contiguous states and parts of Canada and Mexico, the *Booklovers Map of America* lists titles and authors associated with each place. Some titles are illustrated. The map also has inset maps of the important literary centers of New York, Philadelphia, Chicago, and San Francisco. An inset map of the world shows literary places in Canada and the Pacific Ocean. Some works are quoted, including Harriet Beecher Stowe's *Uncle Tom's Cabin* (1852), Oliver Wendell Holmes's *The Autocrat of the Breakfast Table* (1858), Walt Whitman's "O Captain, My Captain," and Sidney Lanier's "The Marshes of Glynn" (1878). Compiler Paul M. Paine (1869–1955), who gathered the information on the map, was head of the Syracuse Public Library from 1915–1942, a newspaper book columnist, textbook writer, and creator of a number of other literary and historical maps.

The Booklovers Map of America, Showing Certain Landmarks of Literary Geography

PAUL M. PAINE
Compiler

New York: R.R. Bowker, 1933
55 x 77 cm
Color
Ethel M. Fair Collection 580

Against an outline map of the forty-eight contiguous states and parts of Canada and Mexico, the *Booklovers Map of America* lists titles and authors associated with each place. Some titles are illustrated. The map also has inset maps of Alaska and of New England, labeled as "The Birthplace of American Literature." Inset text blocks locate authors and titles associated with the important literary centers of New York, Philadelphia, Chicago, and San Francisco. An inset map of the world shows Canada and the Pacific Ocean. This map places more emphasis on works set in Canada and Mexico than do Paine's other versions. Titles shown for Canada include Lucy Maude Montgomery's *Anne of Green Gables*, Henry Wadsworth Longfellow's *Evangeline* (1847), and Charles William Gordon's *Sky Pilot* (1899) and for Mexico, William H. Prescott's *History of the Conquest of Mexico* (1843), Archibald MacLeish's poem *Conquistador* (1938), and H. Rider Haggard's *Montezuma's Daughter* (1920). Compiler Paul M. Paine (1869–1955), who gathered the information on the map, was head of the Syracuse Public Library from 1915–1942, a newspaper book columnist, textbook writer, and creator of a number of other literary and historical maps.

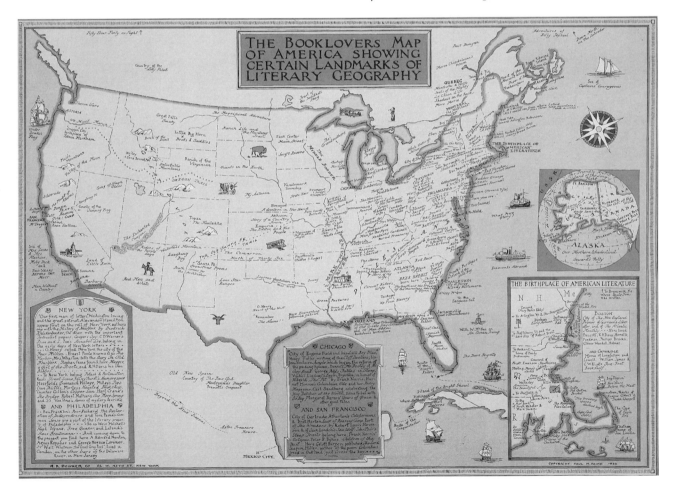

Language of the Land

The Booklovers Map of America

PAUL M. PAINE
Compiler

New York: R.R. Bowker, 1933–1939
54 x 78 cm
Color
Ethel M. Fair Collection 581

Against an outline map of the forty-eight contiguous states and parts of Canada and Mexico, the *Booklovers Map of America* lists titles and authors associated with each place. Some titles are illustrated. The map also has inset maps of Alaska and of New England, labeled as "The Birthplace of American Literature." Inset text blocks locate authors and titles associated with the important literary centers of New York, Philadelphia, Chicago, and San Francisco. An inset map of the world shows Canada and the Pacific Ocean. Quotations on the map come from Harriet Beecher Stowe's *Uncle Tom's Cabin* (1852), Oliver Wendell Holmes's *The Autocrat of the Breakfast-Table* (1858), and Sidney Lanier's "The Marshes of Glynn" (1878). Titles shown for Canada include Lucy Maude Montgomery's *Anne of Green Gables* and Henry Wadsworth Longfellow's *Evangeline* (1847) and for Mexico, Archibald MacLeish's poem *Conquistador* (1938). Compiler Paul M. Paine (1869–1955), who gathered the information on the map, was head of the Syracuse Public Library from 1915–1942, a newspaper book columnist, textbook writer, and creator of a number of other literary and historical maps. The map is a revised version of one published in 1933 (Ethel M. Fair Collection 580).

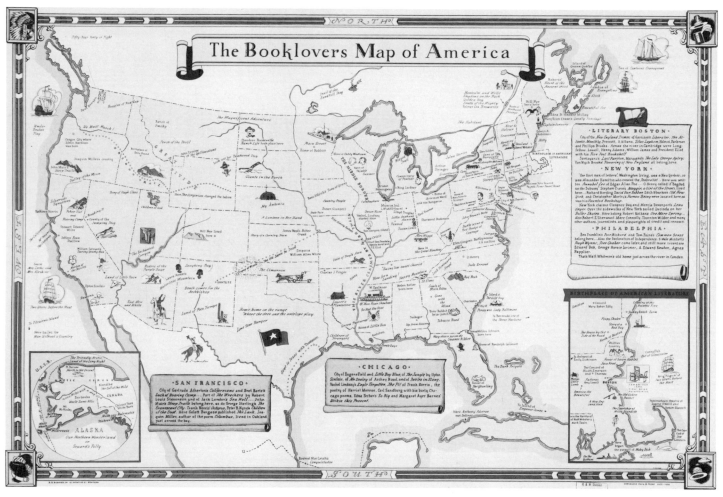

The Booklover's Map of the United States

AMY JONES
Designer and Illustrator

New York: R.R. Bowker, 1949
51 x 66 cm
Color
G3701 .E65 1949 .J6

At the top of *The Booklover's Map of the United States* are portraits of a traditional pantheon of American writers: Washington Irving, James Fenimore Cooper, Ralph Waldo Emerson, Nathaniel Hawthorne, Henry Wadsworth Longfellow, Edgar Allan Poe, Henry David Thoreau, Walt Whitman, and Mark Twain. Insets show the important literary areas of New York City, Chicago, and Boston. Writers who lived much of their lives abroad, such as Henry James, Pearl Buck, Ernest Hemingway, and Gertrude Stein, are listed on a ribbon at the bottom of the map.

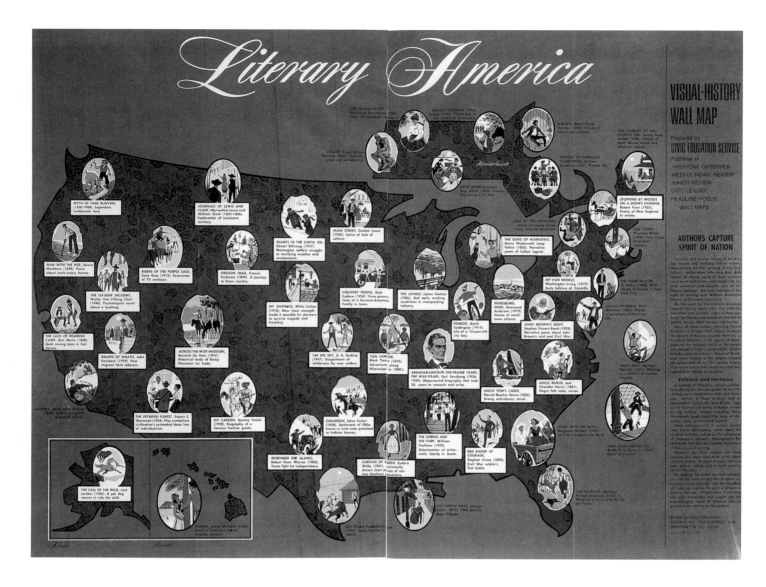

Literary America:
Visual-History Wall Map

Joe Phillips
Illustrator

Washington, D.C.: Civic Education Service,
    1966
67 x 80 cm
Color
G3701 .E65 1966 .C5

Published by an educational organization and intended for classroom use, *Literary America* provides a geographical setting for more than fifty prominent American literary works. Inset maps show Alaska, Hawaii, and Massachusetts. Author, date of publication, and a one-sentence synopsis are given beneath an illustration of an incident from each work. Among the titles depicted are Henry David Thoreau's *Walden* (1854), Robert Frost's "Stopping by Woods on a Snowy Evening" (1923), Walter Van Tilburg Clark's *The Ox-Bow Incident* (1940), Eudora Welty's *A Curtain of Green* (1941), and James Michener's *Hawaii* (1960).

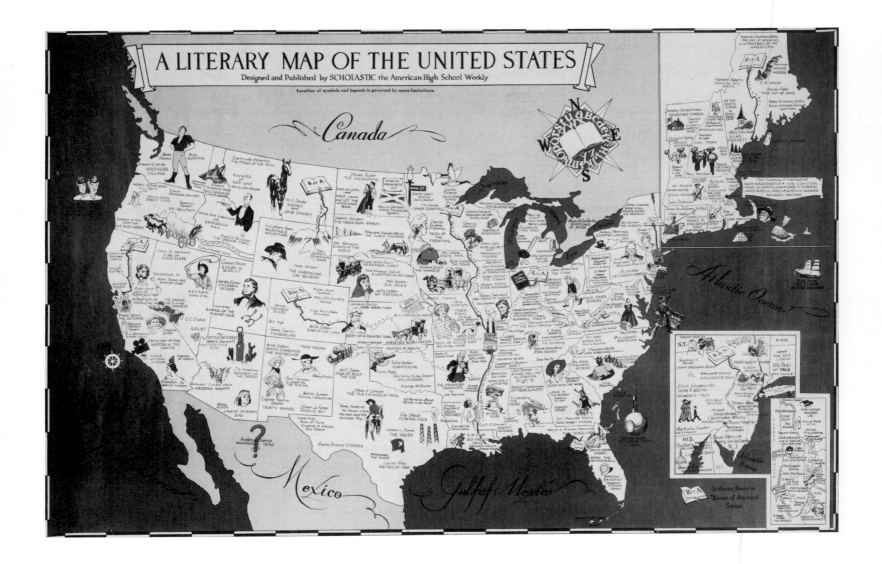

A Literary Map of the United States

Scholastic Corporation, 1940
54 x 83 cm
Color
Muriel H. Parry Collection 510

A Literary Map of the United States, designed and published by *Scholastic* magazine, a weekly publication for high school students, lists titles and authors of books for each of the contiguous forty-eight states. Insets give titles for the New York City area (identified as the publishing center of the United States) and the northeastern and mid-Atlantic states. An inset "The Flowering of New England" (the title of a well-known literary work by Van Wyck Brooks) lists Ralph Waldo Emerson, Nathaniel Hawthorne, Henry Wadsworth Longfellow, Henry David Thoreau, John Greenleaf Whittier, James Russell Lowell, and Oliver Wendell Holmes. Illustrations show characters and scenes from featured books. Also noted are homes of selected authors and rivers described on a related "Rivers of America" series map.

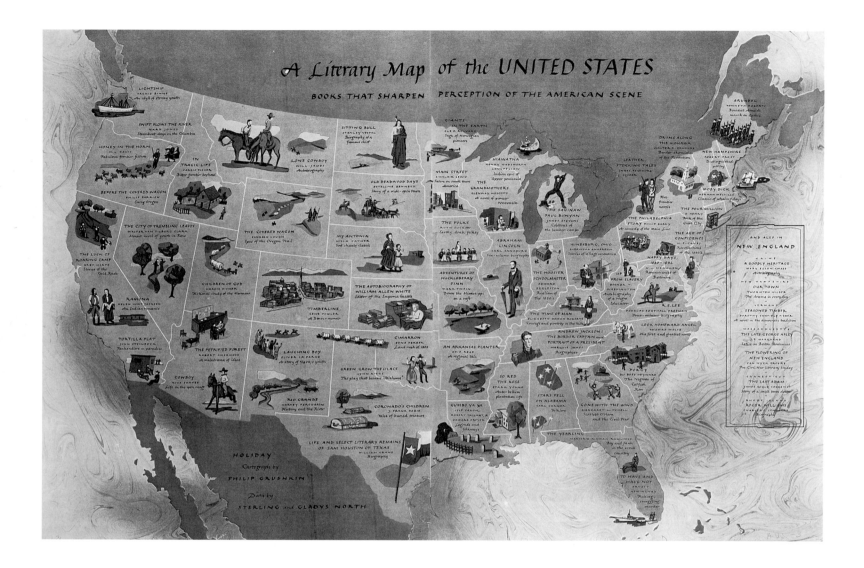

A Literary Map of the United States: Books That Sharpen Perception of the American Scene

STERLING AND GLADYS NORTH
Compilers

PHILIP GRUSHKIN
Cartographer

From *Holiday,* February 1947, pp. 140–141
35 x 53 cm
Color
Muriel H. Parry Collection 509

A Literary Map of the United States, which illustrated a 1947 article in *Holiday* magazine, identifies for each of the contiguous forty-eight states one or more books that have shaped readers' perceptions of that state. A short description of the book follows each title. Examples of the titles selected are *Gone with the Wind* (1936) by Margaret Mitchell for Georgia, *The Yearling* (1938) by Marjorie Kinnan Rawlings for Florida, and *Winesburg, Ohio* (1919) by Sherwood Anderson for Ohio. Most of the titles are accompanied by illustrations of scenes or characters from the books. The map is part of an article subtitled "From Hawthorne to Steinbeck Writers Have Added Another Dimension to Our View of America," which gives a region-by-region overview of major American writers.

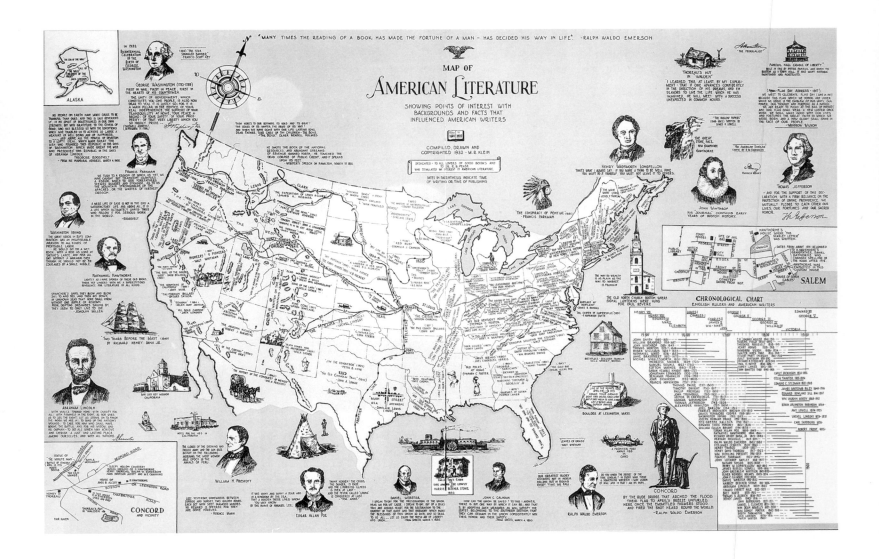

**Map of American Literature,
Showing Points of Interest with
Backgrounds and Facts That
Influenced American Writers**

M[ax] R[alph] Klein
Compiler

Cleveland Heights, Ohio: M. R. Klein, 1932
58 x 91 cm
Color
G3701 .E65 1932 .K51

Produced for the bicentennial of the birth of George Washington in 1932, the map emphasizes history as much as literature. Images of historical figures and of historic sites are prominently featured. Inset maps show locations in Salem, Massachusetts, associated with Nathaniel Hawthorne, and Concord, Massachusetts, places associated with the New England transcendentalist writers. Book titles and names of authors appear on the map at the localities with which the authors or works are associated. At the bottom is a time line relating life dates of famous authors writing in or about America from John Smith to Robert Frost to the reigns of British monarchs up through the then-current George V (reigned 1910–1936). The map also exists in a smaller, black-and-white version (G3701 .E65 1932 .K5).

Language of the Land

Map of Good Stories

PAUL M. PAINE
Compiler

[Syracuse, New York]: Paul M. Paine, 1931
28 x 41 cm
Black and white
G3701 .E65 1931 .P3

Against an outline map of the forty-eight contiguous states and parts of Canada and Mexico, the *Map of Good Stories* lists authors, titles, characters, and events associated with each country, with emphasis on the United States. Titles printed in large, bold type include Nathaniel Hawthorne's *The House of the Seven Gables* (1851), Stephen Crane's *The Red Badge of Courage* (1895), Willa Cather's *My Antonia* (1918), and Bret Harte's "The Luck of Roaring Camp" (1868). An inset shows Alaska, represented by Jack London's *The Call of the Wild* (1903). The edges of the map list titles or characters associated with areas bordering on the United States or the Atlantic and Pacific oceans, such as, to the east Charles Dickens's *David Copperfield* (1849–1850) and Miguel de Cervantes's *Don Quixote* (1605, 1615), and to the west the sea of Herman Melville's Captain Ahab, from *Moby Dick* (1851); Jack London's *The Sea Wolf* (1904); and Joseph Conrad's *Lord Jim*. Compiler Paul M. Paine (1869–1955), who gathered the information on the map, was head of the Syracuse Public Library from 1915–1942, a newspaper book columnist, textbook writer, and creator of a number of other literary and historical maps.

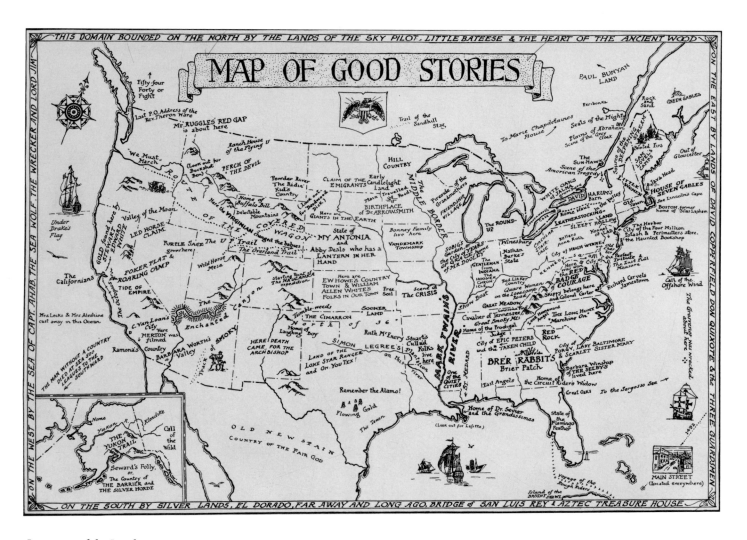

A North Star Map of United States History

Boston: Houghton Mifflin, ca. 1962
58 x 86 cm
Color
Ethel M. Fair Collection 865

On an outline map of the forty-eight contiguous states, *A North Star Map of United States History* locates settings of thirty-two books of American history and biography and features an illustration for each book. Works include *Mark Twain and the River* (1961) and *Thoreau of Walden Pond* (1959) by Sterling North, literary mapmaker and Literary Editor of the *Chicago Daily News* and *New York Post*; *The Fishing Fleets of New England* (1961) by Mary Ellen Chase, Smith college professor and author of novels of New England life; and *Jessie Benton Fremont* (1962) by Marguerite Higgins, Pulitzer Prize-winning war correspondent. The map appears to have been prepared by Houghton Mifflin publishing company to promote a series of books for young readers by prominent authors.

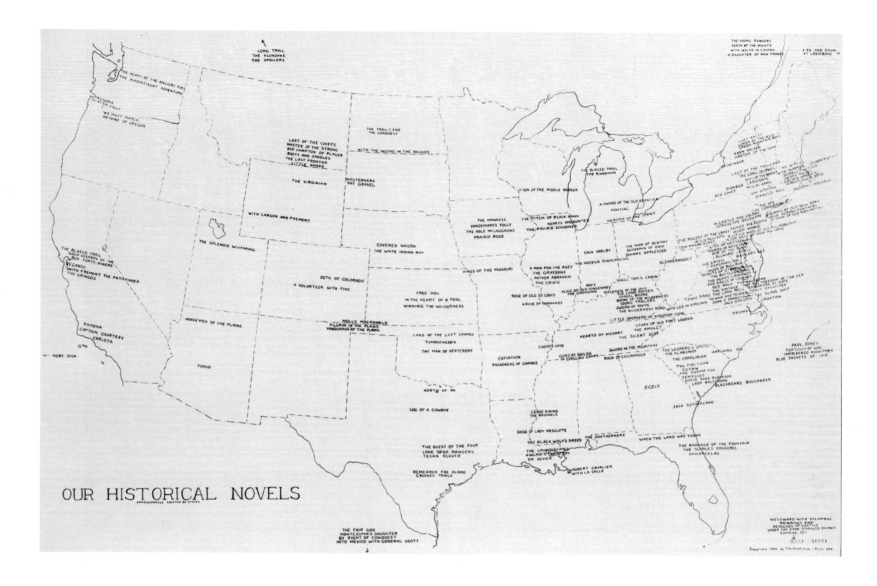

OUR HISTORICAL NOVELS

**Our Historical Novels,
Approximately Located by States**

T.H. McMillan, 1929
39 x 59 cm
Black and White
G3701 .E65 1929 .M3

O n this outline map of the United States and parts of Canada and Mexico, historical novels are identified by title and by geographic location. Authors are not identified on the map. Titles listed include James Fenimore Cooper's *The Last of the Mohicans* (1826), about the French and Indian War, and *The Spy* (1821), a novel of the Revolutionary War; Nathaniel Hawthorne's *The Scarlet Letter* (1850), set in Puritan New England; Harriet Beecher Stowe's *Uncle Tom's Cabin* (1852), a depiction of the horrors of slavery; Helen Hunt Jackson's *Ramona* (1884), a story of Indians at an early California mission; Mary Johnston's *To Have and to Hold* (1900), about Jamestown, Virginia; and Owen Wister's *The Virginian* (1902), a tale of frontier days in Wyoming.

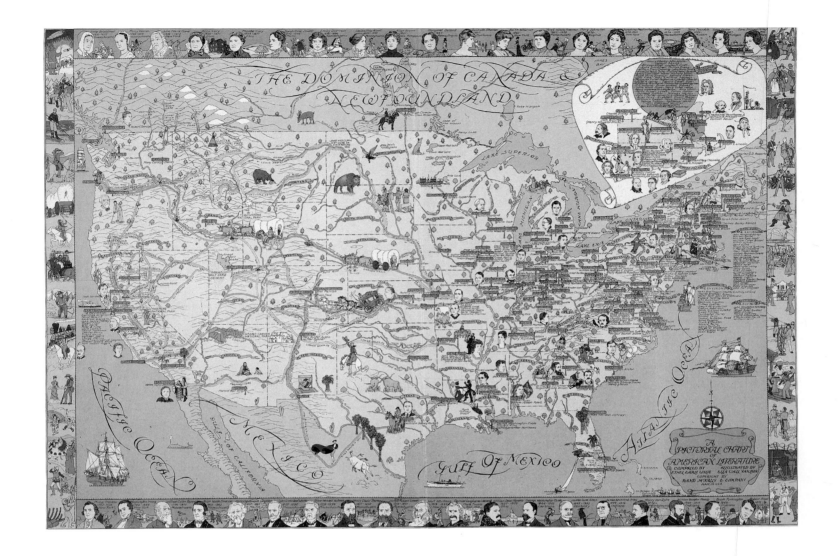

A Pictorial Chart of American Literature

ETHEL EARLE WYLIE
Compiler

ELLA WALL VAN LEER
Illustrator

Chicago: Rand McNally, 1932
58 x 91 cm
Color *(See color section.)*
G3701 .E65 1932 .W9

A Pictorial Chart of American Literature was produced in 1932, when the bicentennial of George Washington's birth created interest in celebrating American achievement. It includes writers who were then contemporary and gives equal representation to America's many outstanding female writers. The top border of the map pictures nineteen female writers and the bottom border shows nineteen male writers along with their dates and the states with which they are associated. The side borders illustrate important events of American history. The body of the map continues a mix of history, natural history, and literature. Along with books and authors, it includes natural wonders such as the Grand Canyon and national parks and sites such as the Oregon Trail and route taken by Lewis and Clark. The map is a companion to *A Pictorial Chart of English Literature* (G5741 .E65 1929 .W9) by the same author and illustrator.

A Pictorial Map Depicting the Literary Development of the United States

Henry J. Firley
Editor

Jean Boys
Illustrator

Chicago: Denoyer-Geppert Company, 1952
100 x 159 cm
Color
G3701 .E65 1952 .D4

The colorful *Pictorial Map Depicting the Literary Development of the United States* includes more than 100 illustrations, approximately 350 titles, and 1000 writers. It also presents nineteen lists of books set in various locales in the forty-eight contiguous states, Alaska, and Mexico. Insets include maps of the Bret Harte Country, New Orleans, New York, and a wreath depicting New England writers Ralph Waldo Emerson, John Greenleaf Whittier, William Cullen Bryant, Henry Wadsworth Longfellow, Oliver Wendell Holmes, Nathaniel Hawthorne, and James Russell Lowell. Images of other authors appear near the locales where they lived, wrote, or set works. Characters and episodes from some titles are illustrated. Further information on the map is contained in Henry J. Firley, *A Glossatteer of World Literature* (PN43 .F5), a manual developed to go with this and two other maps in the Denoyer-Geppert Series, *A Pictorial Map of Mediterranean Mythology and Classical Literature* (G6531 .E6 1959 .F5) and *A Panorama of World Literature* (G3201 .E65 1955 .B6).

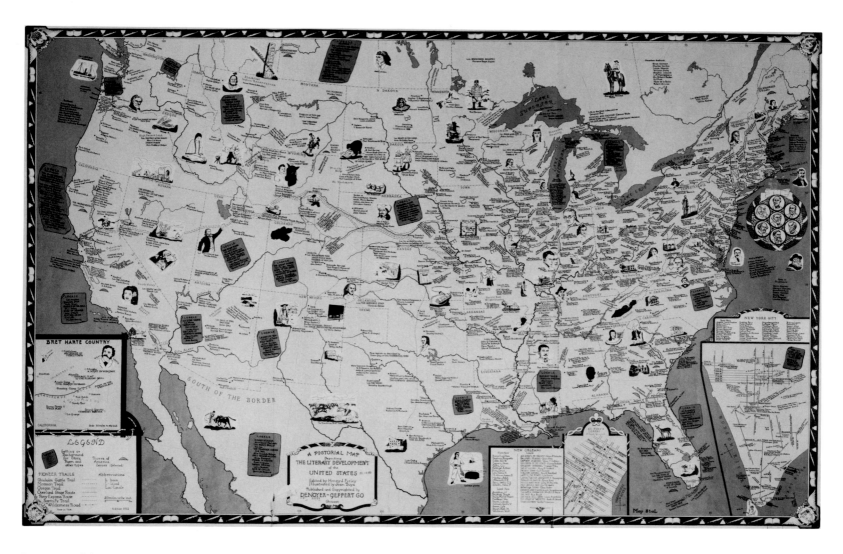

A Pictorial Map of Colonial-Revolutionary American Literature, 1585–1789

HENRY J. FIRLEY
Editor

Chicago: Denoyer-Geppert, 1965
110 x 162 cm
Color *(See color section.)*
G3701 .E65 1789 .D4

A Pictorial Map of Colonial-Revolutionary American Literature, 1585–1789 is two distinct maps on one sheet. One is a color-coded map of the eastern United States that identifies American literature and authors before 1800 and literature written after 1800 that has a colonial-revolutionary setting. The second map identifies important colonial-revolutionary figures, their birthplaces, residences, and the towns they founded. The maps feature numerous illustrations of literary and historic figures and works, each accompanied by a caption or quote. Inserts include a map of England showing places and dates of birth of early American writers, illustrations of well-known early American Indians, a time line relating life dates of British and American writers, and lists of colleges founded in colonial times and key documents in the formation of the United States. This map is as much a historical document as it is a literary one. Editor Henry J. Firley also produced other literary maps for Denoyer-Geppert.

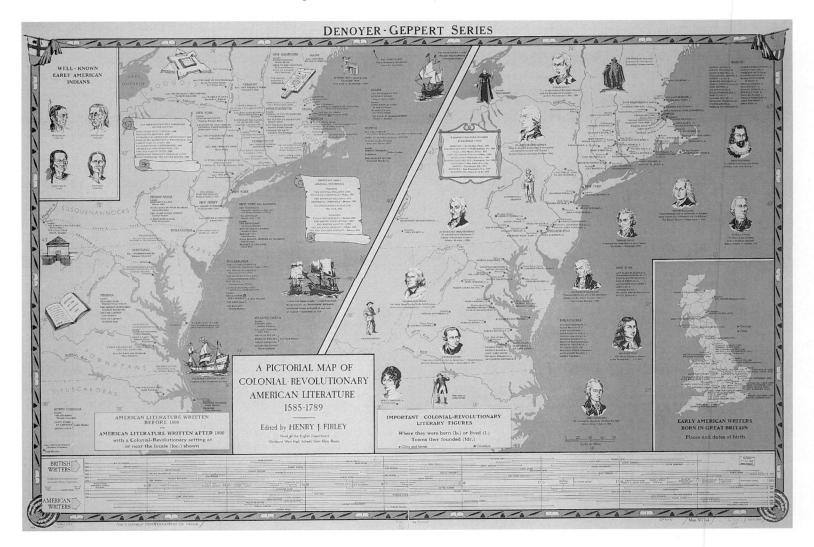

Language of the Land

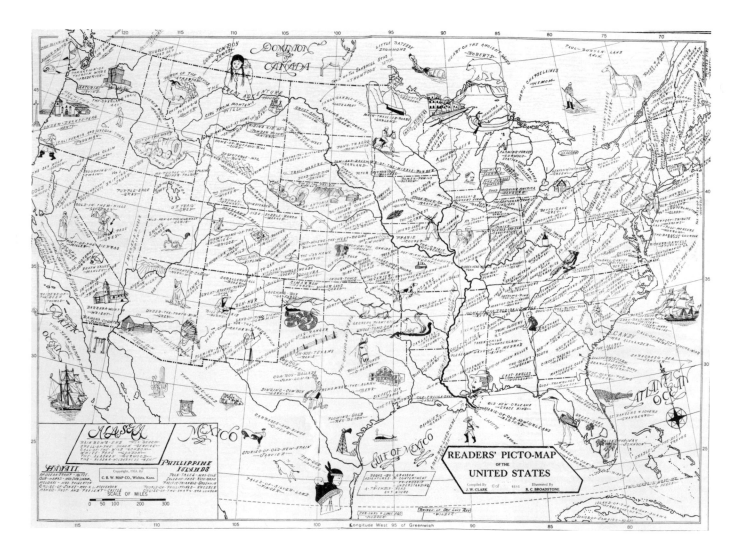

Readers' Picto-Map of the United States

J.W. Clark
Compiler

R.C. Broadstone
Illustrator

Wichita: C.B.W. Map Company, 1933
59 x 83 cm
Black and white
G3701 .E65. 1933 .C5

The *Readers' Picto-Map of the United States* shows the forty-eight contiguous states, southern Canada, and most of Mexico. Insets show Alaska, Hawaii, the Philippine Islands, Jamaica, and some other Caribbean Islands. Book titles and authors are given for each state or country. The map has images of Indians, explorers, ships, covered wagons, and various animals. Titles include classics such as the *Red Badge of Courage* (1905) by Stephen Crane, *House of the Seven Gables* (1851) by Nathaniel Hawthorne, *Walden* (1854) by Henry David Thoreau, and the works of James Fenimore Cooper. Books shown for Mexico and the Caribbean are by non-native authors, such as *The Bright Shawl* (1922) by Joseph Hergesheimer (1880–1954) and *Songs of Jamaica* (1912) by Claude McKay. African American authors James Weldon Johnson, Booker T. Washington, Paul Laurence Dunbar, and W. E. B. Dubois are represented. A number of the terms are misspelled; for example, *The Little Shepherd of Kingdom Come* (1903) by John Fox is spelled "Shepard," Carl Sandburg (1878–1967) is "Sanburg," and *Deliverance* (1904) by Ellen Glasgow is "Deliverence."

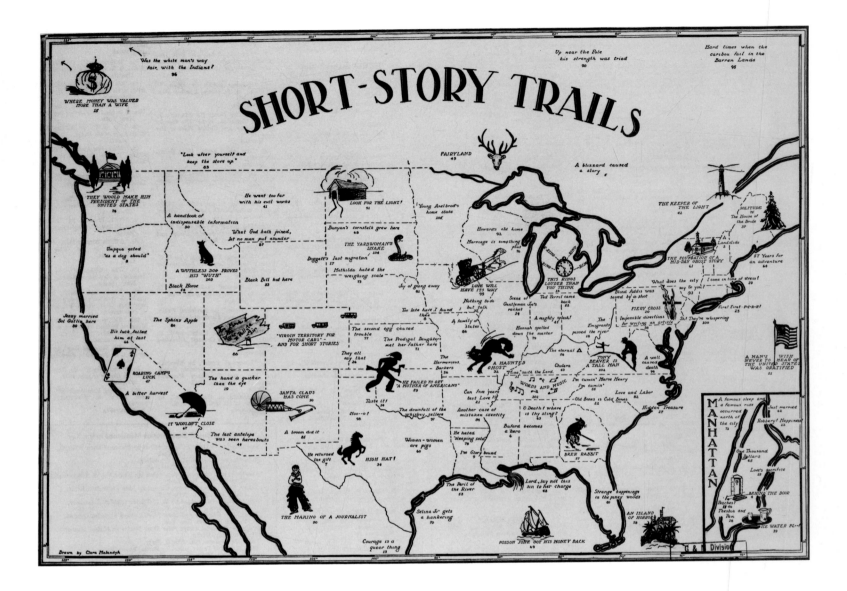

Short-Story Trails

CLARA MOLANDYK
Illustrator

Columbus, Ohio: 10-Cent Books, Inc., ca. 1929
26 x 35 cm
Color
Ethel M. Fair Collection 156

On an outline map of the forty-eight contiguous states, *Short-Story Trails* locates sites for 105 short stories. On the map an incident is described or a quote is given for each work. An inset for Manhattan lists works set there. The numbers on the map are keyed to an alphabetical list of stories on the verso of the map. The key also gives the state in which the story occurred and a publication in which each story may be found. Some works appear in the ten short-story collections listed in an inset. For stories printed in the years just preceding production of the map, magazine citations are included. Featured stories range from classics such as "The Gold Bug" (1843) by Edgar Allan Poe, "An Occurrence at Owl Creek Bridge" (1895) by Ambrose Bierce, and "The Luck of Roaring Camp" (1868) by Bret Harte to fiction that appeared in popular magazines such as *The Saturday Evening Post, Harper's,* and *The Atlantic Monthly* in the 1920s.

Sisters in Crime: Solving Mysteries Coast-to-Coast

BARBARA GREGORICH
Producer

JACQUELINE FEIDLER
Designer

ROBIN MICHAL KOONTZ
Illustrator

Raleigh, North Carolina: Sisters in Crime, 1991
51 x 77 cm
Color
G3701 .E65 1991 .S5

Courtesy of Sisters in Crime

The *Sisters in Crime* map was produced by the organization of that name, a group of female mystery writers and fans with chapters in many states. Founded in 1986 by Sara Paretsky and other writers, the group has as its major purpose raising the level of awareness of women's contributions to the mystery genre. At the center of the design is an outline map of the forty-eight contiguous states, with daggers marking the locations where mysteries written by group members are set. Lines lead from the daggers to forty-five ovals, in each of which a scene from a book is illustrated, along with a description of the incident and the work's title and author. Works depicted include *Death in a Tenured Position* (1981) by Amanda Cross (pseudonym of Carolyn Heilbrun), *The Christie Caper* (1991) by Carolyn G. Hart, *Vane Pursuit* (1989) by Charlotte MacLeod, and *Bum Steer* (1990) by Nancy Pickard.

Regions of the United States

"For all of our enormous geographic range, for all of our sectionalism, for all our interwoven breeds drawn from every part of the ethnic world, we are a nation, a new breed. Americans are much more American than they are Northerners, Southerners, Westerners, or Easterners."

John Steinbeck
Travels with Charley, 1962

APPALACHIA

Literary Map of Southern Appalachia

Parks Lanier, Jr., and
Grace Toney Edwards
Compilers

Radford, Virginia, Radford University, 1982
97 x 65 cm
Color
G3867 .A6 1982 .L3

Courtesy of Parks Lanier, Jr., and Grace Toney Edwards

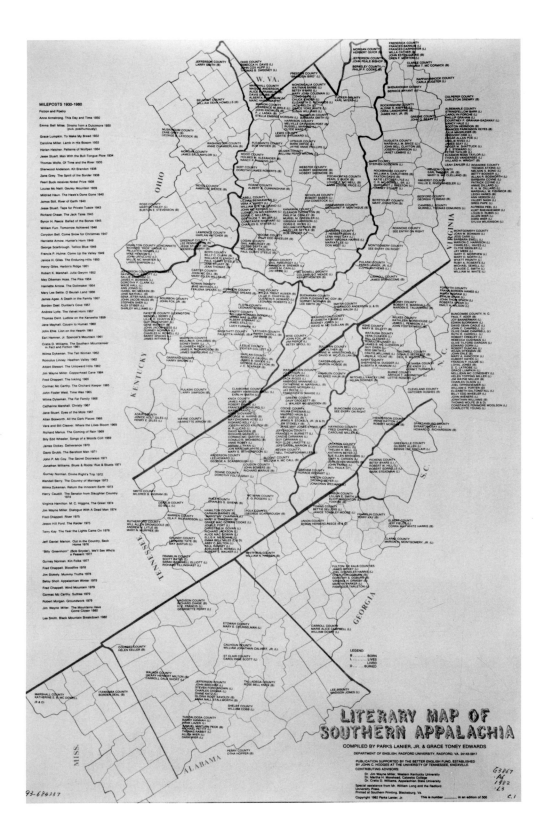

This literary map of southern Appalachia includes portions of ten states—Ohio, West Virginia, Virginia, North Carolina, Kentucky, Tennessee, South Carolina, Georgia, Alabama, and Mississippi. Literary figures are identified by county, and the nature of their relationship to the location is indicated by letters standing for born, lives/lived, and buried. In the margin is a chronologically arranged list of poetry and fiction entitled "Mileposts 1930–1980." Among the more than seventy works listed are Anne Armstrong's *This Day and Time* (1930); Jessie Stuart's *Taps for Private Tussie* (1943); Harriet Arnow's *The Dollmaker* (1954); James Dickey's *Deliverance* (1970); and Lee Smith's *Black Mountain Breakdown* (1980).

NEW ENGLAND

Literary-Pictorial New England

Henry J. Firley
Editor

Ernest Dudley Chase
Illustrator

Chicago: Denoyer-Geppert, 1942
137 x 105 cm (on four sheets)
Color
G3721 .E65 1942 .F5

*L*iterary-Pictorial New England shows literary sites in Maine, New Hampshire, Vermont, Massachusetts, Connecticut, and Rhode Island, some of the earliest states with an important literary tradition. Basically a general map of the area, the chart features superimposed images of ships, churches, colleges, schools, historic sites, and other presumably significant buildings, none of which is identified.

An inset map, "Literary Associations" (shown), depicts important sites in the area, as well as New York City and Long Island. The illustrations depict the homes of authors Ralph Waldo Emerson, Nathaniel Hawthorne, Louisa May Alcott, John Greenleaf Whittier, Sarah Orne Jewett, and Henry Wadsworth Longfellow. Beneath the names of towns and cities are listed writers who were born or lived there or the titles of works they wrote or set there.

Other inset maps show Boston and vicinity, central Boston, and Cambridge and vicinity. Captions on these maps note homes of writers and historic figures, cemeteries where they are buried, and places identified with their works.

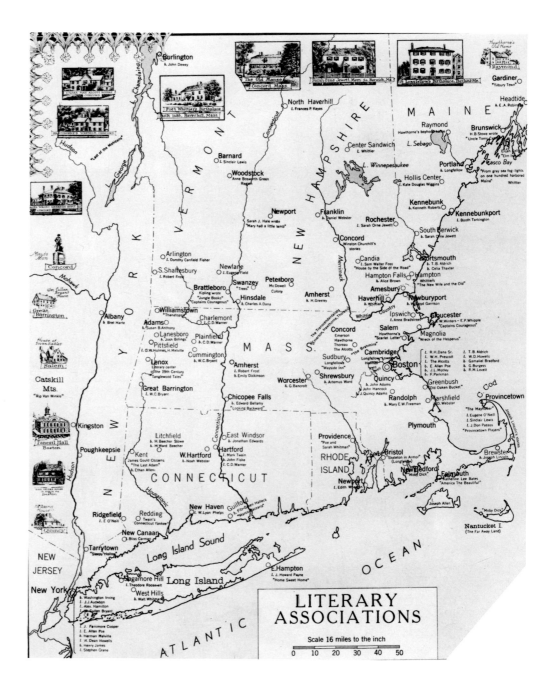

The accompanying "New England Literature Index" gives latitude and longitude for a number of places, the literary associations of which are not given. It also includes keys to the inset maps that list the sites shown on them. The map is one of the earliest that editor Henry J. Firley produced for Denoyer-Geppert.

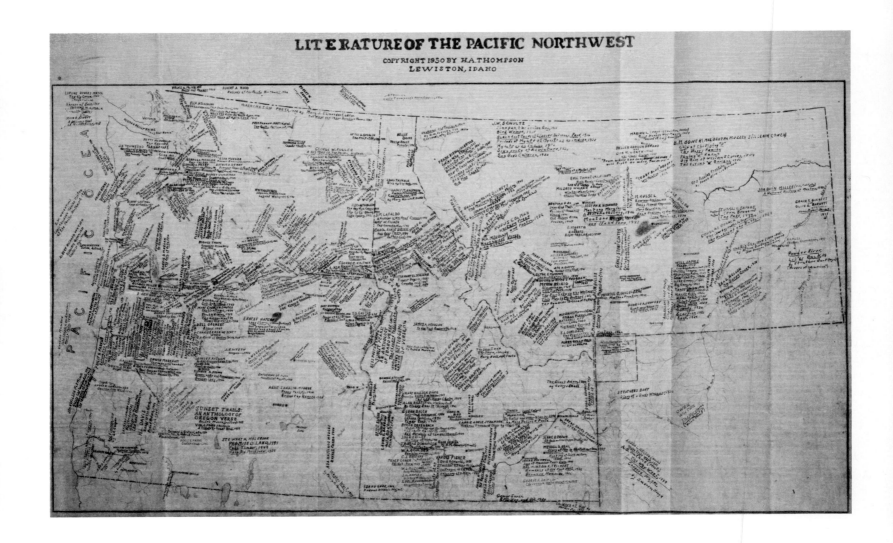

PACIFIC NORTHWEST

Literature of the Pacific Northwest

HARRY ALONZO THOMPSON
Compiler

Lewiston, Idaho: H.A. Thompson, 1950
93 x 157 cm
Black and white
G4241 .E65 1950 .T5

A photostat of a hand-drawn map, *Literature of the Pacific Northwest* shows authors and titles of books associated with Washington, Oregon, Idaho, Montana, and the northwest corner of Wyoming. The map is comprehensive in its coverage of the literary history of the Pacific Northwest from the early 1800s through 1949. Hundreds of authors, both prominent and obscure, are listed along with the titles of their most famous works and, in most instances, the publication dates of the works. Historical figures and a number of local history books are also listed. Authors include Edwin Markham and Joaquin Miller for Oregon, Robert Cantwell and Archie Binns for Washington, Vardis Fisher and Mary Hallock Foote for Idaho, Will James and A[lfred] B[ertram] Guthrie for Montana, and Struthers Burt and Owen Wister for Wyoming. Because fewer authors are given for Wyoming than for the other states, the map may be unfinished. It is not known if the map was ever commercially produced.

SOUTH

The Literary Map of the American South

Molly Maguire
Designer

Linda Ayriss
Illustrator

Los Angeles: Aaron Blake, 1988
53 x 70 cm
Color
G3866 .E65 1988 .A2

Courtesy of Molly Maguire and Aaron Silverman

Intended as an overview of 200 years of southern writing, *The Literary Map of the American South* highlights Virginia, West Virginia, North Carolina, South Carolina, Georgia, Alabama, Arkansas, Kentucky, Mississippi, and Florida. Authors' homes and settings of books indicated on the map are numbered to a key with fuller explanations. Also pictured are important elements of southern literature and culture such as a bust of William Faulkner; a photograph of Martin Luther King, Jr.; the house used as the model for Tara, home of Scarlett O'Hara in *Gone with the Wind* (1936) by Margaret Mitchell; and images of authors Marjorie Kinnan Rawlings, Robert Penn Warren, and Mark Twain. Research and design for the map were performed by Molly Maguire, who produced a series of literary maps in the 1980s.

The South through Its Literature

Nashville: George Peabody College for
   Teachers, 1941
53 x 80 cm
Color
G3866 .E65 1941 .G4

This outline map of thirteen southern states—Virginia, Kentucky, Tennessee, North Carolina, South Carolina, Georgia, Florida, Alabama, Louisiana, Mississippi, Arkansas, Oklahoma, and Texas—lists approximately three hundred literary works and authors. The works are located in the state with which the work or author is most closely identified. Most of the works on the map itself are literary, but the left margin features a list of historical and sociological studies of the South, such as *I'll Take My Stand* (1930) by a group of twelve "Agrarian" writers, including Robert Penn Warren, Donald Davidson, Allen Tate, and John Crowe Ransom; W[ilbur] J[oseph] Cash's *The Mind of the South* (1941); and W[illiam] E[dward] B[urghardt] Du Bois's *Black Folk, Then and Now* (1939). The border of the map contains illustrations suggestive of the South, for example, pine, cotton, tobacco, and magnolia plants, oil wells, plantation houses, and alligators.

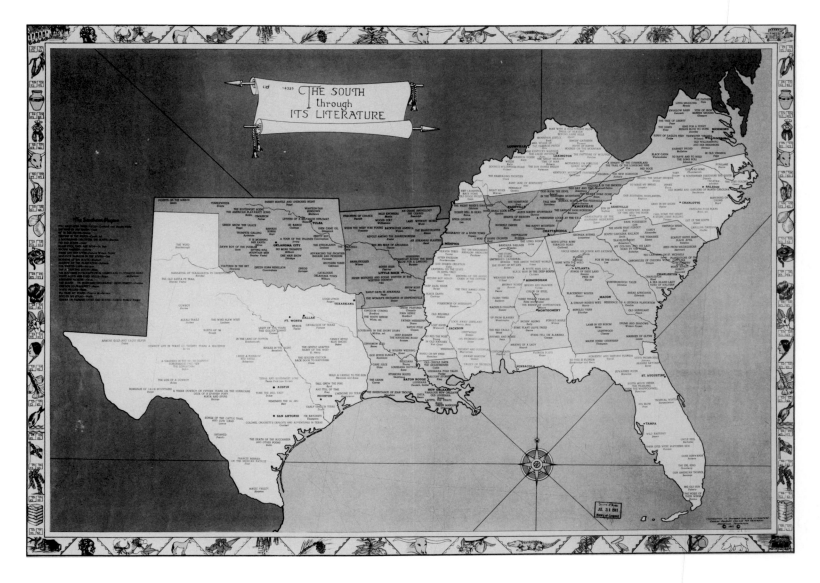

SOUTHWEST

[*Literary Map of the American Southwest*]

Fanita Lanier
Illustrator

Saturday Review of Literature, May 16, 1942,
    pp. 23–24
30 x 44 cm
Color
Ethel M. Fair Collection 149

This literary map of the American Southwest was part of a special *Saturday Review of Literature* issue of May 16, 1942, titled "The Southwest—Inventory and Sampling." One of a series on each region of the United States, the issue featured short stories and articles, including "The Southwest in Fiction," which discusses some of the authors named on the map. The map by Dallas artist Fanita Lanier shows New Mexico, Texas, and Oklahoma, as well as parts of Arizona, Utah, Colorado, Kansas, Missouri, Arkansas, Louisiana, and Mexico. The map displays titles of books near the locations where they were set. Featured works include Conrad Richter's *The Sea of Grass* (1937), Willa Cather's *Death Comes for the Archbishop* (1927), Edna Ferber's *Cimarron* (1930), and Katherine Anne Porter's *Pale Horse, Pale Rider* (1939). The left margin gives a brief literary history of the region from Indian tales through the Spanish captains to the Anglo settlers of the 1800s. The right margin lists thirty-four prominent writers of the era between World War I and World War II, among them Mary Austin, Willa Cather, J. Frank Dobie, Edna Ferber, Marquis James, and Conrad Richter. Illustrations depict a Hopi woman, cowboys, wagon trains, and other Western icons.

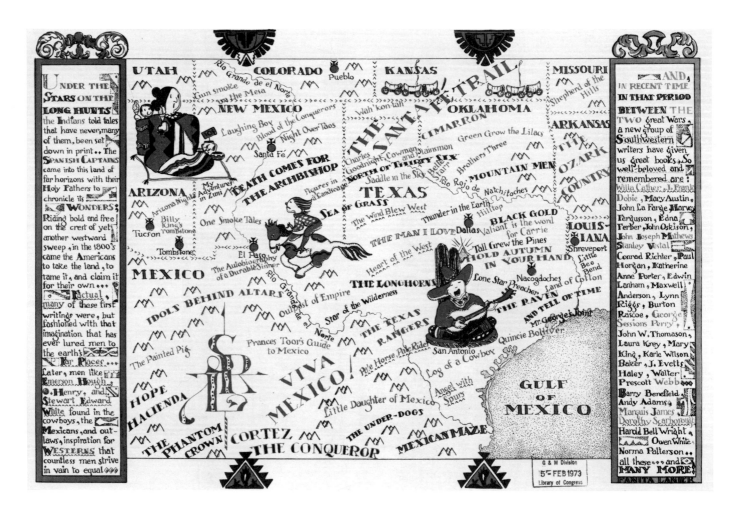

Individual States and Cities

"The United States themselves are essentially the greatest poem...."

Walt Whitman,
Preface to Leaves of Grass, *First Edition, 1855*

ALABAMA

Literary Map of Alabama

KURT LANG
Compiler

[Montgomery?]: Alabama Library
    Association, 1969
82 x 56 cm
Color
G3971 .E65 1969 .L3

Prepared for the 150th anniversary of
the founding of Alabama in 1891,
this map depicts historical sites and
characters as well as selected books and
authors. A scroll in the right margin lists
nineteenth- and twentieth-century
authors; Alabama-born authors are
marked with an asterisk. Among the
authors included are Johnson Jones
Hooper, author of *Adventures of Captain
Simon Suggs*; Sidney Lanier, who wrote
poetry while living in Montgomery and
Prattville; Booker T. Washington, author
of *Up from Slavery* (1901); Tuscumbia
native Helen Keller, author of *The Story
of My Life* (1902); and Monroeville native Harper Lee, author of the Pulitzer
Prize-winning *To Kill a Mockingbird*
(1960).

ALASKA

Alaska's Literary Map

WENDY WITHROW
Compiler

SUSAN PECK
Designer and Illustrator

Anchorage: Alaska Center for the Book, 1994
58 x 76 cm
Color
G4371 .E65 1994 .W5

*A*laska's Literary Map was produced by the state's Center for the Book and sponsored in part by the Alaska Humanities Forum and the National Endowment for the Humanities. It was published as part of the spring 1994 "Writers Rendezvous" at the Anchorage Museum of Art and History, a festival of awards, readings by authors, and seminars and panels celebrating Alaska's literature and literacy. For the most part, the map lists titles of books about Alaska by Alaskans next to the locations with which they are associated. (A few exceptions are made for notable books set in Alaska, for example, Jack London's 1903 novel *The Call of the Wild*.) A note indicates that future editions of the map will include work written by Alaskans on any subject and by non-natives about Alaska. Works noted on the map include *News from the Glacier* (1982) by former Alaska poet laureate John Haines, *A Fatal Thaw* (1993) by Dana Stabenow, *Arctic Wild* (1973) by Lois Crisler, *Alaska Stories* (1984) by John Mitchell, and *Travels in Alaska* (1915) by John Muir. The map is accompanied by a bibliography that gives author, publisher, call numbers, Alaska library system location, and brief descriptions of books featured on the map.

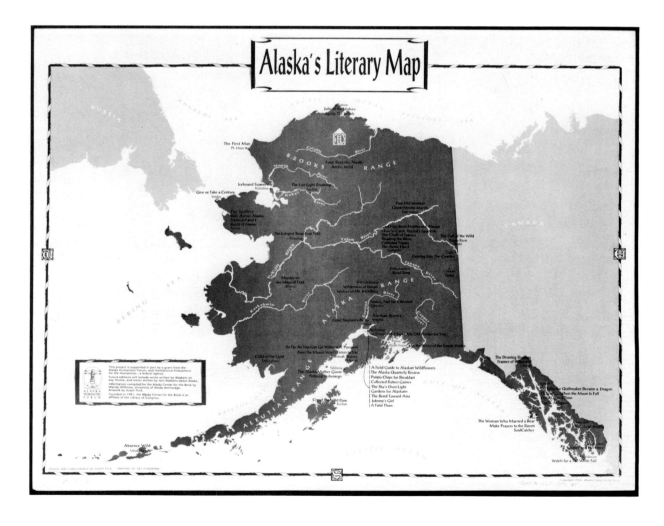

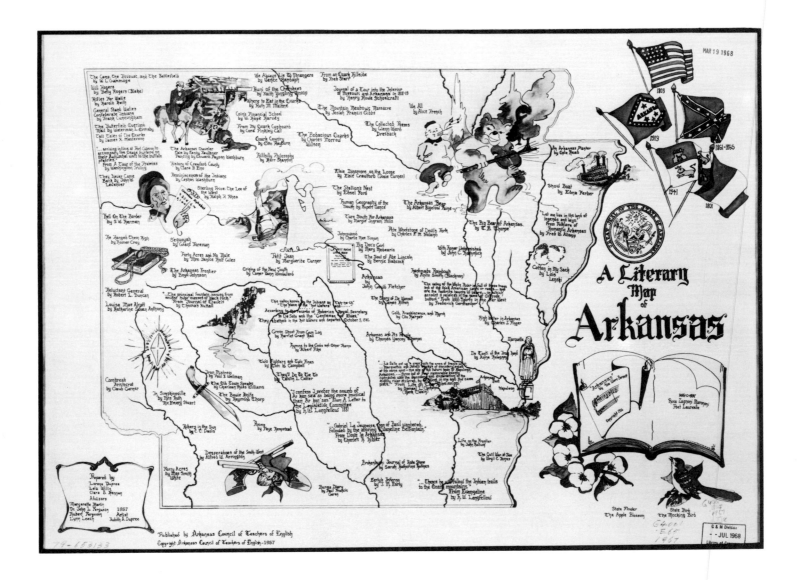

ARKANSAS

A Literary Map of Arkansas

JUDITH DuPREE
Illustrator

Arkansas Council of Teachers of English, 1967
40 x 56 cm
Color
G4001 .E65 1967 .D8

*Courtesy of the Arkansas Council of
Teachers of English and Language Arts*

A Literary Map of Arkansas features books by Arkansas authors such as Opie Read's *An Arkansas Planter* (1896) and Albert Bigelow Paine's *The Arkansaw Bear* (1898). Along with illustrations from works of Arkansas writers, the map includes quotes about Arkansas by out-of-state writers Mark Twain and Henry Wadsworth Longfellow. This map also includes such non-literary elements as state flags and the state seal, song, and bird. A slightly revised and updated version of the map (G4001 .E65 1976 .D8) was produced in 1976.

The Reader's Map of Arkansas

C.D. Wright
Author

Peter Armitage
Designer

Samuel Truitt
Researcher

Fayetteville, Arkansas: University of
Arkansas Press, 1994
42 x 47 cm
Color
G4001 .E65 1994 .W7

Courtesy of C. D. Wright

*T*he Reader's Map of Arkansas was produced by Arkansas native C. D. Wright, a professor at Brown University, in conjunction with *The Lost Roads Project: A Walk-in Book of Arkansas.* This project featured excerpts from the works of twenty-one post-World War II Arkansas writers and photographs appropriate to their work in an exhibition that toured the state for two years. Modeled on Works Project Administration (WPA) posters of the 1930s, the map shows Arkansas's principal towns and cities at its center. On the side margins are double columns alphabetically listing 150 authors along with their life dates, place of birth, genre of work, and up to three titles. The map includes native and adopted writers and is primarily concerned with those for whom creative and aesthetic values are paramount. It does, however, list some biographers, folklorists, journalists, historians, and other writers of nonfiction. Noted writers who spent time in Arkansas include Maya Angelou, Ellen Gilchrist, Albert Pike, Opie Read, Henry Rowe Schoolcraft, Octave Thanet, and Richard Wright.

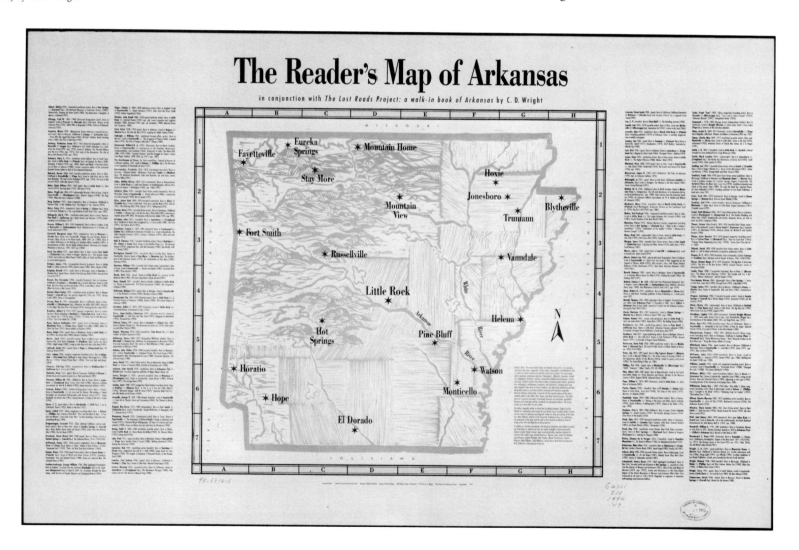

CALIFORNIA

California Literary Map

San Diego: California Association of
    Teachers of English
91 x 62 cm
Black and white
G4361 .E65 1995 .C3

Commissioned by the California
Association of Teachers of English,
the *California Literary Map* features 100
authors of fiction, nonfiction, poetry,
and drama who have made significant
contributions to the literary heritage of
the state. Authors' names are given near
the town associated with them or their
work. Authors pictured include Bret
Harte, John Steinbeck, Allen Ginsburg,
Jack Kerouac, Wallace Stegner, Joan
Didion, Dashiell Hammett, Ray Bradbury, Maxine Hong Kingston, Amy Tan,
and Alice Walker. Lists of authors are
given for Los Angeles, the San Francisco
Bay Area, Oakland, Berkeley, and San
Jose. The map also illustrates natural
and historic sites such as Yosemite and
Redwood national parks, Death Valley,
and the California State Capitol. The
text invites viewers to add their home
towns and favorite authors to the map.

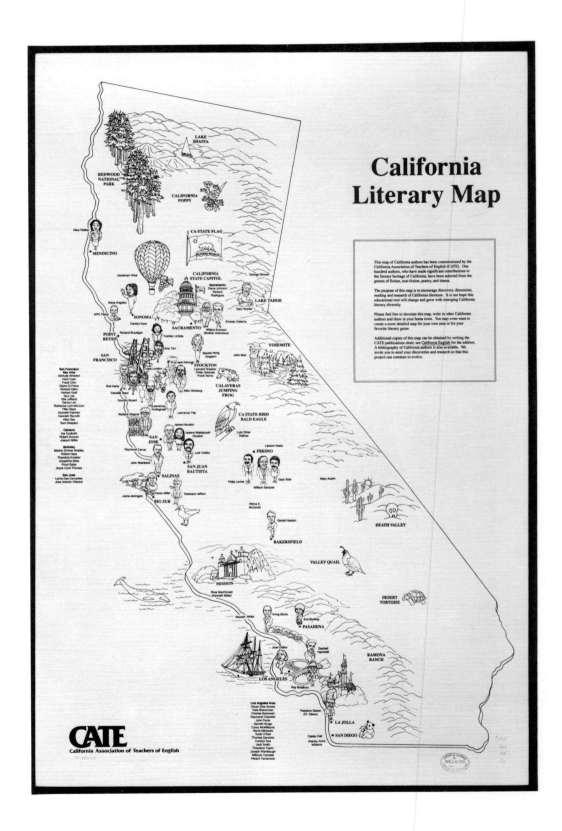

104

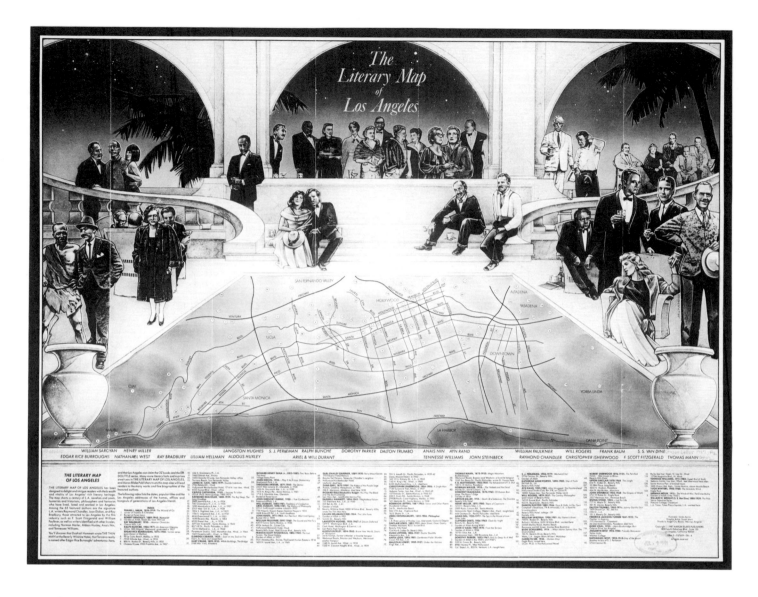

The Literary Map of Los Angeles

MOLLY MAGUIRE
Designer

LINDA AYRISS
Illustrator

Los Angeles: Aaron Blake, 1987
52 x 68 cm
Color
G4364 .L8E65 1987 .A2

Courtesy of Molly Maguire and Aaron Silverman

*T*he Literary Map of Los Angeles charts the homes, offices, and haunts of sixty-five novelists, poets, humorists, and historians who have lived and worked in Los Angeles. The map shows a glamorous Hollywood party, held around a swimming pool that contains street maps of the area, keyed by number to lists below. Among the Los Angeles authors portrayed around the pool are Raymond Chandler, Joan Didion, Dashiell Hammett, and Ray Bradbury. Also shown are some of the many authors attracted to the area by the film industry, for instance, F. Scott Fitzgerald, William Faulkner, and Aldous Huxley. Research and design for the map were performed by Molly Maguire, who produced a series of literary maps in the 1980s.

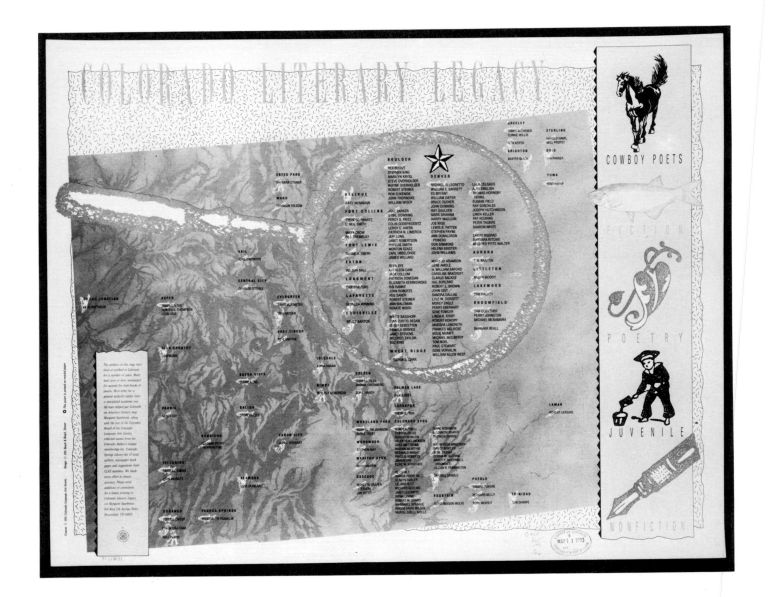

COLORADO

Colorado Literary Legacy

[Denver?]: Colorado Language
 Arts Society, 1991
43 x 47 cm
Color
G4311 .E65 1991 .C6

Courtesy of the Colorado Language Arts Society

The *Colorado Literary Legacy* map identifies authors who have lived or worked in the state and have written for a general audience. Grouped under place names, the authors are marked by symbols representing the types of works they produce. The symbols are: a horse for a group of writers known as the "Cowboy Poets," a fish for writers of fiction, a leaf for poets, a fountain pen for nonfiction writers, and a child for those who write for juveniles. Noted authors with Colorado connections include Damon Runyan, Helen Hunt Jackson, Louis L'Amour, and Leon Uris.

FLORIDA

Florida in Literature

VINCENT MCGUIRE
Compiler

MARTHA BALLARD CODY
Illustrator

Gainesville: V. McGuire, 1956
96 x 71 cm
Green and white
G3931 .E65 1956 .M2

The numerous illustrations on *Florida in Literature* are keyed to a list giving locations associated with 158 literary works published between 1848 and 1954. The many works geared toward young people are indicated by an asterisk. Books identified on the maps include Ernest Hemingway's *To Have and Have Not* (1937), set in the Florida Keys; Zora Neale Hurston's *Their Eyes Were Watching God* (1934) and *Jonah's Vine* (1934), set in Sanford and Maitland, respectively; and Marjorie Kinnan Rawlings's *The Yearling* (1938), set near the St. Johns River. This map is the first in a series of literary maps of Florida produced by Dr. Vincent McGuire, College of Education, University of Florida. Revised versions were produced in 1961 (G3931 .E65 1961 .M2) and 1966 (G3931 .E65 1966 .M2).

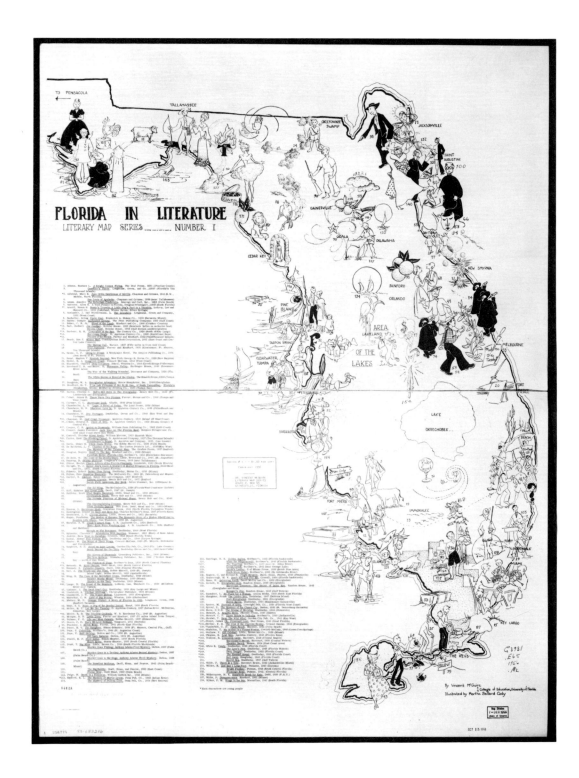

Florida Literary Map, 1994

BERNADINE CLARK ET AL.
Editors

Fort Lauderdale: Florida Center for the
  Book, 1994
42 x 57 cm
Color
G3931 .E65 1994 .F5

*Courtesy of the Florida Center for the Book at
Broward County Library, Fort Lauderdale*

The front of the *Florida Literary Map, 1994* features a colorful map of the state showing its main regions and chief cities. Along the top and bottom margins of the map are images of twenty Florida authors, among them John James Audubon, Marjorie Stoneman Douglas, Madeleine L'Engle, Wallace Stevens, Tennessee Williams, and Richard Wilbur. Some of these authors and others are listed under the categories "Florida Artists Hall of Fame," "Literary Legends," and "Literary Landmarks: Locations Marked with Plaques." "A Gazetteer of Florida Prize-Winning Authors" lists writers who have won major literary prizes such as the Pulitzer Prize, the National Book Award, and the Newberry Prize. On the back of the map an essay, "Paradise for the Written Word: 400 Years of Literary History in Florida" by Kevin McCarthy, gives an overview of Florida's literary heritage. Images of additional authors who lived in Florida such as Zora Neale Hurston, Ernest Hemingway, Marjorie Kinnan Rawlings, and Elizabeth Bishop and of book-related events such as the Miami Book Fair International are interspersed with the text. The map was produced by the Florida Center for the Book, with additional funding from the Florida Humanities Council, the State of Florida Division of Cultural Affairs, and the Lila Wallace-Reader's Digest Fund.

Illustration and design by Mary Porter

Copyright © 1986 by The Georgia Council of Teachers of English
Original concept by Betty Ostrander

GEORGIA

Georgia's Literary Heritage

MARY PORTER
Illustrator and Designer

Athens, Georgia: Georgia Council of
    Teachers of English, 1986
48 x 39 cm
Black and white
G3921 .E65 1986 .G4

Produced by the Georgia Council of Teachers of English, *Georgia's Literary Heritage* records the state's place in the literary world. Names of Georgia-born authors are placed near their birth-places and those of non-native authors near their primary residences. Illustrations suggest the most noted works of some of the writers or dominant themes in their books. Georgia authors featured include poet Sidney Lanier, author of "The Marshes of Glynn"; Conrad Aiken, who won the Pulitzer Prize for *Selected Poems*; Erskine Caldwell, author of *Tobacco Road* (1932) and more than sixty other novels; Carson McCullers, author of *The Heart Is a Lonely Hunter* (1940); James Dickey, who wrote *Deliverance* (1970); short-story writer Flannery O'Connor, author of "A Good Man Is Hard to Find"; and Alice Walker, who won the Pulitzer Prize for *The Color Purple* (1982). The map is accompanied by a booklet that gives biographical information and publishing histories for these and many other Georgia authors.

IDAHO

Idaho by the Book

Tom Trusky and Megan Laxalt
Designers

Boise: Idaho Center for the Book and
   Idaho Council of English Teachers, 1996
37 x 25 cm
Black and white
G4271 .E65 1996 .I3

Idaho by the Book is in the shape of a "tetratetraflexagon," i.e., a specially folded design in which users flex the maps to view three different pages. The pages cover the periods "Pioneers," 1839–1899; "Statehood," 1890–1959; and "Contemporary," 1960–. The map of Oregon, Washington, and Idaho illustrated is from the "Pioneers" section. According to text on the back of the map, authors listed include producers of genres as diverse as poetry, "Christian Romance," children's literature, and "Cyberpunk sagas." Authors given special prominence must have published a minimum of two books, preferably with nationally or internationally recognized publishers. Ernest Hemingway, Edgar Rice Burroughs, and Vardis Fisher are among the authors on the map because they spent significant parts of their adult lives in Idaho; those born in the state, whose names are accentuated in boxed, white-on-black type, include Fisher, Ezra Pound, and Richard M. McKenna. In addition to author information, the maps highlight Idaho's presses, printers, publishers, bookstores, and libraries. Further information is provided on the envelope that encloses the main map.

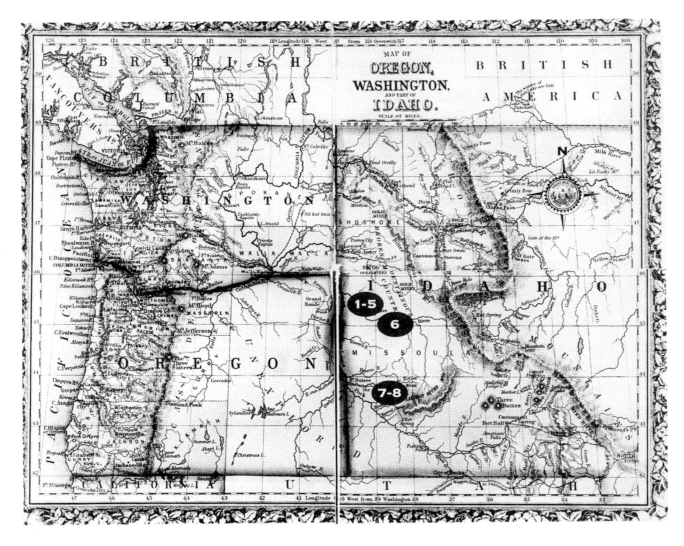

ILLINOIS

Illinois Authors

ELLEN BURKHART, LOUISE LANE,
    AND J. N. HOOK
Compilers

Urbana: Illinois Association of Teachers
    of English, 1952
86 x 56 cm
Color
G4101 .E65 1952 .B8

Courtesy of the Illinois Association of Teachers of English

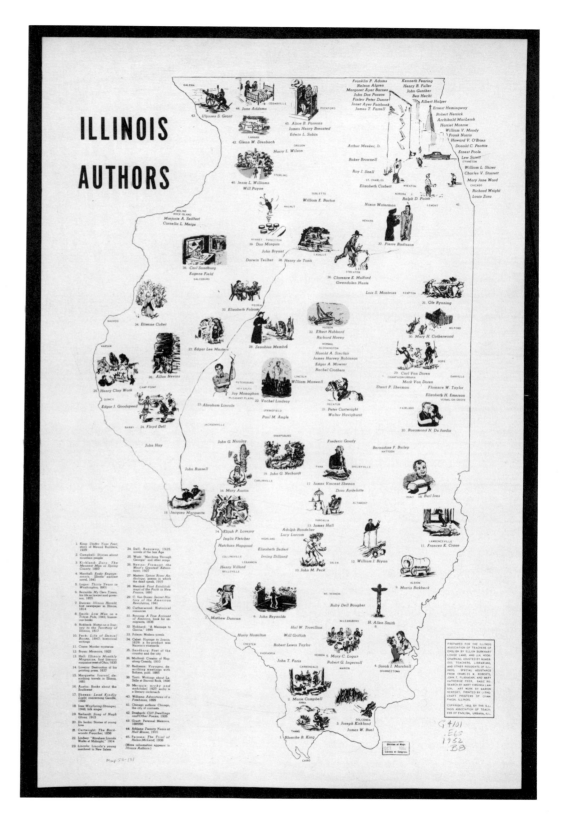

More than 120 noteworthy figures are listed on the colorful *Illinois Authors* map. Those listed include novelists, journalists, poets, song writers, biographers, essayists, historians, and scholars. Specific works of forty-five authors, accompanied by illustrations, are identified by name and publication date, placed near the home of the author. Some of the most noted authors depicted are John Dos Passos, Ernest Hemingway, Richard Wright, Carl Sandburg, and Allan Nevins. Some figures mentioned are famous for their accomplishments in other than literary fields—for example, Abraham Lincoln (1809–1865), Ulysses S. Grant (1822–1885), William Jennings Bryan (1850–1925), and John Hay (1838–1905).

Illinois Authors

Judie Anderson, Arn Arnam,
 and Tom Heinz
Illustrators

Chicago: Chicago Tribune Educational
 Services, 1987
79 x 60 cm
Color *(See color section.)*
G4101. E65 1987 .A5

The central, most prominent portion of *Illinois Writers* is a typical state map showing counties, major cities, and important buildings such as the state capitol and the campus of the University of Illinois at Champaign-Urbana. Writers are listed in boxes to the sides of the map by locality, such as Northern Illinois, Western Illinois, Central Illinois, and Chicago. Pictured at the bottom border is a group of famous authors associated with the state. Included are Nelson Algren, who lived in Chicago for many years and used it as the setting of his novel *The Man with the Golden Arm* (1949); Edna Ferber, who worked for the Chicago *Tribune* and wrote her Pulitzer Prize-winning novel *So Big* (1924) while living in the city; Lorraine Hansberry, born in Chicago, the setting of her play *A Raisin in the Sun* (1959); Ernest Hemingway, who was born in Oak Park and worked in Chicago; Edgar Lee Masters, Petersburg-born author of the *Spoon River Anthology* (1941); and Carl Sandburg, from Galesburg, who wrote *Chicago Poems* (1916) during his residence in that city. The map was a project of the Illinois Center for the Book.

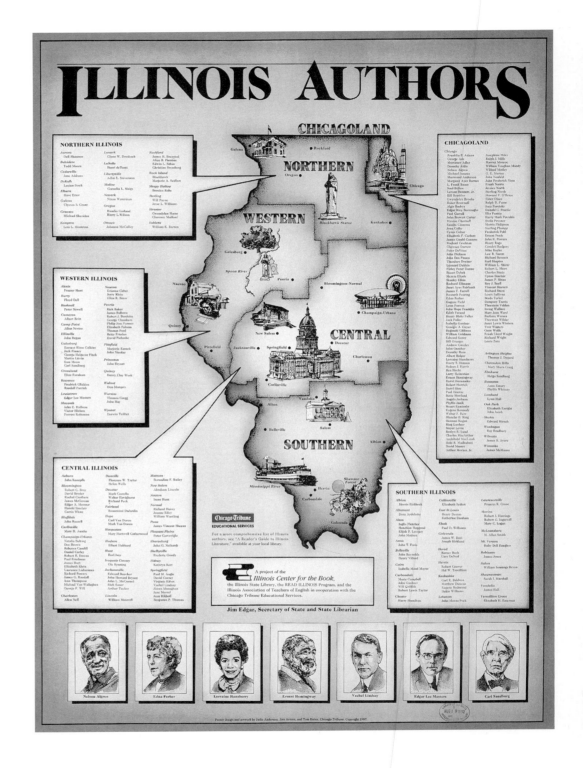

INDIANA

A Literary Map of Indiana

WARREN CASEY
Illustrator

Indianapolis: Indiana Council of Teachers
of English and the Indiana College
English Association, 1956
70 x 48 cm
Color
G4091 .E65 1956 .I5

Against an outline drawing of the state, *A Literary Map of Indiana* displays the names of selected authors, the titles of books, and illustrations of authors, book covers, and scenes from works. Works illustrated include Lew Wallace's *Ben Hur* (1880), "Hoosier Poet" James Whitcomb Riley's *The Old Swimmin'-Hole and 'Leven More Poems* (1883), Booth Tarkington's *Penrod* (1914), and Lloyd C. Douglas's *The Robe* (1942). Other vignettes include the cover of Meredith Nicholson's *House of a Thousand Candles* (1905); the birthplace of George Ade, author of *Fables in Slang* (1900); and images of poets Alice and Phoebe Cary. In the side margins are lists of "Other Hoosier Writers" and "Other Writers for Younger People," as well as images of Lew Wallace's study in Crawfordsville and the Indianapolis home of James Whitcomb Riley. At the bottom of the map is "A Hoosier Bookshelf," showing the spines of twenty-one books by Indiana authors. The map also includes the state seal, flag, tree, and bird.

A Literary Map of Indiana

EDWARD M. BLACKWELL
Illustrator

[Terre Haute]: Indiana Council of
    Teachers of English, 1974
71 x 50 cm
Color
G4091 .E65 1974 .B6

Against an outline drawing of the
state, *A Literary Map of Indiana* displays the names of selected authors, the
title of one of the author's books, and a
vignette showing a scene from the work.
Images of Meredith Nicholson, author
of *House of a Thousand Candles* (1905):
George Ade, author of *Fables in Slang*
(1900); Booth Tarkington, author of *The
Magnificent Ambersons* (1918) and *Penrod* (1914); and "Hoosier Poet" James
Whitcomb Riley, author of *The Old
Swimmin'-Hole and 'Leven More Poems*
(1883) appear at left. Beneath them are
lists of "Other Writers" and "Writers for
Young People." The map also includes
the state seal, flag, and bird.

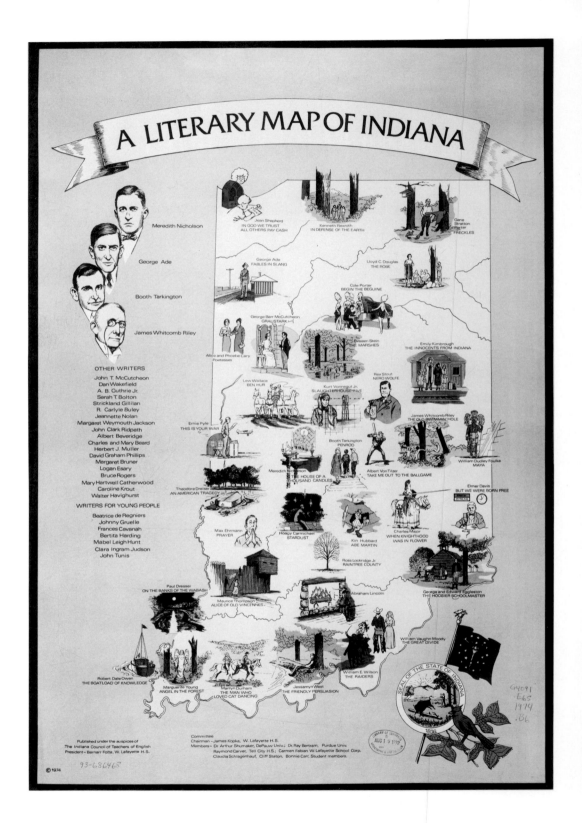

IOWA

Historical and Literary Map of Iowa

Vira E. Morgan
Illustrator

Davenport: Davenport Public Library, 1934
43 x 71 cm
Color
G4151 .S1 1934 .M6

The *Historical and Literary Map of Iowa* emphasizes both aspects of its title. Historic sites such as the path taken by explorer of the West Zebulon Pike (1779–1813) in 1805–1806; the underground railroad route; the trail the Mormons followed to Utah in 1847; and the state's first stage coach and railroad routes are listed along with sites connected with authors. The map features images of Native Americans Black Hawk (1767–1838)—leader of an unsuccessful war against white expansion into his tribe's territory, who died on a reservation in Iowa—and Keokuk (1780–1848)—an ally of the American cause during the War of 1812. Among writers featured on the map are Hamlin Garland, who recounted his experiences growing up near Osage in *Boy Life on the Prairie* (1899); Bess Streeter Aldrich, whose novel *Song of Years* (1939) is set in a town resembling her birthplace, Cedar Falls; novelist and short-story writer Ruth Suckow, born in Hawarden and author of *Iowa Interiors* (1962); Carl Van Vechten, born in Cedar Rapids, the probable setting of his novel *The Tatooed Countess* (1924); Susan Glaspell, a Davenport native who won the Pulitzer Prize in 1930 for her novel *Alison's House*; and Edna Ferber, whose autobiographical books *A Peculiar Treasure* (1939) and *A Kind of Magic* (1963) recount the short period of her childhood she spent in Ottumwa.

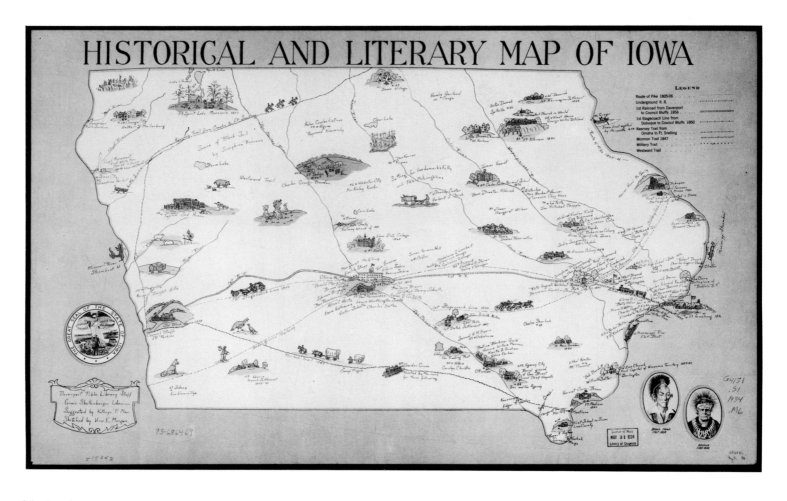

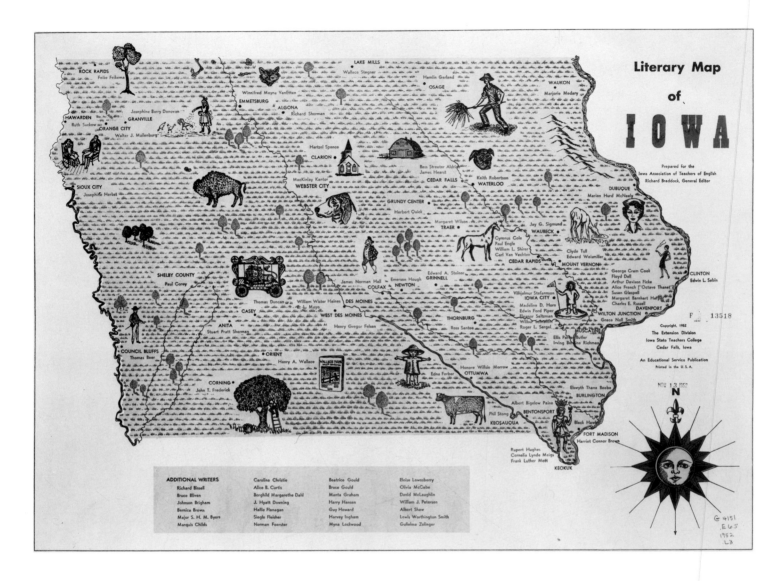

Literary Map of Iowa

Harriet Larkin
Designer

Cedar Falls, Iowa: Iowa State Teachers
   College, 1952
44 x 59 cm
Color
G4151 .E65 1952 .L3

Mↄre than ninety prominent authors are recorded on the *Literary Map of Iowa* produced by the Iowa Association of Teachers of English. Authors featured on the map are listed near places associated with them or their works. For example, Wallace Stegner, born in Lake Mills, set his novella *Remembering Laughter* (1937) in Iowa; MacKinlay Kantor, a native of Webster City, wrote for the town newspaper as a young man; Hamlin Garland recounted his experiences growing up near Osage in *Boy Life on the Prairie* (1899); and Edna Ferber described her childhood days in Ottumwa in *A Peculiar Treasure* (1939) and *A Kind of Magic* (1963). Some works are illustrated without explanatory captions. Additional writers are listed in alphabetical order in the map's bottom margin.

KANSAS

Centennial Literary Map of Kansas, 1861–1961

BEN W. FUSON
Editor

LEONA CRAFT CREAGER
Designer

Topeka: Kansas Association of Teachers of
    English, 1961
51 x 70 cm
Color
G4201 .E65 1961 .F8

The cultural history of the state of Kansas from 1854 to the 100th anniversary of its statehood in 1961 is featured on the *Centennial Literary Map of Kansas.* One hundred noteworthy names, each accompanied by a significant book title and date, appear on this map, placed, where possible, near the writers' residences, birthplaces, or the locales associated with their work. Thirty-five illustrations portray the works or careers of especially noteworthy personalities claimed by Kansas. Some, such as Wyatt Earp (1848–1929) and John Brown (1810–1882), although not primarily writers, are identified with the state through their lives and exploits; the others are noted authors, including Edgar Lee Masters, Gwendolyn Brooks, William Inge, and L. Frank Baum. An additional sixty-five names and book titles of novelists, poets, dramatists, essayists, biographers, journalistic commentators, and scholars connected with Kansas literature also appear. The accompanying guide, *Centennial Bibliography of Kansas Literature* (Z1285 .F87), supplies additional information about each figure mentioned on the map. The book also contains twenty-one lists relating to Kansas literature, such as "Kansas Firsts in Literary History" and "A Reference Bibliography for Kansas Literature."

KENTUCKY

Literary Map of Kentucky

Charles T. Wade
Illustrator

[Paducah, Kentucky]: Kentucky
   Library Association, 1959
38 x 71 cm
Black and White
G 3951 .E65 1959 .W3

The *Literary Map of Kentucky* identifies authors and works associated with the state as well as historical figures such as Abraham Lincoln and Henry Clay. The fifty-seven authors, works, and characters identified are keyed to numbered illustrations on the map. Authors featured include Harriet Arnow, Robert Penn Warren, Jesse Stuart, and James Still. An exact duplicate of the map was issued in 1970 (G3951 .E65 1970 .E7).

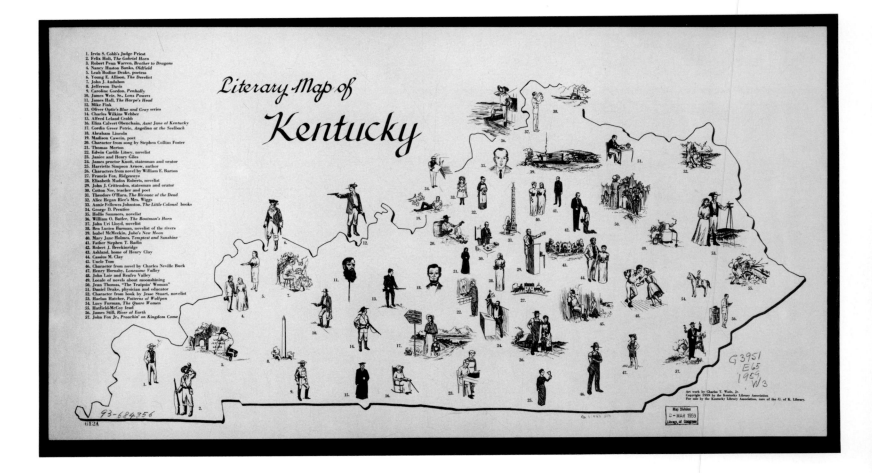

LOUISIANA

Louisiana Literature

MATTHEW J. ARMAND
Designer

Baton Rouge: Louisiana Library Association
and the Louisiana Council of Teachers
of English, 1992
92 x 61 cm
Color
G4011 .E65 1992 .A7

*Courtesy of the Louisiana Library Association and
the Louisiana Council of Teachers of English*

The background of *Louisiana Literature* is a manuscript page from the diary of Sarah Morgan Dawson, who recorded her experiences as a young woman living in Baton Rouge during the Civil War. Superimposed on the background are photographs of Louisiana writers, including Dawson, Kate Chopin, Ernest J. Gaines, Shirley Ann Grau, Robert Penn Warren, Walker Percy, John William Corrington, Arna Wendell Bontemps, Lyle Saxson, Grace King, John Kennedy O'Toole, and George Washington Cable. A list at the bottom of the map features these authors as well as forty other Louisiana writers and their principal works.

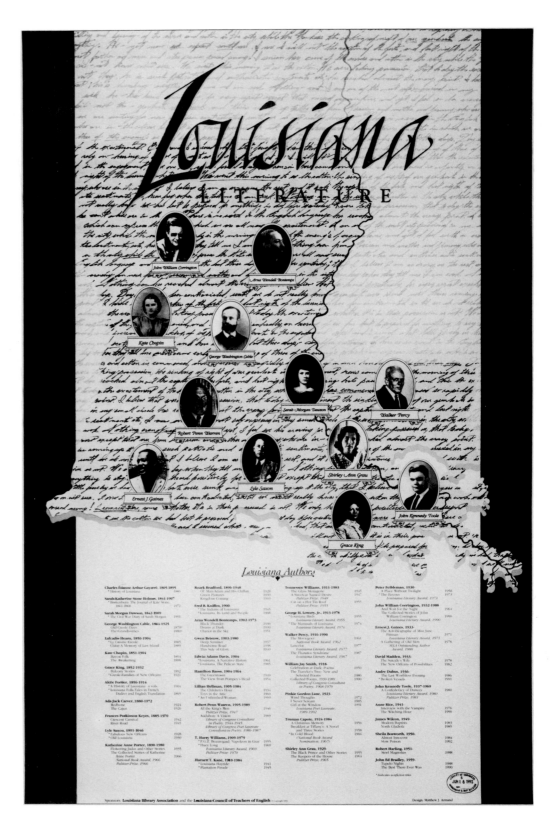

MAINE

Maine Writers

RUTH RHOADS LEPPER
Mapmaker

Maine Council of Teachers of English, 1977
56 x 41 cm
Color
G3731 .E65 1977 .L4

Copyright© 1981, Maine Council for English Language Arts. Used by permission

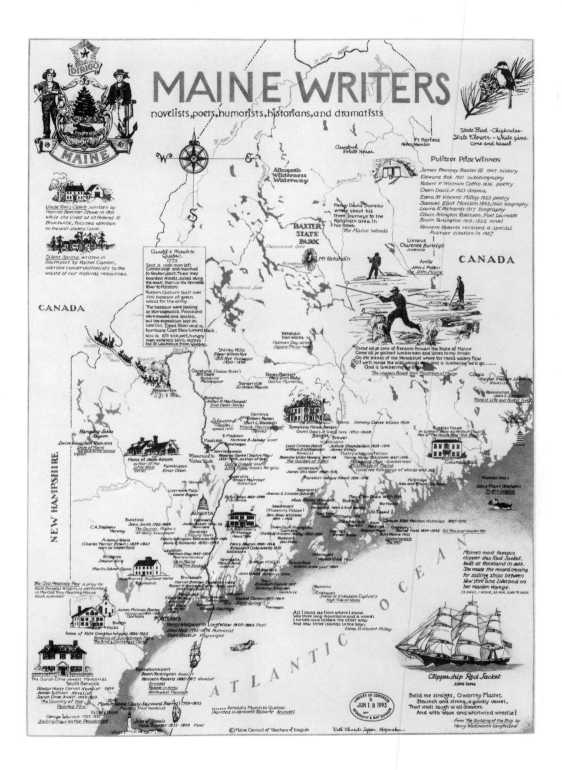

The *Maine Writers* map shows authors who were born, lived, or set their works in the state, as well as images of the homes of writers and scenes from Maine books. Among the important writers with connections to the state are Edna St. Vincent Millay, who was born in Rockland and raised in Camden; Henry Wadsworth Longfellow, who was born in Portland; Rachel Carson, who wrote *Silent Spring* (1962) in the state; Nathaniel Hawthorne, who attended Bowdoin College in Brunswick; and Harriet Beecher Stowe, who wrote *Uncle Tom's Cabin* (1852) in Brunswick. Names of writers, titles of their works, and images from the works are depicted on the map near the locales with which they are associated. Nonliterary information such as the state seal, state bird, and flower appear on the map along with an inset showing the famous march through the state led by Benedict Arnold (1741–1801) on his unsuccessful expedition against Quebec in 1775, an event chronicled by Maine writer Kenneth Roberts in his historical novel *Arundel*. Quotes from Longfellow and Millay are also featured.

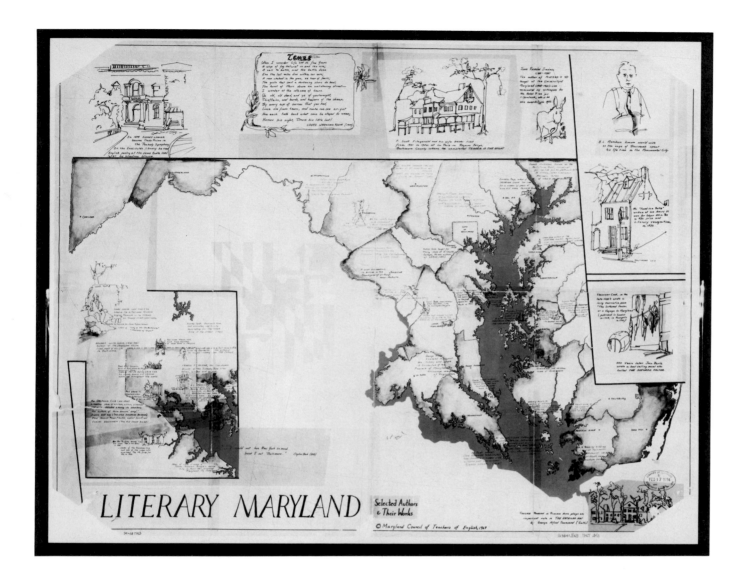

MARYLAND

Literary Maryland: Selected Authors and Their Works

Maryland Council of Teachers of
English, 1967
55 x 73 cm
Color
G3841 .E65 1967 .M3

The main part of *Literary Maryland* shows sites connected with Maryland writers. Illustrations around the edges show the house in which F. Scott Fitzgerald lived while writing *Tender Is the Night* (1934); H. L. Mencken, the "sage of Baltimore"; a Baltimore house in which Edgar Allan Poe wrote "Ms. Found in a Bottle" (1831); and sites associated with poets Ebenezer Cooke, author of "The Sot-Weed Factor" (1708), and Sidney Lanier, who lived in Baltimore and is buried there. In the lower left corner is an inset showing literary sites of Baltimore, such as the old Baltimore *Sun* newspaper building and Poe's grave.

MICHIGAN

Portraits of Literary Michigan

Lansing: Library of Michigan, 1994
61 x 46 cm
Color *(See color section.)*
G4111 .E65 1994 .M5

Courtesy of the Library of Michigan

Portraits of Literary Michigan defines a Michigan author as "someone whose work bears the imprint of time spent in Michigan. The author, native born, adoptive, or just passing through, was affected by the varied Michigan experience." Against an outline of the state, the map depicts twelve Michigan authors above the towns with which they are associated. The authors are Harriet Arnow, Charles Baxter (b. 1947), Joan Blos, Jim Harrison, Ernest Hemingway, Elmore Leonard, Edmund Love, Terry McMillan, Marge Piercy, Henry Schoolcraft, Theodore Roethke, and Robert Traver. Books by additional authors are listed in the margin. There is also a list of other writers with Michigan ties: James Fenimore Cooper, Edna Ferber, Robert Frost, Ring Lardner, Henry Wadsworth Longfellow, and Joyce Carol Oates (b. 1938). The map was produced under the auspices of the Michigan Center for the Book.

MINNESOTA

A Literary Map of Minnesota

EUGENE V. MARTZ
Designer

Minneapolis English Teachers Club, 1954
74 x 58 cm
Color
Ethel M. Fair Collection 456

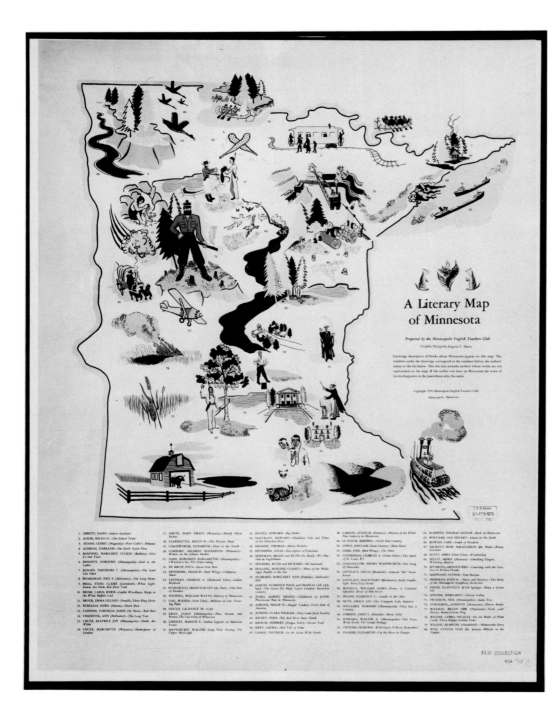

A Literary Map of Minnesota lists eighty writers and book titles keyed to places with which they are connected. Incidents from selected books are illustrated on the map and are keyed to an alphabetical list of authors. Among those shown are Herbert Krause's *The Oxcart Trail* (1954), Esther Shephard's *Paul Bunyan* (1921), Laura Ingalls Wilder's *Those Happy Golden Years* (1953), Charles Lindbergh's Pulitzer Prize-winning *The Spirit of St. Louis* (1953), and Sinclair Lewis's *Main Street* (1920).

Minnesota Writers

Ronald Barron
Compiler

William C. Falwell
Illustrator

Bloomington, Minnesota: Minnesota
    Council of Teachers of English, 1994
88 x 64 cm
Black and white
G4141 .E65 1994 .F3

Courtesy of the Minnesota Council of Teachers of English

Minnesota Writers lists names of sixty writers next to places with which they or their work are associated. In cases where authors spent an equal amount of time in more than one city, they are listed under both. Images of nineteen writers also appear, without identifying captions. Writers with Minnesota connections listed include novelists F. Scott Fitzgerald, born and raised in St. Paul; Sinclair Lewis, born in Sauk Centre, which he immortalized as "Gopher Prairie"; and O. E. Rolvaag, who taught at St. Olaf's College in Northfield; radio host and writer Garrison Keillor, creator of the mythical town of "Lake Woebegone"; playwright August Wilson; and poet Robert Bly, who was born and has lived much of his life in Madison. The map is based on compiler Ronald Barron's *A Guide to Minnesota Writers* (1993), which contains biographical and bibliographical information about significant Minnesota writers.

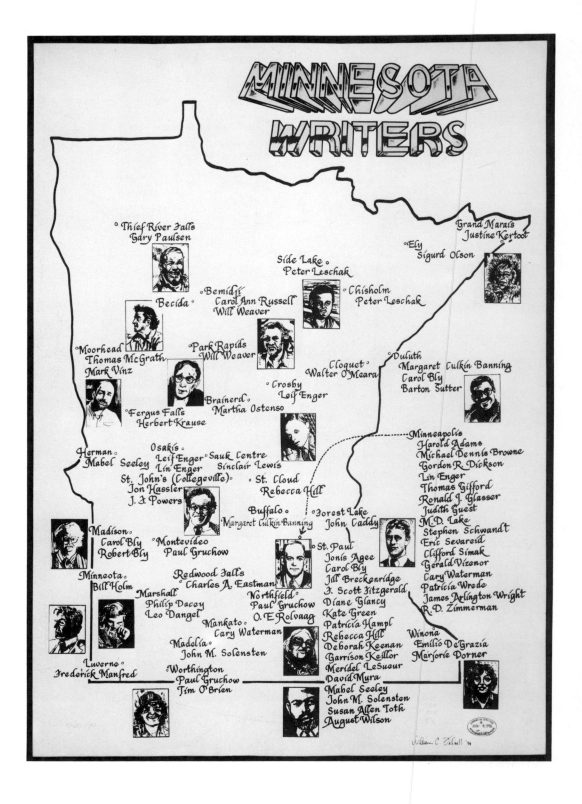

The writers featured on this map have all spent an important part of their lives in Mississippi and have published creative or interpretive literature—fiction, poetry, drama, literary essays—that has received critical attention. These Twentieth-Century writers are identified by the communities with which they are most closely associated.

MISSISSIPPI

Modern Mississippi Writers: A Map of Literary Mississippi

WYATT WATERS
Illustrator

Jackson: University Press of Mississippi, 1992
57 x 51 cm
Color *(See color section.)*
G3981 .E65 1987 .M5

Published with the permission of the University Press of Mississippi

Produced in cooperation with the Mississippi Council of Teachers of English for use in classrooms, the *Modern Mississippi Writers* map is intended to foster pride in the state's writers. The makers have chosen not to feature all the writers of the state, but only twentieth-century writers who spent an important part of their lives in Mississippi and published creative or interpretive literature. The map juxtaposes authors' portraits with illustrations recalling some of their books. Phoenix, the main character in Eudora Welty's story "A Worn Path" (1941), is pictured behind Miss Welty. Walker Percy, author of *The Movie-Goer* (1961) is in front of a theater. Tennessee Williams is associated with the type of plantation house that features in the lives of many of his characters. Behind William Faulkner is a scene showing the Bundren family's journey with Addie's coffin in *As I Lay Dying* (1930). Richard Wright is pictured in front of a scene from his autobiography, *Black Boy* (1945).

MISSOURI

A Literary Map of Missouri

BILL CLEMENSON
Designer

Missouri Association of Teachers of
English, 1955
75 X 55 cm
Color
G4161. E65 1955 .C5

A Literary Map of Missouri features
100 Missouri writers whose names,
along with the title of an important
work, are placed near the locations with
which the authors or their books are
most closely identified. Immediately
below the map are two compilations—
"A List of One Hundred Additional
'Missouri Authors,' 1900–1955" and
"Fifty 'Missouri Authors,' 1780–1900,"
listed along with their noteworthy
works. The listed publications include
biography, history, fiction, verse, drama,
criticism, and travel writing. Among the
more prominent authors featured are
Kate Chopin, Tennessee Williams, T. S.
Eliot, Langston Hughes, Theodore
Dreiser, and Mark Twain.

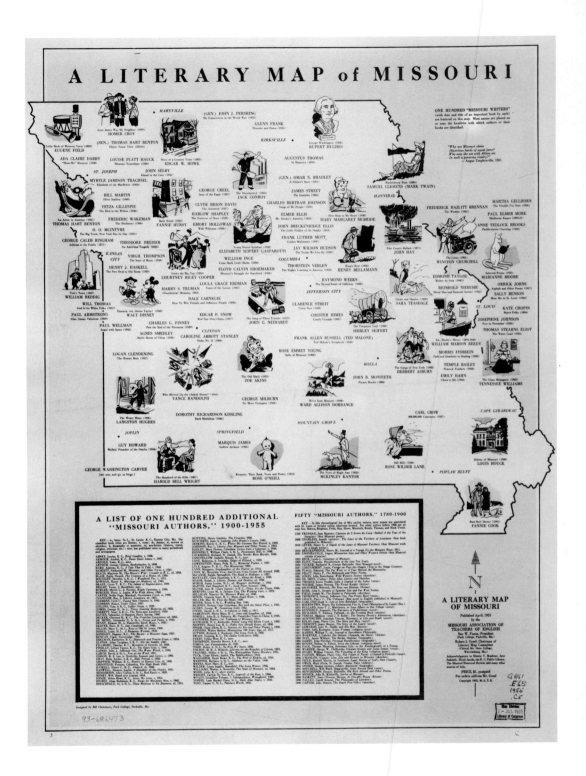

A Literary Map of Missouri

ALLISON C. EMRICK
Illustrator

Warrensburg, Missouri: Ronald W.
    McReynolds and Frank M. Patterson, 1988
92 x 61 cm
Color
G4161 .E65 1988 .M8

A Literary Map of Missouri features a
small outline map of the state on
which various place names are prominently identified. On the left and right
sides of the map are images of well-
known Missouri writers or scenes from
their books. Authors featured are Harry
S. Truman, Langston Hughes, Sara Teas-
dale, Samuel Clemens (Mark Twain),
T. S. Eliot, Marianne Moore, and Laura
Ingalls Wilder. Below the map is an alphabetical list of more than 120 places,
under which are listed more than 400
authors identified with them. The best-
known work of each author and its publication date are given.

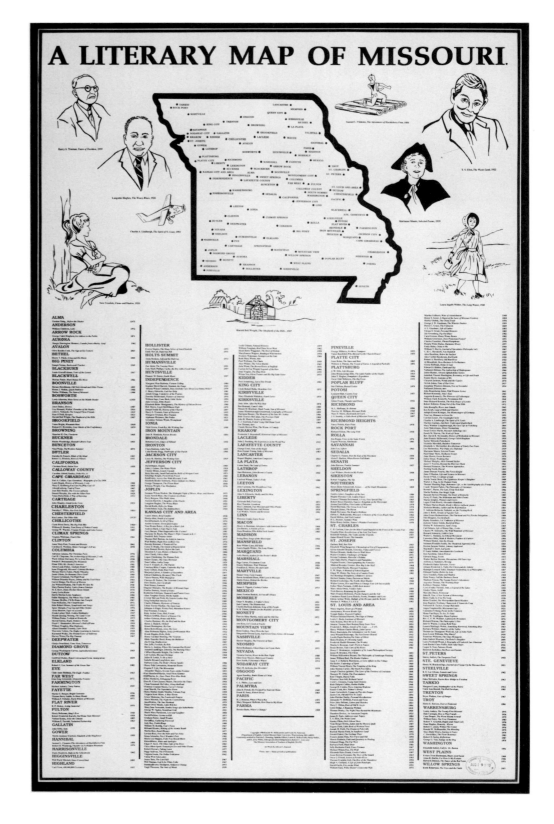

MONTANA

Montana's Literary Heritage

Montana Authors Coalition, 1991
47 x 81 cm
Black and white
G4251 .E65 1991 .M6

Courtesy of the Montana Authors Coalition

Montana's Literary Heritage lists authors and titles next to locations associated with them and their work. Lists of authors and titles for major cities appear in the margins, with blank lines where viewers can add their own favorite writers. The map is illustrated with symbols of Montana's frontier heritage and natural history. Images of the following Montana authors are placed at the far left and right margins: A[lfred] B[ertram] Guthrie, James Welch, B. M. Bower, Richard Hugo, Norman Maclean, Dorothy M. Johnson, Mildred Walker, Ivan Doig, Will James, and Dan Cushman.

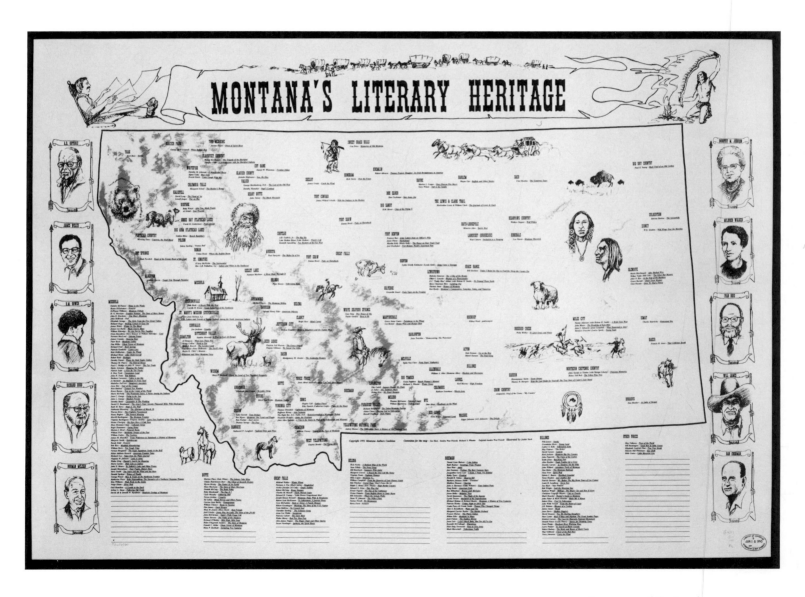

NEBRASKA

Nebraska Authors

DIKA ECKERSLEY
Designer

Omaha: University of Nebraska at Omaha
    and the Nebraska Center for the Book, 1991
46 x 61 cm
Color
G4191 .E65 1991 .E3

Courtesy of the Nebraska Center for the Book, 1991

*N*ebraska Authors was prepared for the First Nebraska Literature Festival, September 27–28, 1991, by the University of Nebraska at Omaha and the Nebraska Center for the Book in cooperation with the Nebraska Humanities Council. It features images by David Routon of six prominent Nebraska authors: John G. Neihardt, Mari Sandoz, Loren Eiseley, Willa Cather, Bess Streeter Aldrich, and Wright Morris. Places associated with each author are listed, followed by three of the author's best-known works, and an inset map locates areas identified with the writers.

NEBRASKA
Centennial
LITERARY MAP
and guide to Nebraska Authors
Map by Jack Brodie
Guide compiled by Bernice Kauffman
Published by
the Nebraska Centennial Commission
in cooperation with
the Nebraska Arts Council.
James Henry Cook
Charley O'Kieffe
Lyman Bryson
VALENTINE
Darien M. Anderson
Zetta C. Tate
Harriette Ashbrook
SCOTTSBLUFF
Gretchen Burnham Sprague
Mari Sandoz
Nellie Snyder Yost
William F. Cody
NORTH PLATTE
Marie Ingold Rose
Wayne C. Lee
George W. Norris
McCOOK
Harry E. Chrisman
Paul R. Beath
Charles Tenney Jackson
Leta M. Edwards
Bess Furman
RED CLOUD
Willa Cather
Mildred R. Bennett
Helen Ferris
Carroll Stewart
Duane Therin
Anne Keeshan
Lynn Montross
James Keogh
NORFOLK
Virgil Geddes
John G. Neihardt
Hawthorne Daniel
Alvin Johnson
Adria Locke Langley
Kenneth Anderson
Frederic Babcock
Sophus Keith Winter
CENTRAL CITY
Grace Abbott
Wright Morris
GRAND ISLAND
Ivan Beede
Keene Abbott
OMAHA
George W. Beadle
William J. Shallcross
LINCOLN
Bess Streeter Aldrich
Clyde Brion Davis
J. Sterling Morton
Hal Borland
Fred Ballard
Francis Lynde Kroll
Weldon Kees
Eugene Manlove Rhodes
Robert H. Davis
Martha McKelvie
Patricia McGerr
LINCOLN
H. B. Alexander
Everett Dick
Mignon G. Eberhart
Loren Eiseley
Ernest K. Gann
Louise and Roscoe Pound
Shirley Schoonover
Dorothy Thomas
OMAHA
Thomas Patton Baird
Marion Marsh Brown
George E. Hyde
Carl Jonas
Helene Magaret
Charles W. Morton
Elia W. Peattie
Robert T. Reilly
1 Pine Ridge—site of Fort Robinson, where Crazy Horse died
2 Scottsbluff National Monument
3 Old Jules Country
4 Ogallala—Nebraska's cowboy capital in trail days
5 Buffalo Bill's "Scout Rest" (North Platte)
6 Bassett—once headquarters for the notorious outlaws Doc Middleton and Kid Wade and the Pony Boys
7 Custer County—home of the pioneer photographer, Solomon D. Butcher
8 Fort Kearny
9 Willa Cather Country
10 Lone Tree Monument at Central City—the "Lone Tree" of Wright Morris's novels
11 John Neihardt Country
12 Homestead National Monument
Copyright 1967 by the Nebraska Centennial Non-Profit Association
Manufactured in the United States of America
G & M Division
OCT 1967
Library of Congress
G4191
E65
1967
B7

Nebraska Centennial Literary Map and Guide to Nebraska Authors

Jack Brodie
Illustrator

[Omaha]: Nebraska Centennial Non-Profit Association, 1967
42 x 59 cm
Color *(See color section.)*
G4191 .E65 1967 .B7

Reprinted with permission of the Nebraska Department of Economic Development, Division of Travel and Tourism, and the Nebraska English Language Arts Council

Produced for the 100th anniversary of the state in 1967, the *Nebraska Centennial Literary Map* is accompanied by a booklet about the state's writers. Despite its title, the map emphasizes Nebraska history as much as literature and its predominant images are of Native Americans, Pony Express Riders, and the State Capitol. Names of authors are printed near the towns with which they or their works are associated. The map features a large image of William F. "Buffalo Bill" Cody, who owned a ranch near North Platte and wrote several books, including The *Life of Hon. William F. Cody* (1879) and *True Tales of the Plains* (1908). Also noted are "Old Jules Country," the setting for the works of Mari Sandoz, and "Willa Cather Country" near Red Cloud, where Cather spent much of her youth and which she later fictionalized as the setting of such works as *The Song of the Lark* (1915), *My Antonia* (1918), and *A Lost Lady* (1923).

Nebraska Literary Map with Native Wildflowers

GERRY COX AND CAROL GULYAS
Compilers

CHAD PINKMAN
Illustrator

JENNIFER DELISLE AND CHRIS HELZER
Designers

Lincoln: Nebraska English Language Arts
    Council, 1996
41 x 89 cm
Color
G4191 .E65 1996 .N4

Courtesy of the Nebraska English/Language Arts Council

Nebraska Literary Map with Native Wildflowers is a topographic map prepared by the Nebraska English/Language Arts Council (NELAC) and the Division of Travel and Tourism of the Department of Economic Development of the state in cooperation with the Nebraska Center for the Book. Funded in part by the Nebraska Humanities Council and the Lincoln Public Schools, the map features writers selected by Nebraska teachers. Places associated with seventy authors are given, along with a color photograph of a wildflower native to each area. Below the map is an alphabetical list of the authors noted on the map, with biographical information on each. Among the prominent Nebraska authors listed are John G. Neihardt, Mari Sandoz, Loren Eiseley, Willa Cather, Bess Streeter Aldrich, Karl Shapiro, Tillie Olsen, Malcolm X, and Wright Morris. More information on these and other Nebraska authors will be found in NELAC's forthcoming *Literary Guide to Nebraska Authors,* intended to accompany the map.

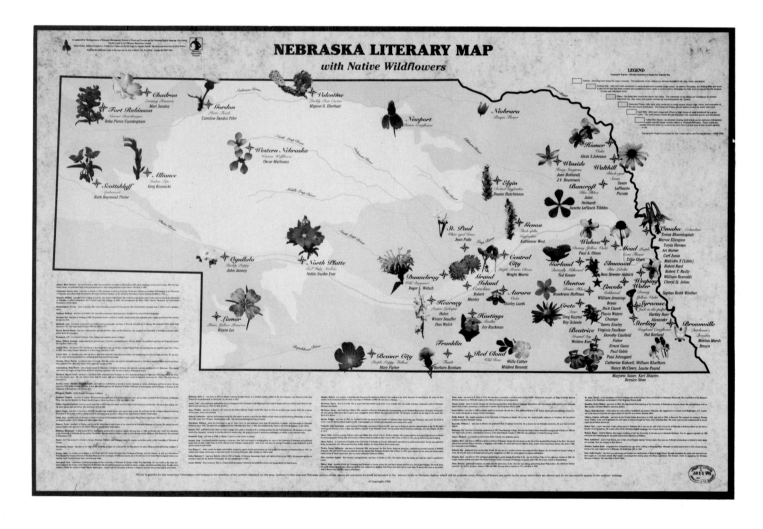

NEVADA

Literary Map of Nevada

MARCIA STEVENS
Illustrator

Las Vegas: Nevada State Library and the
 Nevada State Council of Teachers of English
48 x 34 cm
Color
G4351 .E65 1993 .S9

*Courtesy of the Nevada State Library and the Nevada
Council of Teachers of English*

The *Literary Map of Nevada* lists 272 authors and 2 illustrators who lived in Nevada, wrote there, or wrote about the state. Most of the authors lived in the twentieth century; names of those deceased are italicized. On a outline map of the state are images of Sarah Winnemucca, Mark Twain, Walter Van Tilburg Clark, and Robert Laxalt, as well as depictions of Virginia City, a train, a cowboy, and a mountain sheep. Sarah Winnemucca (Hopkins) wrote about her tribe in *Life Among the Piutes* (1883). Twain (Samuel Clemens) began his writing career in Nevada, publishing his first articles as "Mark Twain" in the *Territorial Enterprise* of Virginia City in 1863. His *Roughing It* (1872) recounts his attempts at mining in the state. Clark spent much of his life in Reno and Virginia City and set his novels *The City of Trembling Leaves* (1945), *The Oxbow Incident* (1940), and *The Track of the Cat* (1949) in Nevada. Laxalt writes about Basque Americans living in Nevada in *Sweet Promised Land* (1986) and *The Governor's Mansion* (1994). Quotes from Robert Laxalt and Mark Twain are also featured.

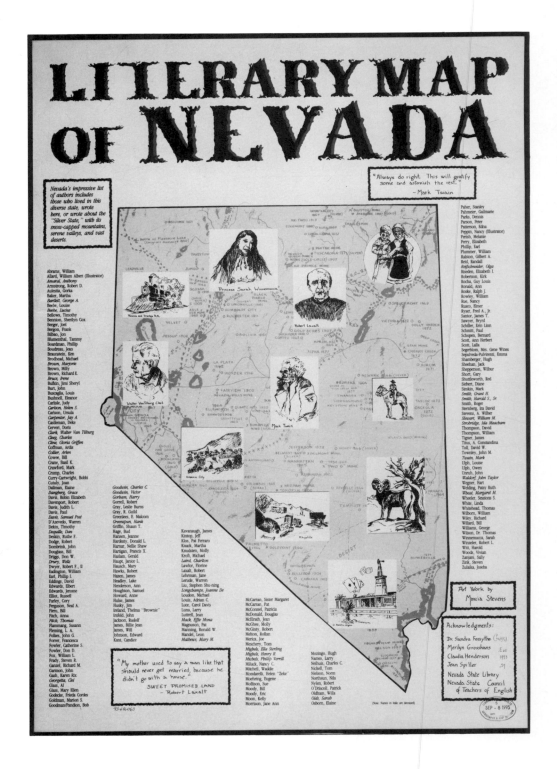

NEW JERSEY

A Literary Map of New Jersey

A. G. HULL
Cartographer

Moorestown: Moorestown Woman's Club,
    1927
71 x 53 cm
Color
G3811 .E65 1927 .H8

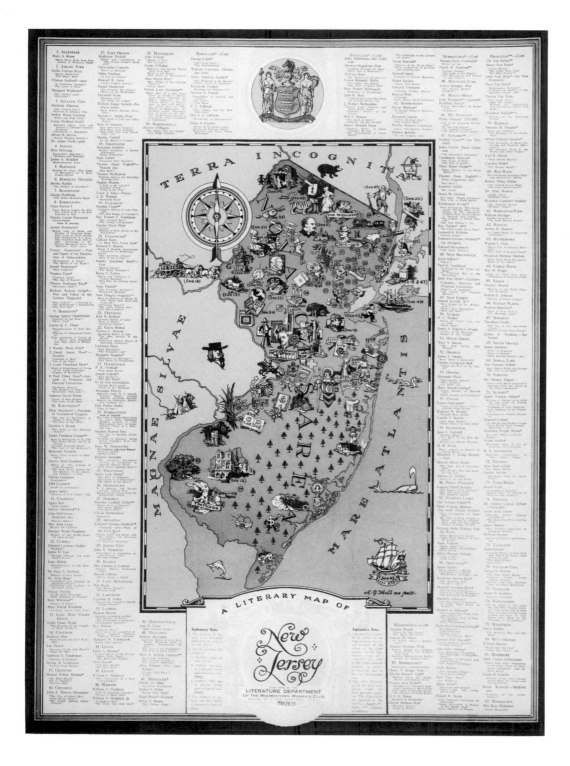

A Literary Map of New Jersey records eighty-two authors who spent time in the state by listing the towns in which they lived and their works. The bordering state of Pennsylvania is marked as "Magnae Silva" or "Great Wood" and New York as "Terrae Incognita" or "Unknown Territory." James Fenimore Cooper, the first major American novelist, was born in Burlington, where his birthplace is a museum. Other noted authors who have spent time in New Jersey are Walt Whitman, who lived in Camden during his later years and died there in a house now open to visitors, and Stephen Crane, who wrote *Maggie, A Girl of the Streets*, one of his most noted works, while living in Clifton in the 1890s. Scottish writer Robert Louis Stevenson conceived the idea for *Treasure Island* (1883) while visiting in Manasquan, and New Brunswick was the birthplace of Joyce Kilmer, the author of "Trees."

NEW MEXICO

[A Literary Map of New Mexico]

RICHARD C. SANDOVAL
Illustrator

From *New Mexico Magazine*, March/April
1974
42 x 27 cm
Color
Muriel H. Parry Collection 564

Reprinted with permission from New Mexico Magazine

This New Mexico map, originally part of an article on the state's literature in *New Mexico Magazine*, locates ninety-five novels set in the state. Numbers key the titles to the names of authors and the publication dates of works. Especially significant works such as *Death Comes for the Archbishop* (1927) by Willa Cather and *The Sea of Grass* by Conrad Richter are printed in boldface. The map features illustrations from some of the novels. Quotes from non-New Mexican writers Jane Austen and Bernard Malamud attesting to the value of novels are given in the lower right corner. Also featured is a quote from Lawrence Clark Powell's *Heart of the Southwest*: "A good work of fiction is a better guide to a region than a bad work of fact."

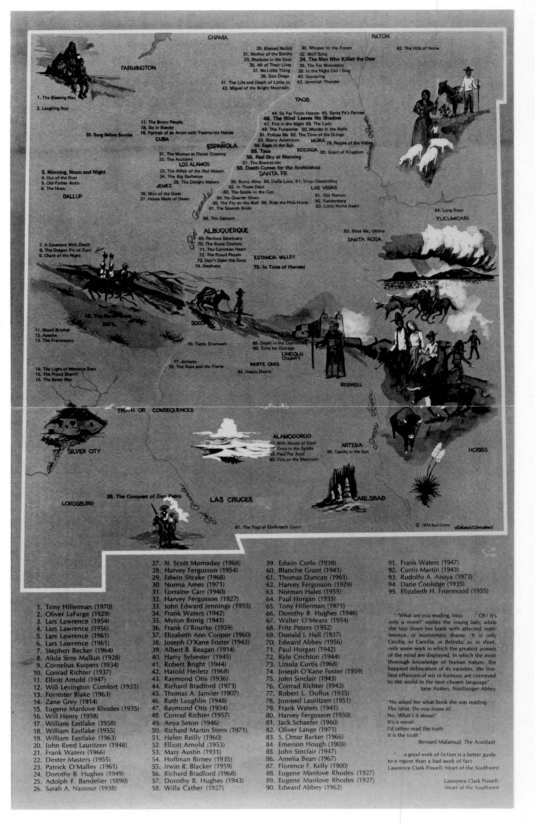

1. Tony Hillerman (1970)
2. Oliver LaFarge (1929)
3. Lars Lawrence (1954)
4. Lars Lawrence (1956)
5. Lars Lawrence (1961)
6. Lars Lawrence (1961)
7. Stephen Becker (1964)
8. Alida Sims Malkus (1928)
9. Cornelius Kuipers (1934)
10. Conrad Richter (1937)
11. Elliott Arnold (1947)
12. Will Levington Comfort (1931)
13. Forrester Blake (1963)
14. Zane Grey (1914)
15. Eugene Manlove Rhodes (1935)
16. Will Henry (1958)
17. William Eastlake (1958)
18. William Eastlake (1955)
19. William Eastlake (1963)
20. John Reed Lauritzen (1948)
21. Frank Waters (1966)
22. Dexter Masters (1955)
23. Patrick O'Malley (1961)
24. Dorothy B. Hughes (1949)
25. Adolph F. Bandelier (1890)
26. Sarah A. Nassour (1938)

27. N. Scott Momaday (1968)
28. Harvey Fergusson (1954)
29. Edwin Shrake (1968)
30. Norma Ames (1971)
31. Lorraine Carr (1940)
32. Harvey Fergusson (1927)
33. John Edward Jennings (1955)
34. Frank Waters (1942)
35. Myron Brinig (1941)
36. Frank O'Rourke (1959)
37. Elizabeth Ann Cooper (1960)
38. Joseph O'Kane Foster (1942)
39. Albert B. Reagan (1914)
40. Harry Sylvester (1945)
41. Robert Bright (1944)
42. Harold Heifetz (1968)
43. Raymond Otis (1936)
44. Richard Bradford (1973)
45. Thomas A. Janvier (1907)
46. Ruth Laughlin (1948)
47. Raymond Otis (1934)
48. Conrad Richter (1957)
49. Anya Seton (1946)
50. Richard Martin Stern (1971)
51. Helen Reilly (1960)
52. Elliott Arnold (1953)
53. Mary Austin (1931)
54. Hoffman Birney (1935)
55. Irwin R. Blacker (1959)
56. Richard Bradford (1968)
57. Dorothy B. Hughes (1943)
58. Willa Cather (1927)

59. Edwin Corle (1938)
60. Blanche Grant (1941)
61. Thomas Duncan (1961)
62. Harvey Fergusson (1929)
63. Norman Hales (1955)
64. Paul Horgan (1935)
65. Tony Hillerman (1971)
66. Dorothy B. Hughes (1946)
67. Walter O'Meara (1954)
68. Fritz Peters (1952)
69. Donald J. Hall (1937)
70. Edward Abbey (1956)
71. Paul Horgan (1942)
72. Kyle Crichton (1944)
73. Ursula Curtis (1968)
74. Joseph O'Kane Foster (1959)
75. John Sinclair (1943)
76. Conrad Richter (1942)
77. Robert L. Duffus (1935)
78. Jonreed Lauritzen (1951)
79. Frank Waters (1941)
80. Harvey Fergusson (1950)
81. Jack Schaefer (1960)
82. Oliver Lange (1971)
83. S. Omar Barker (1966)
84. Emerson Hough (1903)
85. John Sinclair (1947)
86. Amelia Bean (1967)
87. Florence F. Kelly (1900)
88. Eugene Manlove Rhodes (1927)
89. Eugene Manlove Rhodes (1927)
90. Edward Abbey (1962)

91. Frank Waters (1947)
92. Curtis Martin (1943)
93. Rudolfo A. Anaya (1972)
94. Dane Coolidge (1935)
95. Elizabeth H. Friermood (1955)

"'What are you reading, Miss ___.' 'Oh! It's only a novel!' replies the young lady, while she lays down her book with affected indifference, or momentary shame. 'It is only Cecilia, or Camilla, or Belinda,' or, in short, only some work in which the greatest powers of the mind are displayed, in which the most thorough knowledge of human nature, the happiest delineation of its varieties, the liveliest effusions of wit or humour, are conveyed to the world in the best chosen language."
Jane Austen, *Northanger Abbey*

"He asked her what book she was reading.
The Idiot. Do you know it?
No. What's it about?
It's a novel.
I'd rather read the truth.
It is the truth."
Bernard Malamud, *The Assistant*

"... a good work of fiction is a better guide to a region than a bad work of fact ..."
Lawrence Clark Powell, *Heart of the Southwest*

Lawrence Clark Powell,
Heart of the Southwest

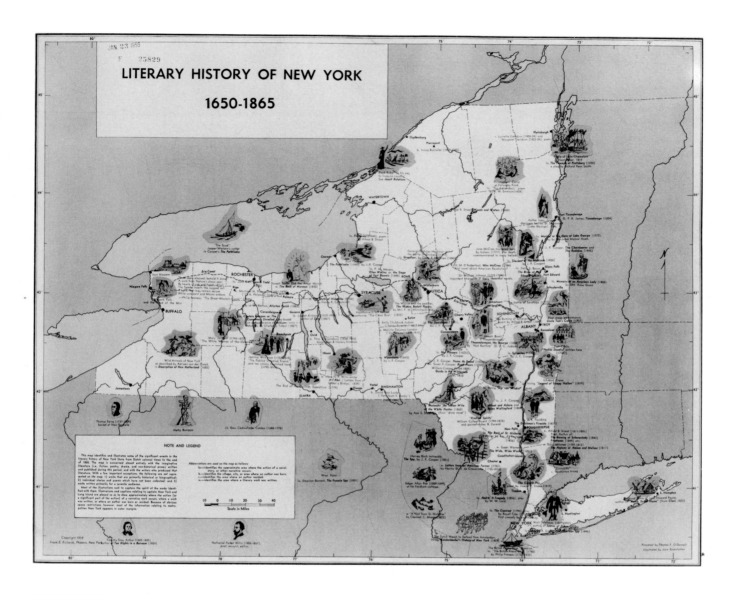

NEW YORK

Literary History of New York 1650–1865

THOMAS FRANCIS O'DONNELL
Compiler

JANE BASENFELDER
Illustrator

Phoenix, New York: Frank E. Richards, 1959
39 x 49 cm
Color
G3801 . E65 1865 .O3

Language of the Land

The *Literary History of New York* identifies and illustrates some of the most significant literary works written in or about the state between Dutch colonial times and the end of the Civil War. The focus of the map is on imaginative literature—fiction, poetry, and drama—rather than on historical and biographical works or juvenile literature. Illustrations of episodes in books are placed so as to show where the action of a narrative work occurs. Information relating to New York City appears in the map's outer margins. Works depicted include Royal Tyler's *The Contrast* (1790), Washington Irving's "The Legend of Sleepy Hollow" (1819), James Fenimore Cooper's *The Spy* (1821), and Walt Whitman's *Leaves of Grass* (1855). The map is one of a three-part series that also includes *Literary History of New York 1866–1928* (G3801 .E65 1928 .O3) and *Literary History of New York 1929–1959* (not in the Library of Congress collections).

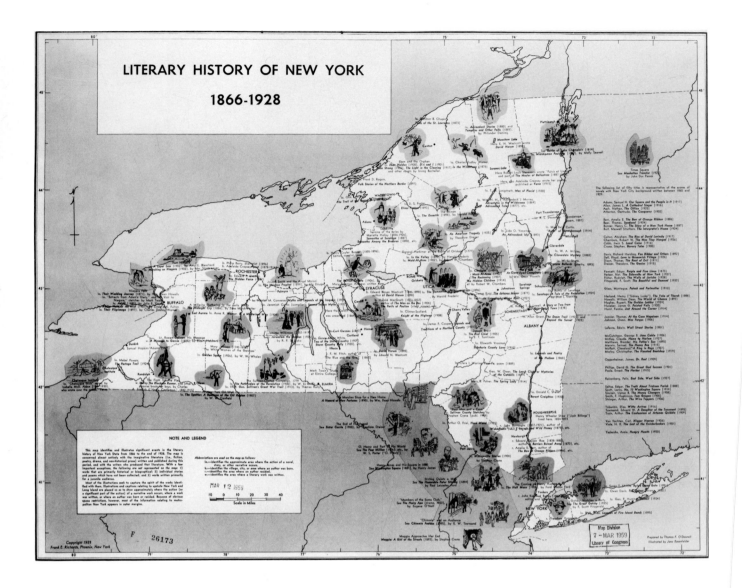

Literary History of New York
1866–1928

THOMAS FRANCIS O'DONNELL
Compiler

JANE BASENFELDER
Illustrator

Phoenix, New York: Frank E. Richards, 1959
39 x 50 cm
Color
G3801 .E65 1928 .O3

The *Literary History of New York* identifies and illustrates some of the most significant literary works written in or about the state between 1865 and 1928. The focus of the map is on imaginative literature—fiction, poetry, and drama—rather than on historical and biographical works or juvenile literature. Illustrations of episodes in books are placed so as to show where the action of a narrative work occurs. Works depicted include Henry James's *Washington Square* (1881), Stephen Crane's *Maggie, A Girl of the Streets* (1893), Theodore Dreiser's *Sister Carrie* (1900), and F. Scott Fitzgerald's *The Great Gatsby* (1925). Information relating to New York City appears in the map's outer margins, including a list of fifty novels with a New York City setting written between 1865 and 1929. The map is one of a three-part series that includes *Literary History of New York 1650–1865* (G3801 .E65 1865 .O3) and *Literary History of New York 1929–1959* (not in the Library of Congress collections).

NEW YORK CITY

The Literary Map of N.Y.

Molly Maguire
Designer

Linda Ayriss
Illustrator

Los Angeles: Aaron Blake, 1988
71 x 59 cm
Color
G3804 .N4 .2M3E65 1988 .A2

Courtesy of Molly Maguire and Aaron Silverman

*T*he Literary Map of N.Y. shows key twentieth-century New York City novelists, poets, editors, and critics who have defined in significant ways the spirit of modern America. The map features a street map of the city showing the residences of important authors as well as literary locales such as cafes, hotels, and magazine offices. A major design element features the Algonquin Hotel, 59 West Forty-fourth Street, meeting place in the 1920s of the famous Round Table, a literary circle founded by Dorothy Parker, Robert Benchley, and Robert Sherwood. At the bottom of the map are images of authors who lived and worked in the city (*l-r*): Eugene O'Neill, John Cheever, Dorothy Parker, Langston Hughes, Dylan Thomas, Susan Sontag, Norman Mailer, Marianne Moore, and James Baldwin. Research and design for the map were performed by Molly Maguire, who produced a series of literary maps in the 1980s.

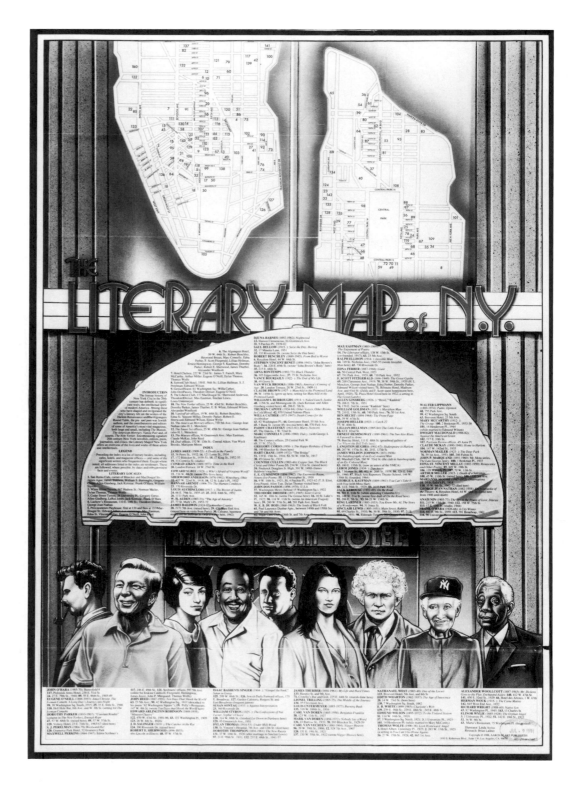

NORTH CAROLINA

A Literary Map of North Carolina

PRIMROSE [MRS. FRANCIS PASCHAL]
Designer

Raleigh: North Carolina English Teachers
     Association, 1950
52 x 84 cm
Color
G3901 .E65 1950 .N6

On an outline of the state, *A Literary Map of North Carolina* features illustrations relating to the work of forty North Carolina authors. Works depicted include Thomas Wolfe's *Look Homeward Angel* (1929); Hatcher Hughes's Pulitzer Prize-winning play *Hell-Bent for Heaven* (1924); Greensboro native O. Henry's short story "Cabbages and Kings"; Rebecca Cushman's *Swing Your Mountain Gal* (1934), a collection of stories about the Appalachian mountain area of the state; and Paul Green's *The Lost Colony* (1937), an outdoor drama about the first English colony, on Roanoke Island. The map also features the state seal and the state flag, tree, and bird, as well as an illustration of the ship that brought the Roanoke Island settlers to America. A scroll contains a list of winners of the Mayflower Award. At the top of the map is a quotation from Sir Walter Raleigh, the Elizabethan author and adventurer who sponsored the Roanoke colony and is sometimes considered the state's founder: "To Seeke New Worlds, For Golde, For Prayse, For Glory." At the bottom of the map is a row of books, with the names of more than sixty additional writers with North Carolina connections.

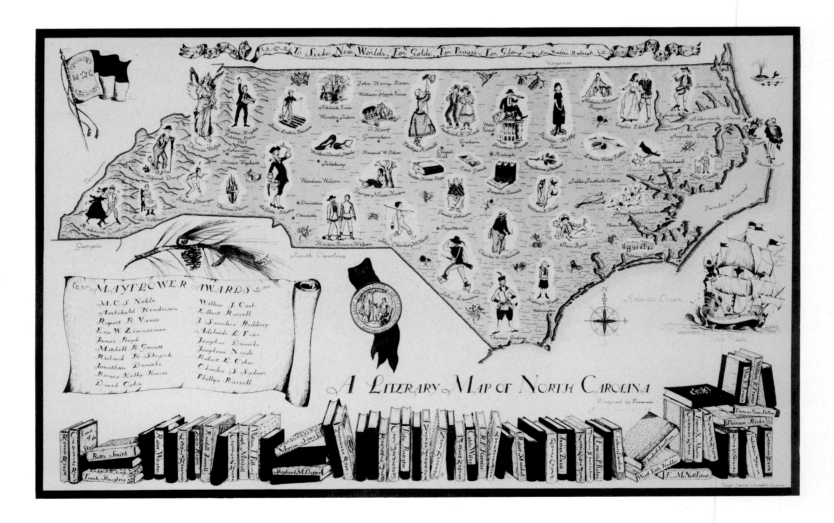

Malone's New Literary Map of North Carolina

E.T. Malone, Jr.
Compiler and Illustrator

Chapel Hill: Literary Lantern Press, 1990
38 x 97 cm
Color
G3901 .E65 1990 .M3

Courtesy of E.T. Malone, Jr., Literary Lantern Press

Malone's New Literary Map of North Carolina identifies the most noted writers associated with the state's counties, towns, and cities. The map was entirely hand-drawn by E. T. Malone, Jr. The colorful illustrations, which originally appeared in North Carolina newspapers and magazines, show various literary scenes and figures. Lists of writers for larger centers such as Chapel Hill, Durham, Charlotte, and Raleigh are in the bottom margin. The map is comprehensive and includes people with North Carolina connections ranging from movie director and producer Cecil B. DeMille (1881–1959) to journalists David Brinkley (b. 1920) and Charles Kuralt (1934–1997) to novelist Thomas Wolfe. Part of a planned series of literary maps of southern states, the map was endorsed by the North Carolina English Teachers Association.

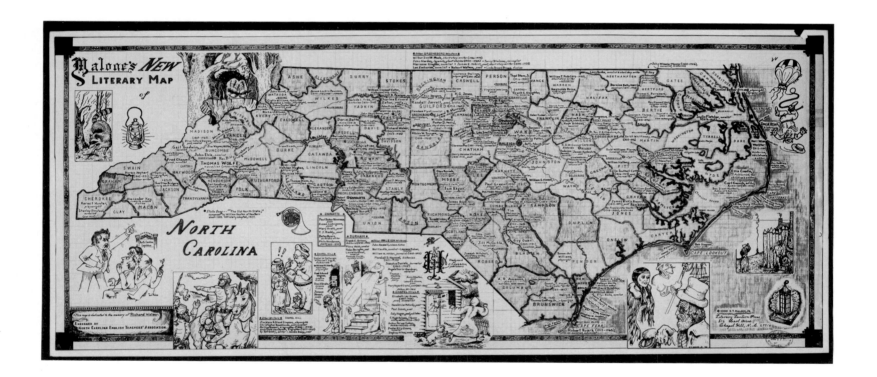

NORTH DAKOTA

North Dakota Literary Trails

CHARLOTTE S. ROSVOLD AND
CATHARINE PHILLIPS
Illustrators

Mayville, North Dakota: Hazel Webster
  Byrnes, c. 1932
43 x 57 cm
Black and white
G4171 .E65 1932 .B9

*N*orth Dakota Literary Trails shows an outline map of the state with rivers and railroads indicated. Images of Indians, buffalo, and covered wagons decorate the map, which gives book titles and authors associated with the state. Among those listed are *History of the Expedition* (1814) by Meriwether Lewis and William Clark and Theodore Roosevelt's *The Winning of the West* (1889–1896).

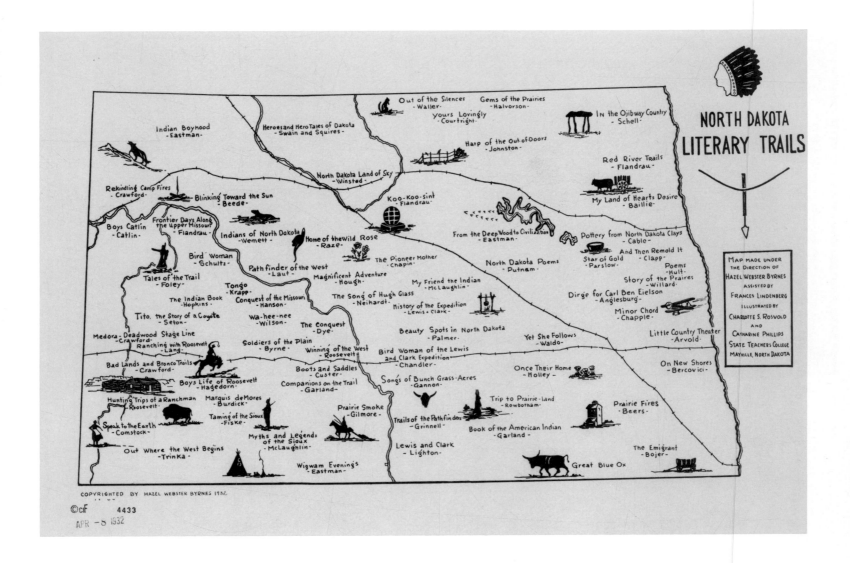

NORTH DAKOTA WRITERS

Wales
Pembina
Walhalla
Kenmare
St. Thomas
Cando
Grafton
Souris R.
Minot
Williston
Grand Forks
Keene
Sanish
Parshall
Velva
Ft. Totten
Ft. Union
McKenzie Co.
Ft. Stevenson
Sheyenne
Mayville
Missouri R.
Fessenden
New Rockford
Finley
Trail Co.
Killdeer
Ft. Atkinson/
Berthold
Ft. Mandan
Sykeston
Carrington
Little
Washburn
Sentinel Butte
Ft. Clark
Jamestown
Fargo
Dickinson
Driscoll
Cleveland
Enderlin
Sheldon
Medora
Ft. Abraham
Lincoln
Bismarck
Cannonball R.
Missouri R.
James R.
Wahpeton
Mott
Strasburg
Lidgerwood
Lemmon
Ft. Yates

Captain Meriwether Lewis
Fort Mandan

Captain William Clark
Fort Mandan

Theodore Roosevelt
Medora

Eric Sevareid
Velva

Era Bell Thompson
Driscoll

Larry Woiwode
Sykeston

Louis L'Amour
Jamestown

Maxwell Anderson
Grand Forks

Thomas McGrath
Sheldon

Louise Erdrich
Wahpeton

North Dakota Writers

NANCY MAXWELL
Editor

Bismarck: North Dakota Center for the
    Book, 1994
28 x 43 cm
Black and white
G4171 .E65 1994 .L3

Courtesy of the North Dakota Center for the Book,
North Dakota Humanities Council, and North Dakota
State Library

The *North Dakota Writers* map appears in a pamphlet prepared by the North Dakota Center for the Book in cooperation with the State Historical Society of North Dakota to supplement the *Language of the Land* exhibit when it appeared in the state. The map was also sponsored by the North Dakota Humanities Council and the North Dakota State Library. The cover lists writers who have either lived in or written about North Dakota, organized by the locations with which they were associated. A two-page spread inside the pamphlet shows a map of the state, with principal cities and towns. Around the map are images of ten writers and places connected with them or their works. Authors shown include Meriwether Lewis and William Clark of the famous expedition that explored the region; playwright Maxwell Anderson; prolific Western writer Louis L'Amour; poet Thomas McGrath; poet and novelist Louise Erdrich; and novelist Larry Woiwode.

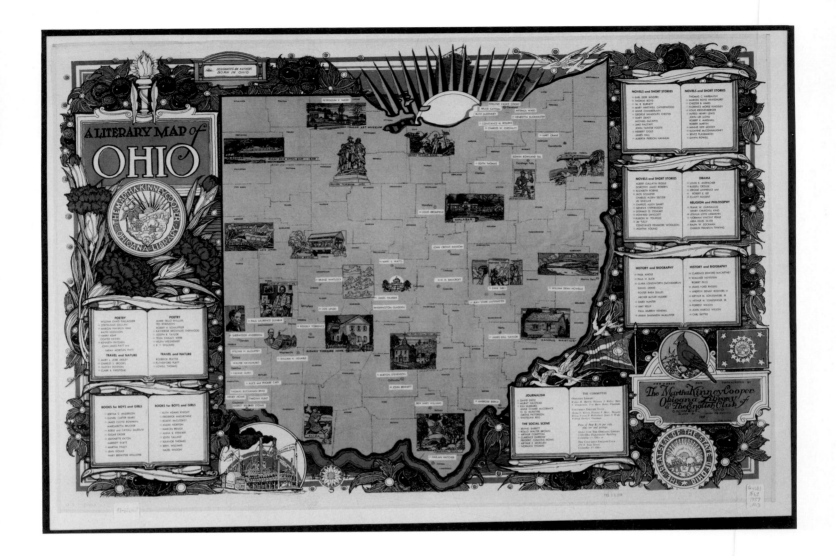

OHIO

A Literary Map of Ohio

MARK RUSSELL
Designer

Columbus: Martha Kinney Cooper Ohioana
   Library Association and the English Club
   of Columbus, Ohio, 1957
59 x 89 cm
Color
G4081 .E65 1957 .M3

Courtesy of the Ohioana Library Association

Against an outline showing the counties in the state, *A Literary Map of Ohio* shows major authors' names near the locales in which they lived. Authors born in Ohio are distinguished by a rising sun. Noted Ohio-born writers listed on the map include Alice and Phoebe Cary, Paul Lawrence Dunbar, Zane Grey, Hart Crane, Charles W. Chesnutt, William Dean Howells, Ambrose Bierce, and Sherwood Anderson. Around the borders, names of authors with Ohio connections are grouped according to the genre of their works, such as "Books for Boys and Girls," "Novels and Short Stories," "Poetry," "Travel and Nature," "History and Biography," and "Drama." No writer is depicted on the map but insets feature details such as a scene from *Uncle Tom's Cabin* by Harriet Beecher Stowe, who lived in Cincinnati, and a scene from a Zane Grey Western. The map is also found in the Ethel M. Fair Collection, 578.

A Literary Map of Ohio

Donald Wentz
Designer

Columbus: Martha Kinney Cooper Ohioana
   Library Association, 1983
58 x 89 cm
Color
G4081 .E65 1983 .M3

Courtesy of the Ohioana Library Association

Against an outline showing the counties in the state, *A Literary Map of Ohio* shows major authors' names near the locales in which they lived. Authors born in Ohio are distinguished from others by an asterisk. Noted Ohio-born writers listed on the map include Paul Lawrence Dunbar, Zane Grey, James Thurber, Hart Crane, Charles Waddell Chesnutt, William Dean Howells, Ambrose Bierce, and Sherwood Anderson. Around the borders, authors with Ohio connections are grouped according to the genre of their works, such as "Fiction," "Religion," "Journalism," or "History." No writer is depicted on the map, but insets feature details such as Thurber's humorous dog drawings; a scene from *Uncle Tom's Cabin* by Harriet Beecher Stowe, who lived in Cincinnati; and a scene from a Zane Grey Western.

Ohioana Ohio Literary Map

BENTON MAHAN
Designer

Columbus: Ohioana Library Association, 1995
49 x 83 cm
Color
G4081 .E65 1995 .M3

Courtesy of the Ohioana Library Association

Against an outline showing the counties in the state, the *Ohioana Literary Map* shows major authors' names near the locales in which they lived; Ohio-born authors are distinguished by an asterisk. Awards the authors won are listed near their names. Ohio-born writers listed on the map include Paul Lawrence Dunbar, Zane Grey, James Thurber, Hart Crane, William Dean Howells, Ambrose Bierce, Sherwood Anderson, Nikki Giovanni, and Rita Dove. Around the borders, authors with Ohio connections are grouped according to the genre of their works, such as "Fiction," "Drama," "Humor," "Children's Books," "Poetry," "Religion," "Journalism," "Theology," or "History." Drawings on the map feature authors and their characters and details such as Thurber's humorous dog drawings; Uncle Tom's Cabin from the book by Harriet Beecher Stowe, who lived in Cincinnati; and a scene from a Zane Grey Western.

144

OKLAHOMA

Literary Map of Oklahoma

J. RICHARDSON
Illustrator

SUZANNE MOUNGER
Designer

Oklahoma City: Oklahoma Center for the
    Book, 1994
61 x 91 cm
Color
G4021 .E65 1994 .O4

Copyright© 1994, Oklahoma Center for the Book.
Used by permission

The *Literary Map of Oklahoma* features some of the writers who have shaped Oklahoma's literary heritage. An outline of the state is superimposed over a drawing of settlers entering Oklahoma to claim land. Ovals scattered around the drawing show twenty-one writers, among them John Berryman, Ralph Ellison, John Hope Franklin, Tony Hillerman, and N. Scott Momaday. Beneath the oval is information on the genres in which the writers worked, cities with which they are associated, and awards they won.

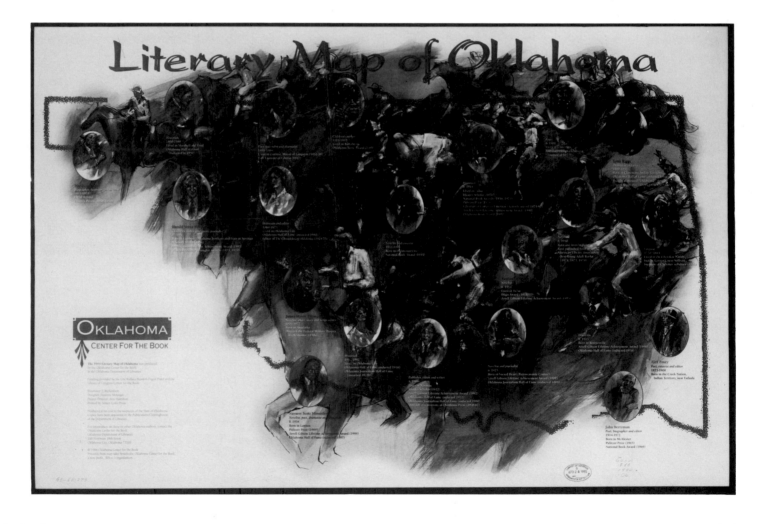

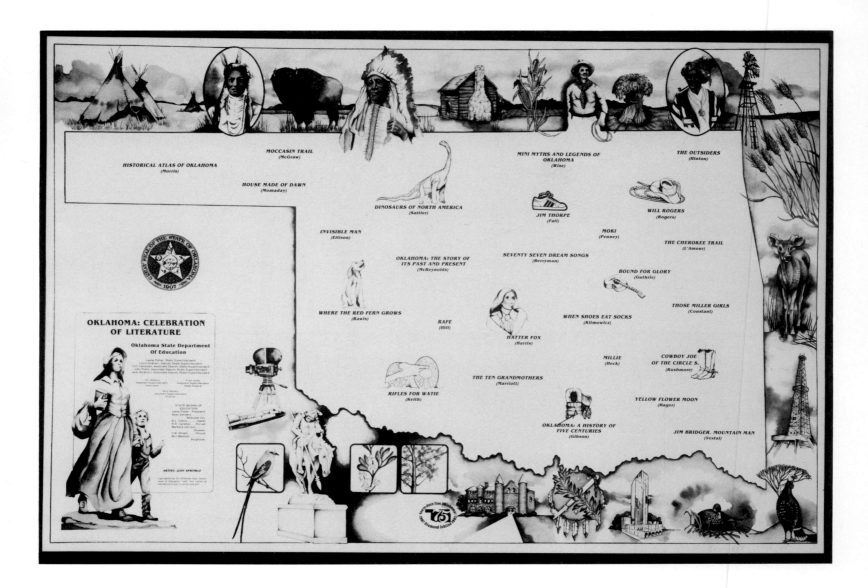

Oklahoma: Celebration of Literature

Judy Sprinkle
Illustrator

Norman: Oklahoma State Department of
   Education, 1983
57 x 88 cm
Color
G4021 .E65 1983 .O4

Oklahoma: Celebration of Literature, produced for the state's seventy-fifth anniversary in 1983, features an outline map on which the state's prominent authors and their works are listed at the sites associated with those works. The map includes other aspects of the state in addition to literature. The border depicts Indians, buffalo, oil wells, crops, statues, and buildings, all important in Oklahoma's history and development. The most noted native writer is novelist Ralph Ellison, author of *Invisible Man* (1952), who grew up in Oklahoma City. Other Oklahoma writers include humorist Will Rogers, from Claremore, and Edna Ferber (1887–1968), who spent time in the state researching her novel *Cimarron* (1930), which traces the early history of the state.

OREGON

Oregon Literary Map

JOHN TURLEY
Illustrator

Portland: Oregon Council of Teachers of
    English, 1989
63 x 88 cm
Color *(See color section.)*
G4291 .E65 1989 .O7

Courtesy of the Oregon Council of Teachers of English

The *Oregon Literary Map* identifies authors who are associated with various places in the state. Oral traditions of Native Americans are represented by a special symbol. Around the borders are images of ten noted Oregon writers: science-fiction writer Ursula K. Le Guin (b. 1929); Ken Kesey, whose novel *Sometimes a Great Notion* (1964) is based on his experience at an Oregon logging camp; Primus St. John, author of *Skins on the Earth* (1976); Walter Morey, author of *Gentle Ben* (1965); poet William Stafford, who won the 1963 National Book Award for *Traveling Through the Dark*; H. L. Davis, winner of a Pulitzer Prize for his novel *Honey in the Horn* (1935); Frances Fuller Victor, poet and historian, who wrote the two-volume *History of Oregon* (1886, 1888); Barry Lopez, author of *Of Wolves and Men*; young people's author Beverly Cleary, who wrote *Henry Huggins* (1950); and Chief Joseph of the Nez Percé, known for his speech "I Will Fight No More Forever." Sketches of cowboys, wild animals, the Lewis and Clark Expedition, skiers, wagon trains, and a replica of the Globe Theatre used for the Oregon Shakespeare Festival enliven the map.

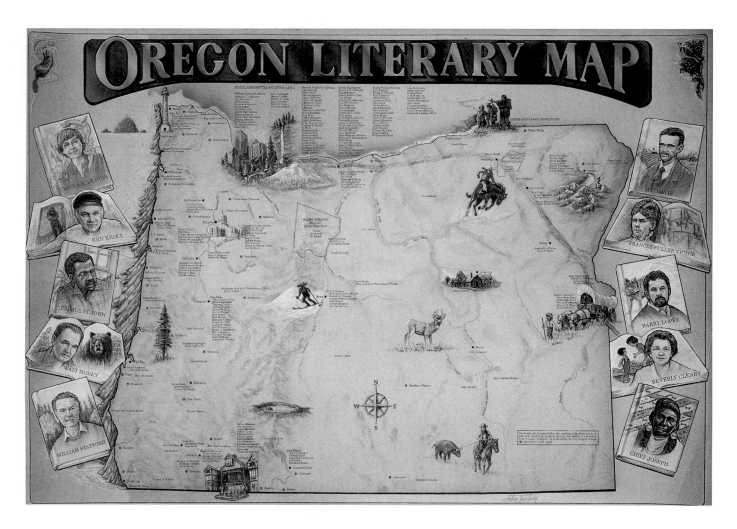

PENNSYLVANIA

Literary Map of Pennsylvania

Pennsylvania Council of Teachers of
   English, 1965
53 x 70 cm
Color
G3821 .E65 1965 .S9

Courtesy of the Pennsylvania Council of Teachers of English

First produced by the Pennsylvania Council of Teachers of English in 1959 and updated in 1965, the *Literary Map of Pennsylvania* records authors who were born, lived, or set their works in the state. A key at the bottom distinguishes among these kinds of writers and also indicates their genres of writing and prizes won. A scroll at right lists forty-one authors of the Philadelphia area, since colonial days an important publishing center where authors have visited, lived, and worked. Philadelphia natives include novelists Owen Wister, Joseph Hergeshiemer, Richard Harding Davis, and Charles Brockden Brown, and playwright Clifford Odets. A similar scroll at left lists thirty-one authors of the Pittsburgh area, including George S. Kaufman, who wrote many Broadway hits; Margaret Deland, who depicted the area in her novels; and William McGuffey, who compiled the famous nineteenth-century readers. Names of other authors and titles of their works are scattered over the map.

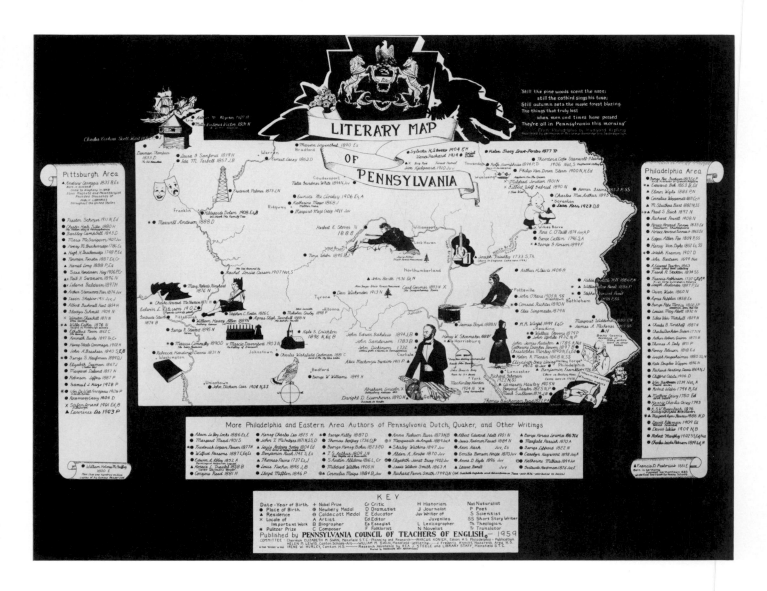

PHILADELPHIA

A Disproportionate Map of Points of Literary Interest in Philadelphia

ARNOLD ROTH
Illustrator

Philadelphia, c. 1960
43 x 50 cm
Black and white
Ethel M. Fair Collection 864

Courtesy of the Free Library of Philadelphia

Prepared by Philadelphia artist Arnold Roth and presented to the Free Library of Philadelphia, *A Disproportionate Map of Points of Literary Interest in Philadelphia* locates twenty-nine historic literary landmarks in Philadelphia, which in the eighteenth century became the first publishing center in the United States. Sites indicated include homes of publishers and editors such as Henry C. Carey (1793–1879), who published American editions of the works of Charles Dickens and Sir Walter Scott, and Edward R. Bok (1863–1930), an influential early editor of the *Ladies Home Journal* magazine. Sites include homes of authors, such as Owen Wister, author of *The Virginian* (1902), and Edgar Allan Poe, who wrote the first drafts of the later published poems "The Raven" (1845) and "The Bells" (1849) while living in Philadelphia between 1838 and 1843. Also marked are the graves of Benjamin Franklin, noted for *Poor Richard's Almanack* (issued annually from 1732 to 1757) and his *Autobiography* (1868), and Charles Brockden Brown, America's first professional novelist, known for *Wieland* (1798), a Gothic romance. Sites of libraries and universities are also marked. Illustrations for each of the items on the list are keyed to the list by numbers.

SOUTH CAROLINA

A Map of South Carolina Writers

Edwin C. Epps
Consultant in Charge

John and Nancy Peeples Dennis
Illustrators

Spartanburg, South Carolina: South Carolina
   Council of Teachers of English, 1993
45 x 59 cm
Black and white
G3911 .E65 1991 .S6

*Courtesy of the South Carolina Council of
Teachers of English*

A Map of South Carolina Writers features twenty-four authors who were chosen by a vote among South Carolina's Southern literature specialists. The authors' writing encompasses a wide range of genres, including journalism, translation, poetry, plays, fiction, and works for young people. Those depicted on the map include John C. Calhoun, William Gilmore Simms, Henry Timrod, Mary McLeod Bethune, DuBose Heyward, James Dickey, Josephine Humphreys, and Pat Conroy. An accompanying booklet, *A Literary Map of South Carolina,* edited by Beverly Spears, contains biographical sketches of each author and bibliographies of works by and about them.

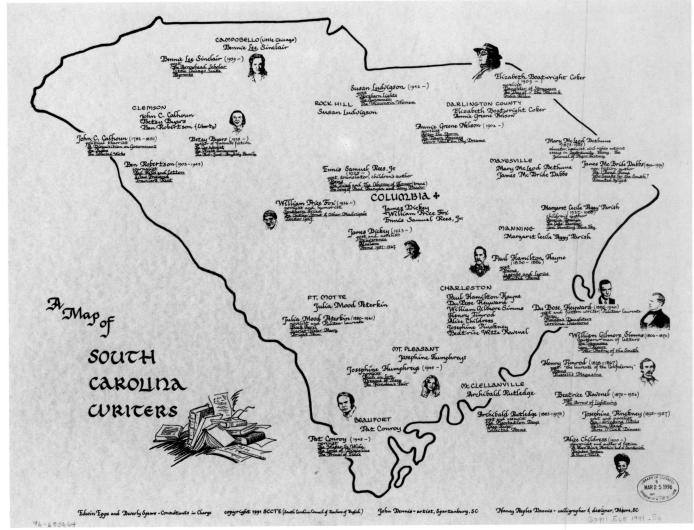

TENNESSEE

Tennessee Literary Map

ELIZABETH MIMS HOFFMAN AND
    ROBERT J. SPIRKO
Illustrators

Morristown, Tennessee: Tennessee Council
    of Teachers of English, 1996
53 x 71 cm
Color
G3961 .E65 1996 .H6

Courtesy of the Tennessee Council of Teachers of English

*T*ennessee Literary Map is illustrated with characters and scenes from various works that make up the state's literary heritage. On the map around forty authors and important works are identified, including James Weldon Johnson's *God's Trombones* (1927), Robert Penn Warren's *All the King's Men* (1946), Arna Wendell Bontemps's *100 Years of Negro Freedom* (1961), James Agee's *A Death in the Family,* (1957), Wilma Dykeman's *The Tall Woman* (1962), Shelby Foote's *The Civil War,* (1958–74) and Alex Haley's *Roots* (1975). An inset lists prominent Tennessee literary figures: Maggie Vaughn, Poet Laureate; Harriet Insignares, Ambassador of Letters; and Wilma Dykeman, State Historian. Additional authors and works are listed in the map's bottom margin. Produced in honor of the bicentennial of the state, the map was sponsored by the Tennessee Council of Teachers of English, the Tennessee State Library and Archives, and the Women's National Book Association, with support from the Tennessee 200 State Bicentennial Planning Committee. The map is based on the 1976 *Tennessee Literature* (G3961 . E65 1976 .H6) but features more women, contemporary, and minority writers than the previous version. It is accompanied by *Selected Lists of Tennessee Writers*, a pamphlet giving biographical and bibliographical information about the state's writers, both those on the map and others.

Tennessee Literature

John W. Warren and Adrian McLaren
Compilers

Elizabeth Mims Hoffman
Illustrator

Memphis: Tennessee Council of Teachers
    of English, 1976
53 x 71 cm
Color *(See color section.)*
G3961 . E65 1976 .H6

Courtesy of the Tennessee Council of Teachers of English

*T*ennessee Literature is illustrated with characters and scenes from various works that make up the state's literary heritage. On the map more than forty authors and important works are identified. These works include Robert Penn Warren's *All the King's Men* (1946), Arna Bontemps's *Chariot in the Sky* (1951), James Agee's *A Death in the Family,* (1957), Nikki Giovanni's *Gemini* (1971), and Alex Haley's *Roots* (1975). In addition, locations of movies, television productions, and outdoor dramas set in the state are identified, as are historical landmarks and ballads that are a part of the state's folklore. Directly below the map is a list of ten famous sayings by Tennesseans.

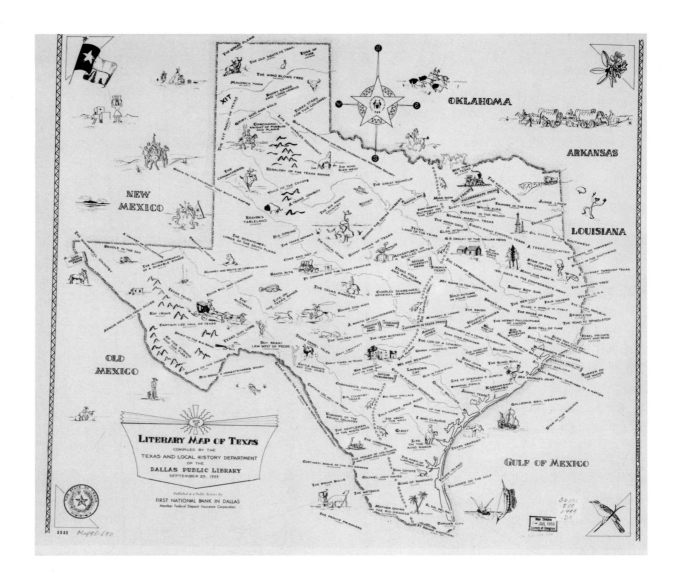

TEXAS

Literary Map of Texas

Dallas: First National Bank in Dallas, 1955
59 x 71 cm
Color
G4031 .E65 1955 .D3

Compiled by the Texas and Local History Department of the Dallas Public Library, the *Literary Map of Texas* was published as a public service by a local bank. Scattered around the map at the appropriate locations are approximately two hundred authors and titles with Texas associations, offering a comprehensive literary history of the state. Illustrations refer to some works. Among the books and authors listed are *A Vaquero of the Brush Country* (1929) by J. Frank Dobie, *The Heart of the West* (1907) by O. Henry (William Sydney Porter), *Giant* (1952) by Edna Ferber, and *Pale Horse, Pale Rider* (1939) by O. Henry's cousin Katherine Anne Porter. The map also lists publishers located in the state, the majority being presses associated with educational institutions such as Baylor and Southern Methodist universities.

UTAH

Literary Utah

ROBERT BISSLAND
Designer

Slanting Rain Graphic Design, 1990
39 x 31 cm
Color
G4341 .E65 1990 .S5

*L*iterary Utah features portraits of twelve major authors superimposed on a topographic map of the state. Writers pictured are May Swenson, Margaret Rostowski, Fawn Brodie, Barbara Williams, Ivy Ruckman, Bernard De-Voto, Dean Hughes, Zane Gray, Juanita Brooks, David Lee, Edward Abbey, and Wallace Stegner. Quotes from some of these authors about Utah and the Rocky Mountain area are also featured on the map. The margins contain a list of eighteen place names and approximately one hundred authors associated with them. The map is accompanied by a seventy-four-page bibliographic guide sponsored by the Utah Council of Teachers of English, the Utah Endowment for the Humanities, and Utah State University. The guide, which lists approximately three hundred authors and their works, also features an index grouping writers by town.

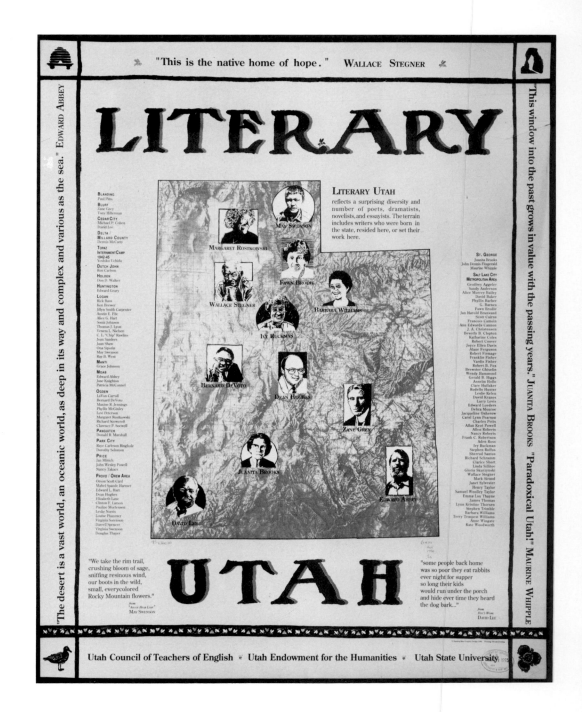

Language of the Land

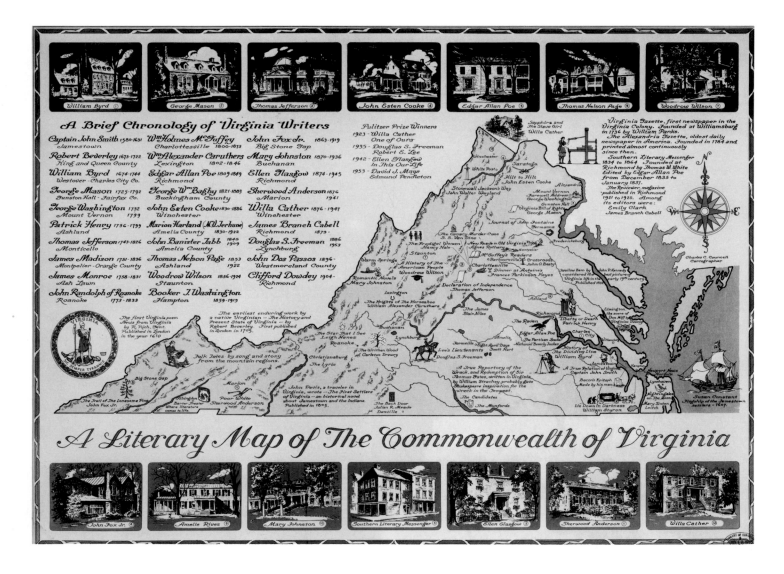

A Literary Map of The Commonwealth of Virginia

VIRGINIA

A Literary Map of the Commonwealth of Virginia

Richmond: Virginia Association of Teachers of English, 1957
52 x 73 cm
Color
G3881 .E65 1957 .V5

Courtesy of the Virginia Association of Teachers of English

A Literary Map of the Commonwealth of Virginia offers a brief chronology of Virginia writers from early explorer John Smith to historian and novelist of the Civil War Clifford Dowdey, with a listing of the places where they lived. Top and bottom borders picture homes of notable writers, keyed by number to places on the map. Pulitzer Prize recipients from Virginia are also listed, along with the winning books. Important Virginia publications such as early newspapers and the *Southern Literary Messenger*, once edited by Edgar Allan Poe, are also featured. The map portrays historical figures and artifacts, for example, the ship *Susan Constant*, which brought settlers to Jamestown in 1607.

20th Century Virginia Authors

Jere Kittle and Debra Bull
Designers

Richmond: Virginia Center for the Book,
  1994
64 x 48 cm
Color
G3881 .E65 1994 .V5

Prepared by the Virginia Center for the Book in cooperation with the Virginia Foundation for the Humanities and Public Policy and the Library of Virginia, *20th Century Virginia Authors* features some of the hundreds of writers who have shaped Virginia's literary heritage. At the top of the map is an outline of Virginia, with numbered photographs of twelve prominent authors who have spent time in the state: Sherwood Anderson, James Branch Cabell, Willa Cather, John Dos Passos, Rita Dove, John Fox, Jr., Ellen Glasgow, Earl Hamner, Jr., Mary Johnston, William Styron, Peter Taylor, and Tom Wolfe. A numbered key below gives information on places where these authors lived, the genres in which they worked, their major works, and awards they won. At right, information is given for an additional forty-seven writers, some of whom are pictured. An accompanying booklet entitled *20th Century Virginia Authors: A Guide to the Literary Map* contains background information on the map and pictures and biographical sketches of fifty-eight modern writers.

WASHINGTON

Washington Writers

Washington State Council of Teachers of
English, 1988
57 x 87 cm
Color
G4281 .E65 1988 .W3

*Courtesy of the Washington State Council of Teachers
of English*

Drawn in a light, cartoon style, *Washington Writers* contains a compass, mythical sea animals, ships, and other elements common to Renaissance maps. The map illustrates the mountains, rivers, lakes, and other topographical features of Washington state, as well as major cities. Writers are not listed directly on the map but are given alphabetically by genre in shields on the left of it. The shields list well-known writers such as Seattle-born Mary McCarthy, author of *The Group*; Tom Robbins, author of *Even Cowgirls Get the Blues*, who worked for Seattle newspapers; Beat Generation poet Gary Snyder, who won the Pulitzer Prize in 1975; and short-story writer Raymond Carver, who grew up in Yakima. Also pictured or mentioned are historical characters, such as the state's first governor; Chief Seattle (1786–1866), the Native American who befriended the first pioneers in the Seattle area and for whom the city is named; and early explorers of the area Meriwether Lewis (1774–1809), William Clark (1770–1838), James Cook (1728–1779), and George Vancouver (1758–1798).

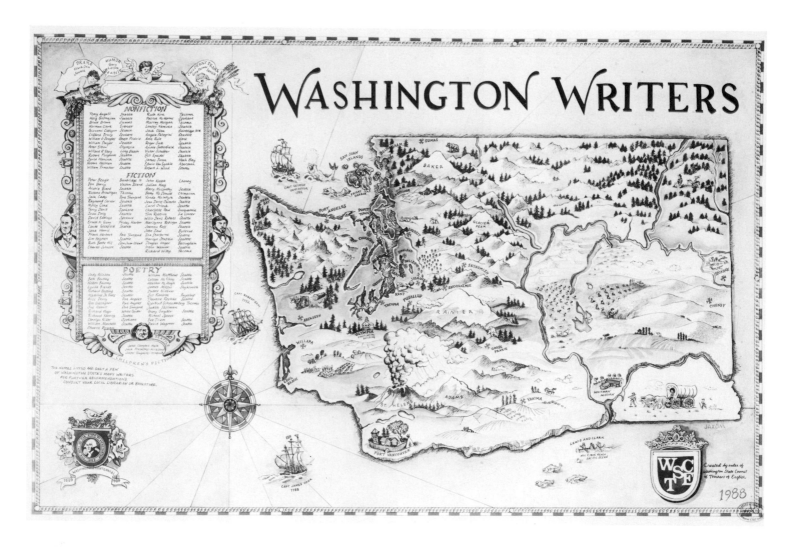

WISCONSIN

Wisconsin Authors

DUANE AND MAUREEN ROEN
Compilers

KIRK TINGEBLAD
Illustrator

Wisconsin Council of Teachers of English,
 1978
74 X 59 cm
Black and white
G4121 .E65 1978 .T5

*W*isconsin Authors features thirty-seven major Wisconsin authors, the towns with which they or their work are associated, and an illustration based on each author's life or work. Books illustrated include *Little House in the Big Woods*, by Laura Ingalls Wilder, born in Pepin; the Pulitzer Prize-winning *So Big*, by Edna Ferber, a book about her childhood in Appleton; the Pulitzer Prize-winning *The Bridge of San Luis Rey* (1938) by Thornton Wilder, born in Madison; and *Misty of Chincoteague* (1947) by Marguerite Henry, who lived in Milwaukee in her youth. The borders of the map provide lists of "Other Adult Writers" and "Other Juvenile Writers." The map is accompanied by *Wisconsin Authors* (Wisconsin Council of Teachers of English service bulletin no. 37, September 1978), which lists life dates, Wisconsin ties, and major works for authors whose works are illustrated on the map as well as many others. It also contains a bibliography of Wisconsin literature. Works suitable for young readers are marked.

WYOMING

Wyoming Literary Map

EUGENE V. MORAN
Compiler

KEN CLUBB
Illustrator

Laramie: University of Wyoming, 1984
49 x 61 cm
Color
G4261 .E65 1984 .M6

*Courtesy of Eugene V. Moran, Professor Emeritus,
University of Wyoming*

The *Wyoming Literary Map* shows a colorful outline of the state featuring titles of books and names of authors of fiction or poetry who are associated with Wyoming, with the best known highlighted in yellow boxes. Around the borders are color images of selected authors who lived in Wyoming or set works there: Western writer Louis L'Amour, who used the state as the locale for a number of novels; Ernest Hemingway, who spent summers in Wyoming; William "Buffalo Bill" Cody, founder of the city of Cody, who wrote about the Rocky Mountain area; Washington Irving, whose *The Adventures of Captain Bonneville, U.S.A.* (1837) occurs in Wyoming; Vladimir Nabokov, who wrote parts of *Lolita* there; Mark Twain, who includes a chapter set in Wyoming in *Roughing It* (1872); Zane Grey, author of *Wyoming* (1932); novelist Mary Roberts Rinehart, who had a summer home in the state; Dee Brown, author of *Fort Phil Kearny*; Owen Wister, who spent his summers in Wyoming and set *The Virginian* (1902) there; humorist Bill Nye, founder of the Laramie *Boomerang*; and Mary O'Hara, author of *My Friend Flicka* (1941), who lived on a ranch near Laramie. Compiled by University of Wyoming professor Eugene V. Moran, the map was funded by the Burlington Northern Railroad and intended for use in Wyoming English classrooms.

Color Illustrations

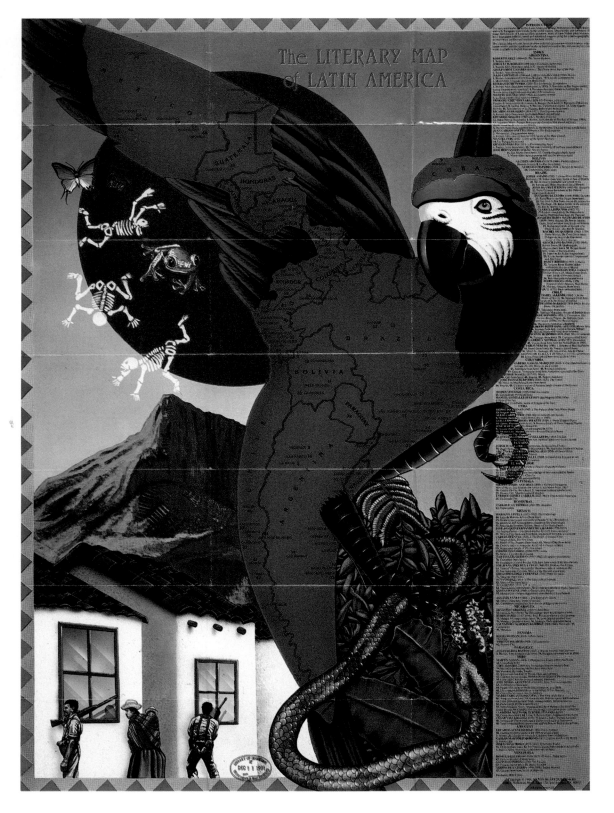

This map by the Aaron Blake Company reflects the increasing attention being given in the 1980s and 1990s to non-European literature, in particular to works from Latin America, Canada, Asia, and Africa.

The Literary Map of Latin America, 1988
Courtesy of Molly Maguire and Aaron Silverman

(See p. 27.)

Language of the Land

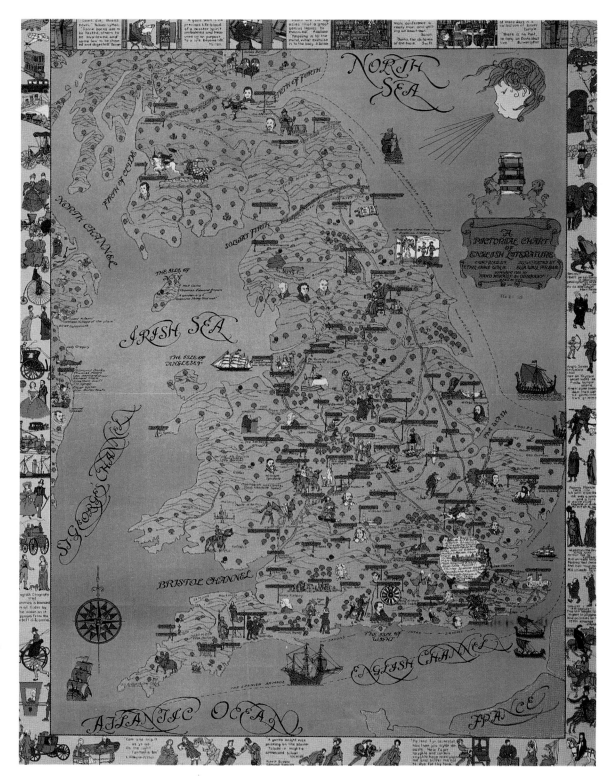

Many American-produced literary maps of the 1920s feature British writers, demonstrating the dominance of that literary tradition in the American imagination before the 1970s.

A Pictorial Chart of English Literature, 1929

(See p. 59.)

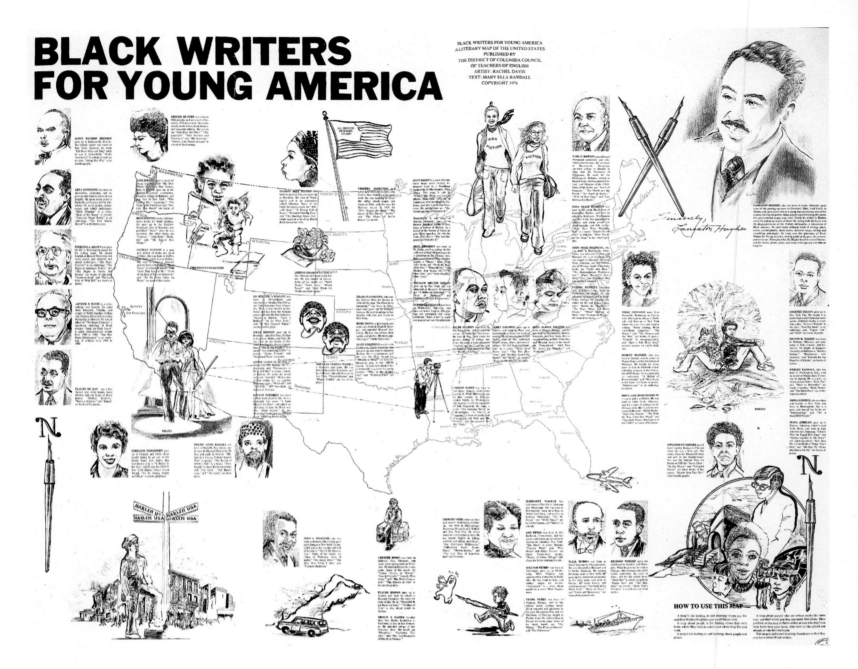

Produced by the District of Columbia Council of Teachers of English for the U.S. Bicentennial, *Black Writers for Young America* is the only map in the Library's collections devoted exclusively to African American authors.

Black Writers for Young America, 1976

(See p. 72.)

Although they are among the earliest examples in the Library's holdings, the literary maps produced by Paul M. Paine are visually among the finest in their use of color and of illustrations of authors and scenes from books.

The Booklovers Map of America, Showing Certain Landmarks of Literary Geography, 1926

(See p. 74.)

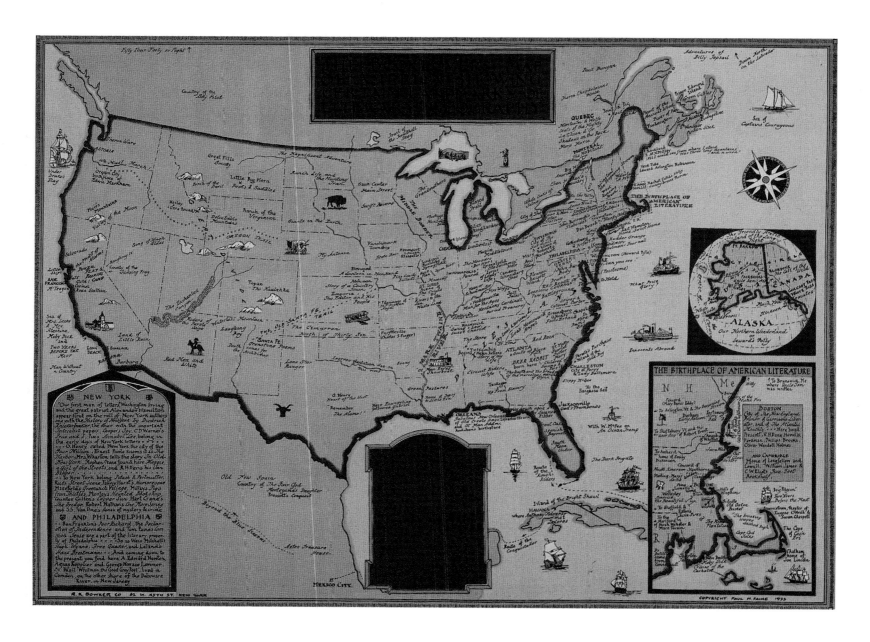

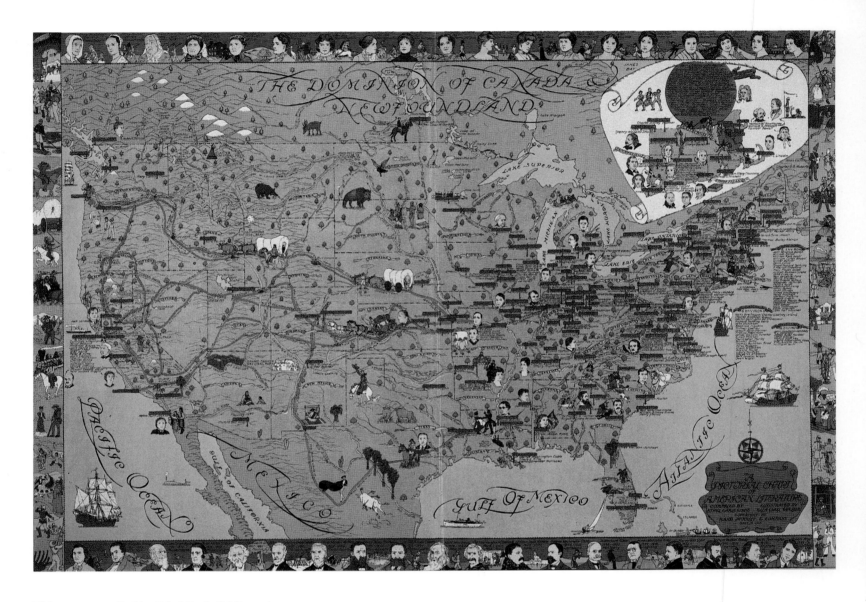

This map compiled by Ethel Earle Wylie and illustrated by Ella Wall Van Leer, the creators of *A Pictorial Chart of English Literature*, is one of the earliest to give America's women writers a prominent place.

A Pictorial Chart of American Literature, 1932

(See p. 84.)

A prolific literary-map producer of the
1940s, 1950s, and 1960s, Henry J. Firley
compiled colorful and highly detailed maps
such as this one for classroom use.

*A Pictorial Map of Colonial-Revolutionary
American Literature, 1585–1789, 1965*

(See p. 86.)

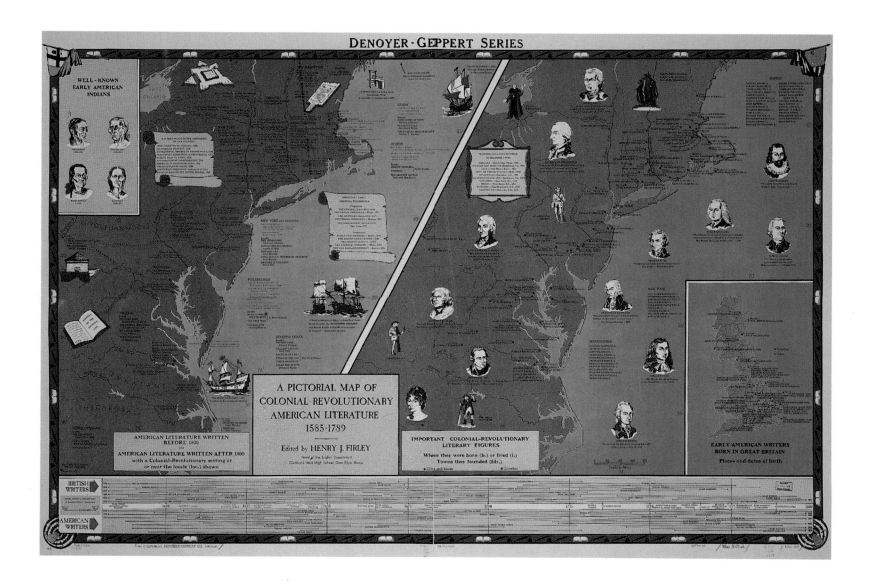

Language of the Land

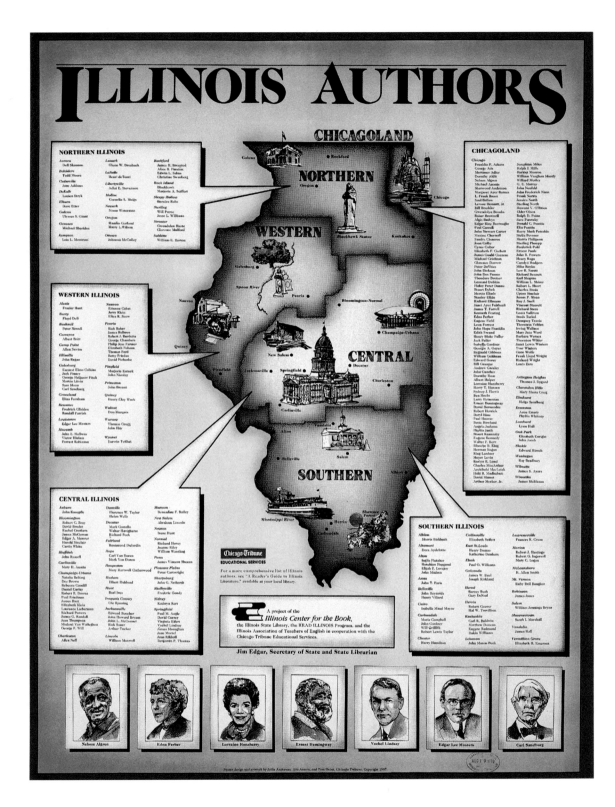

In contrast to an earlier Illinois map of the 1950s, this map features many more authors, in particular more women and black writers, in keeping with a trend toward greater diversity in the literary canon that developed in the 1980s.

Illinois Authors, 1987

(See p. 112.)

Language of the Land

Prepared by the Michigan Center for the Book, *Portraits of Literary Michigan* is one of the literary maps produced in the 1990s in connection with the tour of the *Language of the Land* exhibit.

Portraits of Literary Michigan, 1994
Courtesy of the Library of Michigan

(See p. 122.)

This map was created to celebrate Mississippi's rich literary heritage and foster pride in that heritage among the state's school children.

Modern Mississippi Writers: A Map of Literary Mississippi, 1992
Published with the permission of the University Press of Mississippi

(See p. 125.)

Language of the Land

Nebraska Centennial Literary Map and guide to Nebraska Authors

1 Pine Ridge — site of Fort Robinson, where Crazy Horse died
2 Scottsbluff National Monument
3 Old Jules Country
4 Ogallala — Nebraska's cowboy capital in trail days
5 Buffalo Bill's "Scout Rest" (North Platte)
6 Bassett — once headquarters for the notorious outlaws Doc Middleton and Kid Wade and the Pony Boys
7 Custer County — home of the pioneer photographer, Solomon D. Butcher
8 Fort Kearny
9 Willa Cather Country
10 Lone Tree Monument at Central City — the "Lone Tree" of Wright Morris's novels
11 John Neihardt Country
12 Homestead National Monument

Map by Jack Brodie
Guide compiled by Bernice Kauffman

Published by the Nebraska Centennial Commission in cooperation with the Nebraska Arts Council.

Copyright 1967 by the Nebraska Centennial Non-Profit Association
Manufactured in the United States of America

Created for the one hundredth anniversary of its statehood, Nebraska's map reflects the pride of its residents in their cultural heritage and celebrates the regionalism that has long been a predominant feature of American literature.

Nebraska Centennial Literary Map and Guide to Nebraska Authors, 1967
Reprinted with permission of the Nebraska Department of Economic Development, Division of Travel and Tourism, and the Nebraska English Language Arts Council

(See p. 130.)

Language of the Land

171

Like many of the literary maps in the
Library's collections, this map of Oregon
was produced by the state's Council of
Teachers of English.

Oregon Literary Map, 1989
Courtesy of the Oregon Council of Teachers of English

(See p. 147.)

Language of the Land

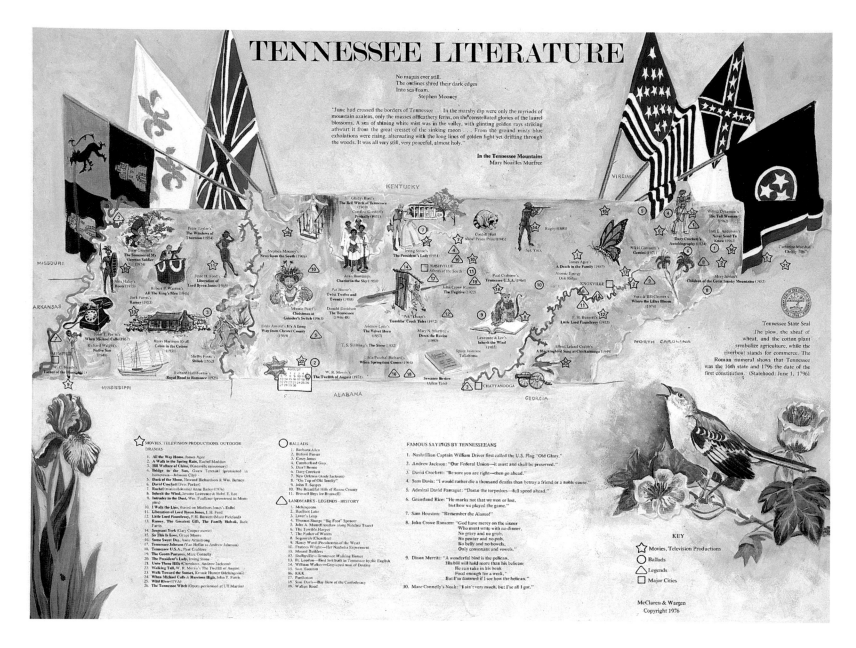

The line between the literary and the historical is often amorphous; like a number of the Library's maps, this one includes representations of the state flag, flower, and bird, and historic figures and monuments.

Tennessee Literature, 1976
Courtesy of the Tennessee Council of Teachers of English

(See p. 152.)

Language of the Land

This colorful map, produced by a book
store, gives readers the thrill of recognizing
characters and episodes from all thirteen of
the books in the Oz series by L. Frank Baum.

The Wonderful World of Oz, 1988
Courtesy of Books of Wonder, New York

(See p. 188.)

Language of the Land

This map by Molly Maguire, who produced a series of literary maps in the 1980s for the Aaron Blake Company, can be used to trace the sites of the incidents in the Sherlock Holmes books by Arthur Conan Doyle.

The Sherlock Holmes Mystery Map, 1987
Courtesy of Molly Maguire and Aaron Silverman

(See p. 207.)

Language of the Land

175

Drawn in a style that mirrors the jackets of
spy thrillers, the *Ian Fleming Thriller Map*
features locations that James Bond, Agent
007 of the British Secret Service, visits in
his exploits.

The Ian Fleming Thriller Map, 1987
Courtesy of Molly Maguire and Aaron Silverman

(See p. 211.)

Language of the Land

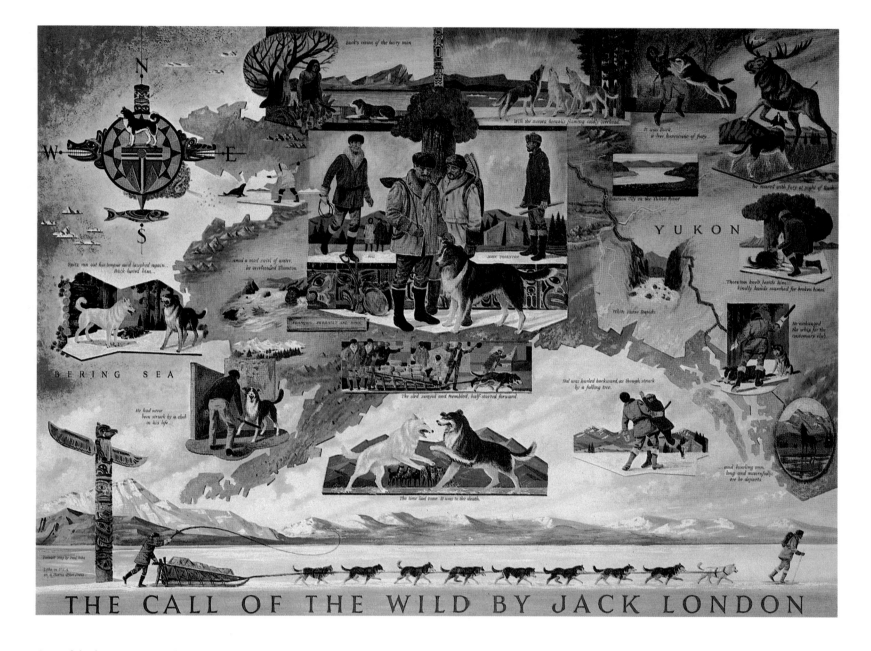

THE CALL OF THE WILD BY JACK LONDON

One of the later maps produced for the Harris-Intertype Corporation's popular calendars, *The Call of the Wild* colorfully portrays scenes from the best-selling 1903 adventure novel based on Jack London's own adventures during the Klondike gold rush.

The Call of the Wild by Jack London, 1962

(See p. 229.)

Language of the Land

Created by well-known advertising artist
Everett Henry, *The Voyage of the Pequod*
is one of twelve maps produced by the
Harris-Seybold Corporation for annual
calendars demonstrating and promoting the
lithographic equipment it manufactured.

The Voyage of the Pequod from the Book
Moby Dick by Herman Melville, 1956

(See p. 230.)

The oldest map in the Library's collections that was not originally in a book, this bird's-eye view map shows the tourist attractions in the hometown of William Shakespeare as they were in the early twentieth century.

Stratford on Avon, 1908

(See p. 243.)

Language of the Land

Produced by artist Everett Henry for the Harris-Intertype Company, this map is an example of the type that give viewers the thrill of seeing representations of familiar characters and scenes from a well-known story.

The Adventures of Huckleberry Finn from the Book by Mark Twain, 1959

(See p. 256.)

Language of the Land

One of the earliest maps in the Library's collections, the highly detailed *Ancient Mappe of Fairyland* depicts motifs from various European fantasy traditions—fairy tales, nursery rhymes, Arthurian legends, children's books, and Celtic, Norse, and Greco-Roman mythology. This detail shows the Holy Mountain Monsalvat, part of the legend of the Holy Grail.

An Ancient Mappe of Fairyland, Newly Discovered and Set Forth, ca. 1920

(See p. 271.)

Language of the Land

Specific Books and Authors

"Everything one invents is true, you may be perfectly sure of that! Poetry is as precise as geometry." **Gustave Flaubert**
quoted in Eudora Welty, "Place in Fiction"

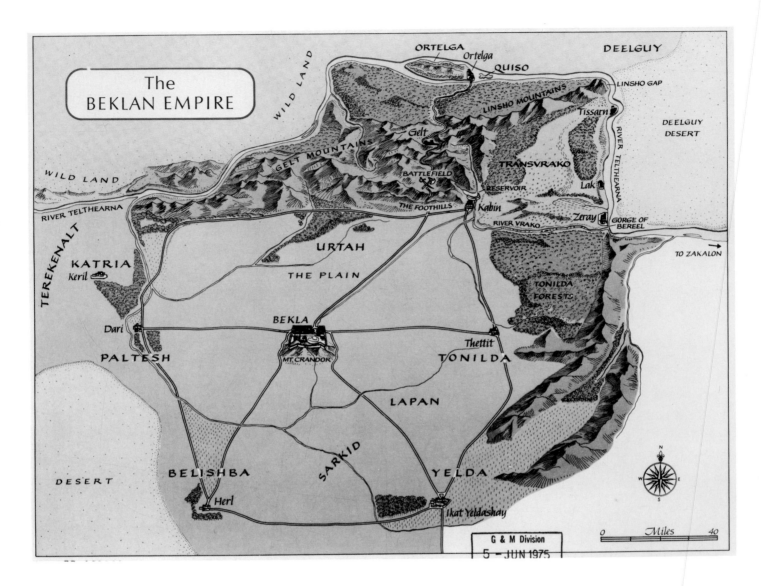

The map labels visible include: ORTELGA, Ortelga, QUISO, DEELGUY, WILD LAND, LINSHO GAP, Tissarn, LINSHO MOUNTAINS, DEELGUY DESERT, Gelt, GELT MOUNTAINS, TRANSVRAKO, RIVER TELTHEARNA, BATTLEFIELD, RESERVOIR, Lak, Kabin, THE FOOTHILLS, RIVER VRAKO, Zeray, GORGE OF BEREEL, KATRIA, Keril, URTAH, THE PLAIN, TONILDA FORESTS, TO ZAKALON, Dari, BEKLA, Thettit, MT. CRANDOR, TONILDA, PALTESH, LAPAN, SARKID, YELDA, BELISHBA, Herl, Ikat Yeldashay, DESERT, G & M Division 5 - JUN 1975, Miles 0 40

RICHARD ADAMS

The Beklan Empire

Rafael Palacios
Illustrator

New York: Simon and Schuster, 1974
20 x 27 cm
Color
G9930 1974 .P3

The Beklan Empire map, which appeared as endpapers in the novel *Shardik* (1975) by Richard Adams, locates places mentioned in the book. The adventure novel is set in the mythical Beklan Empire, whose inhabitants, the Ortelgans, have been enslaved. Inspired by worship of a giant bear, Shardik, they are able to drive off their oppressors. At the center of the empire is the city of Bekla, on top of Mt. Crandor. Roads from it lead to the cities of Thettit, Dari, Herl, Kabin, and Ikat Yeldashay. Also shown are the Gelt Mountains, the Tonilda Forests, the Telthearna and Vrako rivers. The Wild Land and the Deelguy Desert, areas that border the empire, also appear.

Language of the Land

APPOLONIUS OF RHODES

Argonautica

Abraham Ortelius
Illustrator

Library of Congress, ca. 1956
In Latin
50 x 70 cm
Black and white
G5672 .M4 .E65 1932 .T3

*A*rgonautica shows the setting of the poem (3rd c. BC) of that name by Apollonius of Rhodes. A leading figure in the cultural life of the Hellenistic period, Appolonius held the post of Royal Librarian at the Library of Alexandria from around 270 to 245 BC. Written in four books in a style influenced by that of Homer, the poem retells the legend of Jason's quest of the golden fleece. The map depicts the area of the eastern Mediterranean Sea where the voyage of Jason and the Argonauts took place. Inset maps show Thessaly, Thrace, and all of Europe. An illustration at the top of the map shows the golden fleece, hanging on a tree guarded by fire-breathing oxen and a dragon. Latin inscriptions tell what happened at various places. The map is a reproduction published by the Library of Congress of a plate from *Theatrum Orbis Terrarum* (1598) by Abraham Ortelius.

JANE AUSTEN

The Jane Austen Map of England

MOLLY MAGUIRE
Designer

CAROL KIEFFER POLICE
Illustrator

Los Angeles: Aaron Blake, 1987
52 x 70 cm
Color
G5751 .E65 1987 .A15

Courtesy of Molly Maguire and Aaron Silverman

*T*he *Jane Austen Map of England* depicts places featured in the novels of Jane Austen, author of *Sense and Sensibility* (1811), *Pride and Prejudice* (1813), *Mansfield Park* (1814), *Emma* (1816), *Northanger Abbey* (1818), and *Persuasion (1818)*. The map shows locations in southern England that played a role in Austen's novels or her own life keyed by number to a list of the novels. Enlarged maps of Bath and London, important settings for the books, are enclosed in ovals surrounded by pink ribbons. The central image shows the drawing room of Lady Catherine de Bourgh, the grande dame who attempts to thwart the marriage of Elizabeth Bennett and Mr. Darcy in *Pride and Prejudice*. Research and design for the map were performed by Molly Maguire, who produced a series of literary maps in the 1980s.

JAMES M. BARRIE

Peter Pan's Never Land

Anaheim, California: Walt Disney
    Productions, 1953
27 x 41 cm
Color
G9931 .A5 1953 .D5

©The Walt Disney Company

*P*eter Pan's Never Land promoted Walt Disney's 1953 animated film version of the classic children's story *Peter Pan* (1904) by James M. Barrie. The central portion of the map shows the topography of Never Land, the magical island to which the characters flee, with such landmarks as Skull Rock, Peter's Hideout, the Indian Camp, and Pirate Cove. Around the border are scenes from the film showing the characters such as Peter Pan; Wendy; her brothers Michael and John; the Lost Boys, Peter's gang; Captain Hook and his diabolical pirate crew; and the crocodile that stalks Hook. The map also advertises the "Peter Pan Beauty Bar With Chlorophyll," introduced by Colgate-Palmolive Company as a tie-in with the film. Soap users could obtain the map by mailing in three soap wrappers and fifteen cents.

L. FRANK BAUM

The Wonderful World of Oz

Dick Martin
Illustrator

New York: Ozma, Inc., 1988
56 x 81 cm
Color *(See color section.)*
G9930 1986 .M3

Courtesy of Books of Wonder, New York

*T*he Wonderful World of Oz is based on the stories created by L[yman] Frank Baum. His most famous work, *The Wizard of Oz* (1900), became a best-seller and was produced as a play in 1902 and as a classic film in 1939. However, the book was only the first in a series of thirteen books about Oz, including *The Emerald City of Oz* (1909), *Tik-Tok Man of Oz* (1914), and *The Scarecrow of Oz* (1915). These books introduce to the Oz story additional characters and episodes, which are reflected on this map.

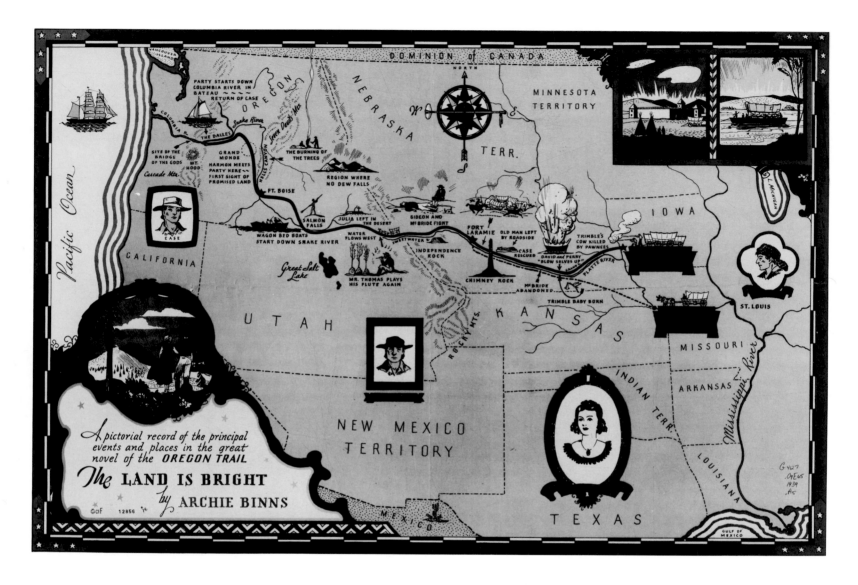

ARCHIE BINNS

A Pictorial Record of the Principal Events and Places in the Great Novel of the Oregon Trail: The Land Is Bright by Archie Binns

GEORGE ANNAND
Illustrator

New York: Charles Scribners and Sons, 1939
45 x 65 cm
Color
G4127 .07E65 1939 .A5

This map records events in Archie Binns's book *The Land Is Bright* (1939), which recounts the misfortunes of a wagon train en route to the West along the Oregon Trail. The map shows territory of the United States from the Mississippi River to the Pacific Ocean. The route to Oregon followed by the settlers in the course of the book is traced on the map, and key events of the story are noted in words and pictures. Insets depict characters from the book—Nancy Ann Greenfield, the heroine, and her suitors McBride, Gideon, and Case—and key places—Fort Laramie and the spot where the wagons cross the Mississippi River.

THE BRONTËS

The Brontë Way

RODICA PRATO
Illustrator

1993
25 x 31 cm
Color
G5753 .W37 .E65 1994 .P7 Vault

Courtesy of Rodica Prato

*T*he Brontë Way, an original artwork which illustrated a January 1994 *Travel and Leisure* magazine article on the Brontë country, traces a tourist route through landmarks of the West Yorkshire countryside that was the home of Charlotte, Emily, and Anne Brontë and forms the setting of most of their works. Illustrations on the maps locate such important sites as the writers' Haworth home, now the Brontë Parsonage Museum, and the Brontë Falls, to which the sisters loved to walk. Other sites identified include the ruins of Wycoller Hall, the model for Ferndean, Mr. Rochester's home in Charlotte's *Jane Eyre* (1847); Pondon Hall, the original of Thrushcross Grange; and Top Withens, the original of Wuthering Heights, both in Emily's 1847 novel of that name. The map features insets of the famous portrait of his sisters that Branwell Brontë (1817–1848) painted around 1835 and a map of England locating the Brontë sites.

Haworth and the Brontë Country, Yorkshire

Geoffrey Conning
Designer and Illustrator

Haworth, Yorkshire: Brontë Parsonage
    Museum, 1963
63 x 48 cm
Color
G5754 .H285 .E65 1963 .C6

Courtesy of the Brontë Parsonage Museum

*H*aworth and the Brontë Country, Yorkshire shows landmarks of the West Yorkshire countryside of England that was the home of authors Charlotte, Emily, and Anne Brontë and forms the setting of most of their major work. Illustrations on the maps locate such important sites as the writers' birthplace in Thornton; their Haworth home, now the Brontë Parsonage Museum; Roe Head School, which they attended; the main street and church of Haworth; and Top Withens, the model for Wuthering Heights in Emily's novel of that name. At bottom right is a genealogical chart of the Brontë family. Around the edges and on scrolls in the body of the map are quotations from Emily's poems.

ROBERT BURNS

Official Tourist Map, Burns Country: Ayrshire, Dumfries, and Galloway

Tenterden, Kent, U.K.: Estate Publications,
    ca. 1986
61 x 76 cm
Color
G5773 .A9E635 1986 .E8

Reproduced with the permission of Estate Publications

Reproduced with the permission of Estate Publications, this map of places associated with Scottish national poet Robert Burns was produced in conjunction with the Dumfries and Galloway Tourist Board, the Ayrshire and Burns Country Tourist Board, the Burns Federation, and the Burns Cottage. It shows the Burns Heritage Trail, a tour around Ayr, Dumfries, and Galloway to places where Burns lived and worked. Burns was born in a cottage in Alloway, now a museum preserving his letters, songs, and other relics, and was educated in Alloway and Ayr. In 1791 he settled in Dumfries, where his house is now a museum, and is buried in a mausoleum in St. Michael's churchyard there. Illustrations show a portrait of Burns; the Brig 'o' doon, where Burns's character Tam o' Shanter on his gray mare outstripped the warlocks and hags, with the Burns monument in the background; the Burns house, Dumfries; and Souter Johnnie's cottage with statues of characters from Burns's poem "Tam o' Shanter." A legend in English, German, French, Dutch, and Spanish locates roads, railways, ferries, national parks, footpaths, and canals.

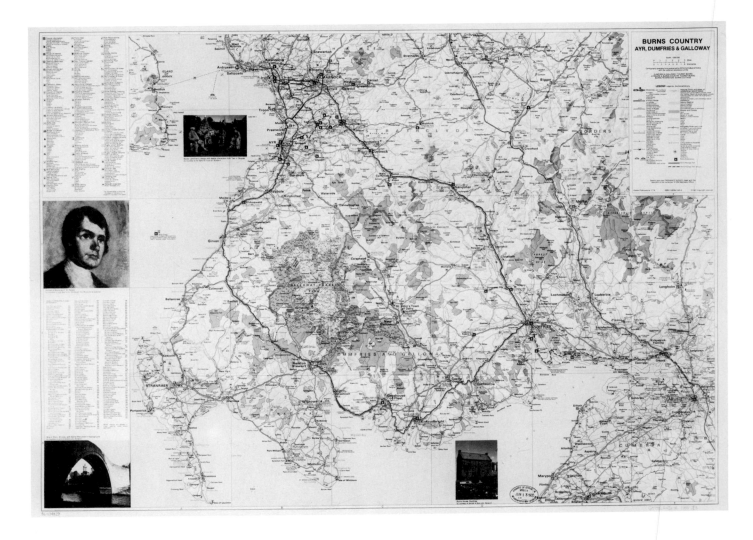

JAMES BRANCH CABELL

Poictesme

PETER KOCH
Illustrator

Chicago: Argus Books, 1929
56 x 74 cm
Color
Ethel M. Fair Collection 336

Poictesme, the location of works by Virginia author James Branch Cabell, is a medieval kingdom in southern France, to the west of Provence. Its one major river, the Duardenez, flows through the country before entering the Gulf of Aiguesmortes in the southeast. It has two major forests, the Forest of Acaire and the Forest of Bovoin. Between Acaire and the Duardenez is Amneran Heath, an area haunted by witches. Another landmark is Storisende, the castle of the Counts of Poictesme. Cabell's books dealing with Poictesme are *Jurgen: A Comedy of Justice* (1919), *Figures of Earth: A Comedy of Appearance* (1921), *The High Place: A Comedy of Disenchantment* (1923), and *The Silver Stallion: A Comedy of Redemption* (1927). Further information on Poictesme can be found in Alberto Manguel and Gianni Guadalupi, *The Dictionary of Imaginary Places* (see "Literary Atlases" section).

LUIS DE CAMÕES

Carta da geografica dos Lusiadas, poema epico de Luis de Camões
(Map of the Lusiadas, an epic poem by Luis de Camões)

A. C. Borges de Figuierdo
Designer and Illustrator

Lisbon: 1883
45 x 92 cm
Color
G3201 .E65 155– .F5 Vault

Carta da geografica dos Lusiadas shows places mentioned in the *Lusiadas* (1572), an epic poem by Luis de Camões that is considered the highest achievement of Portuguese literature. De Camões himself served the Portuguese Empire as a soldier in India and China. Based on the discovery of a sea route to India by Vasco da Gama in 1497–98, the poem celebrates the founding of the Portuguese Empire in the East and other episodes of Portuguese history. The name of the epic refers to the ancient Roman region of Lusitania, which included modern Portugal. Written in ten cantos, the poem is modeled on Virgil's *The Aeneid*. Mythological figures such as Jupiter, Venus, and Bacchus appear in the poem along with the giant Adamastor, an invention of Camões. Red lines on a world map trace de Gama's voyage along the east coast of Africa, into the Indian Ocean, and on to India. Blue lines trace the voyage of Ferdinand Magellan. Inset maps show the Iberian Peninsula, Italy, Greece, Arabia, India, and Southeast Asia.

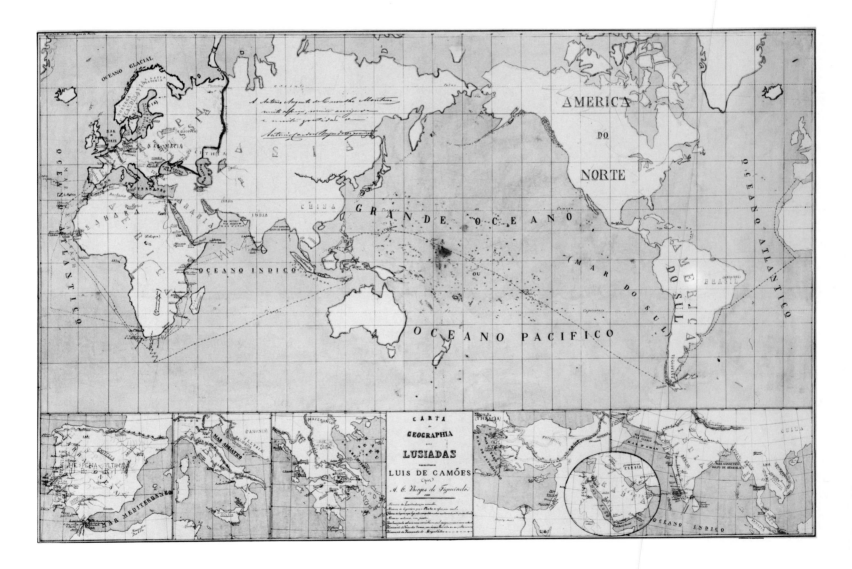

Language of the Land

RAYMOND CHANDLER

The Raymond Chandler Mystery Map of Los Angeles

MOLLY MAGUIRE
Designer

ALICE CLARKE
Illustrator

Los Angeles: Aaron Blake, 1985
51 x 61 cm
Color
G4364 .L8E65 1987 .A21

Courtesy of Molly Maguire and Aaron Silverman

*T*he *Raymond Chandler Mystery Map of Los Angeles* traces sites connected with the works of Raymond Chandler, American novelist and screenwriter famous for his tough, literate crime stories featuring private detective Philip Marlowe. An image at top left shows the hard-boiled Marlowe with the body of a dead young woman on the floor. The map highlights Los Angeles and its surrounding areas of Santa Monica (Bay City), Hollywood, and Lake Arrowhead that are the setting of Chandler's stories from *The Big Sleep* (1939) to *Playback* (1958). A key at the bottom of the map gives further information on the connections between the places and Chandler's works. Research and design for the map were performed by Molly Maguire, who produced a series of literary maps in the 1980s.

JAMES FENIMORE COOPER

Carte dressée pour la lecture du Puritain d' Amérique, roman de J. Fenimore Cooper

(Map prepared for the reading of *Puritan of America,* a novel by J. Fenimore Cooper)

ARISTIDE MICHEL PERROT
Cartographer

Paris: Charles Gosselin, ca. 1829
In French
13 x 16 cm
Black and white
G3721 .E65 1829 .P4

*C*arte dressée pour la lecture du Puritain d' Amérique, roman de J. Fenimore Cooper* probably illustrated a French edition of *The Wept of Wish-Ton-Wish* (1829) by James Fenimore Cooper. Author of the popular "Leather-stocking Tales" of the early American frontier and one of the first American writers to achieve international recognition, Cooper was popular in Europe, particularly in France, where his work influenced novelists such as Honoré de Balzac. *The Wept of Wish-Ton-Wish* is a novel of Puritan life during the period of King Philip's War (1675–1676), the bloodiest of the seventeenth-century conflicts between English colonists and

the Indians. Led by Philip, Chief of the Wampanoag tribe, Indian warriors destroyed settlements on the western frontiers of New England. Based in part on true accounts of pioneers captured by Indians, the book is about the Heathcotes, settlers on the Connecticut frontier whose home is destroyed by Indians who carry off their daughter. After years in captivity, during which she almost forgets her family and marries a Narragansett chief, the girl is returned, but dies soon after. The map traces family patriarch Mark Heathcote's route when he emigrates from Massachusetts, following a sea route from Plymouth and around Cape Cod, then up the Connecticut River to Hartford. He settles in a nearby valley named Wish-Ton-Wish after the first bird seen by the English colonists. The title refers to the wept-for daughter, whose tombstone reads "The Wept of Wish-Ton-Wish."

The Last of the Mohicans by James Fenimore Cooper

KEN RILEY
Illustrator

Cleveland: Harris-Intertype, 1963
52 x 68 cm
Color
G3802 .G4E65 1757 .R5

*T*he Last of the Mohicans by James Fenimore Cooper shows scenes from the classic 1826 novel of the French and Indian War by James Fenimore Cooper, author of the popular "Leather-stocking Tales" of the early American frontier and one of the first American writers to achieve international recognition. Frontiersman Natty Bumppo, or "Hawkeye," hero of this novel and other Cooper works such as *The Pioneers* (1823) and *The Deerslayer* (1841), appears at bottom right, holding his long rifle. Alice and Cora Munro, Major Heywood, Chingachgook, and his son Uncas, the last of the Mohicans, appear in other scenes. These vignettes show the flight to Fort William Henry, surrender of the fort to French general Montcalm, the death of Magua, and other famous episodes from the book. An inset map shows the area around New York's Lake George, where most of the novel's action takes place.

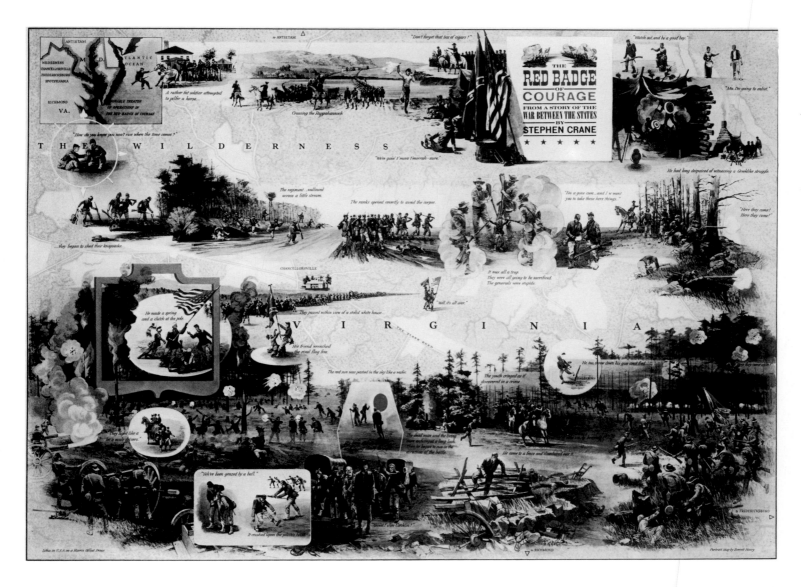

STEPHEN CRANE

The Red Badge of Courage from a Story of the War Between the States by Stephen Crane

Everett Henry
Illustrator

Cleveland: Harris-Intertype, 1961
47 x 64 cm
Color
G3884 .C36. S5 1961 .H4

A gainst an outline of Virginia, *The Red Badge of Courage* map shows scenes from the 1895 novel by Stephen Crane in which he describes the Civil War experiences of young recruit Henry Fleming. A small inset map in the upper left corner shows the eastern Virginia area in which the action of the novel takes place.

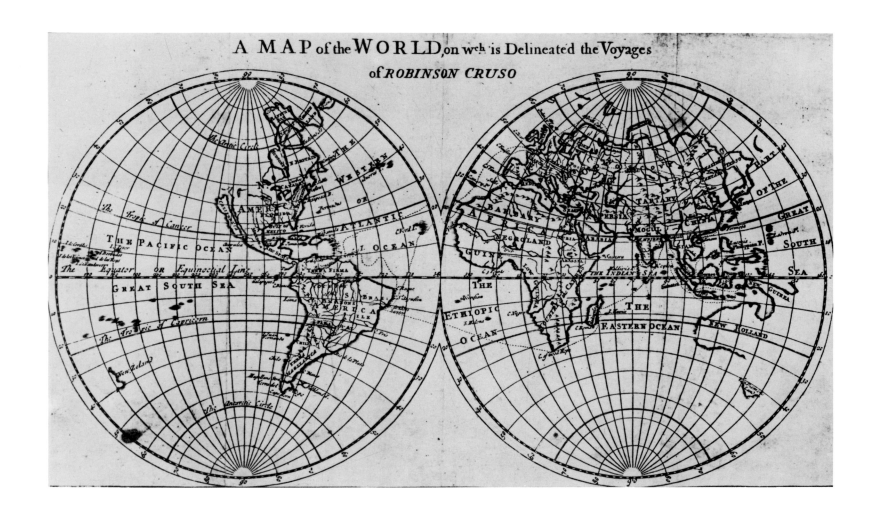

A MAP of the WORLD, on wᶜʰ is Delineated the Voyages of ROBINSON CRUSO

DANIEL DEFOE

Map of the World on w[hi]ch is Delineated the Voyages of Robinson Cruso [sic]

London: 1719
27 x 33 cm
Black and white photocopy
G3201 .E65 1719 .M3

This map is a photocopy of the frontispiece map of volume 2 of the first edition of *The Farther Adventures of Robinson Crusoe: Being the Second and Last Part of His Life* (1719), by Daniel Defoe, a sequel to his popular *The Life and Adventures of Robinson Crusoe* (1719). Defoe wrote two sequels following the success of the first book, the other being *Serious Reflections during the Life and Surprising Adventures of Robinson Crusoe* (1720), but the sequels were never as well regarded as the original book. In *The Farther Adventures*, Crusoe goes back to the desert island as a colonist and has more of the kind of adventures that befell him in the first book. Dotted lines on the map trace journeys made by Crusoe after his original rescue from the island.

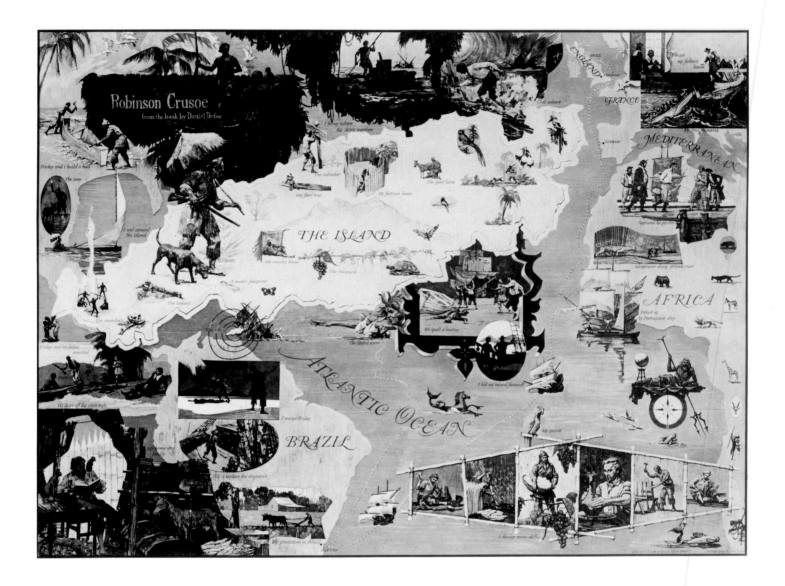

Robinson Crusoe from the Book by Daniel Defoe

KEN RILEY
Illustrator

Cleveland: Harris-Intertype, 1964
45 x 60 cm
Color
G9930 1964 .R5

The *Robinson Crusoe* map is based on the most famous work of English author Daniel Defoe. Published in 1719, *The Life and Adventures of Robinson Crusoe* recounts the fictional adventures of a Yorkshire native shipwrecked on a desert island. Inspired by the true story of Alexander Selkirk (1676–1721), a Scottish sailor who spent four solitary years on an island off Chile, the book became immensely popular. The map illustrates episodes from the book, such as Crusoe's first meeting with his eventual companion Friday.

Language of the Land

CHARLES DICKENS

Map of the London of Dickens

Frances Loomis, ca. 1935
24 x 43 cm
Black and white photostat
G5754 .L7 .E65 1865 .L6

The *Map of the London of Dickens* is a photostat of a hand-drawn map. It identifies nineteenth-century London locations mentioned in the works of English novelist Charles Dickens. The map locates the homes of characters and places they visit and describes incidents in Dickens's novels such as *The Pickwick Papers* (1836–1837), *Oliver Twist* (1837–1839), *Nicholas Nickleby* (1838–1839), *Martin Chuzzlewit* (1843–1844), and *David Copperfield* (1849–1850).

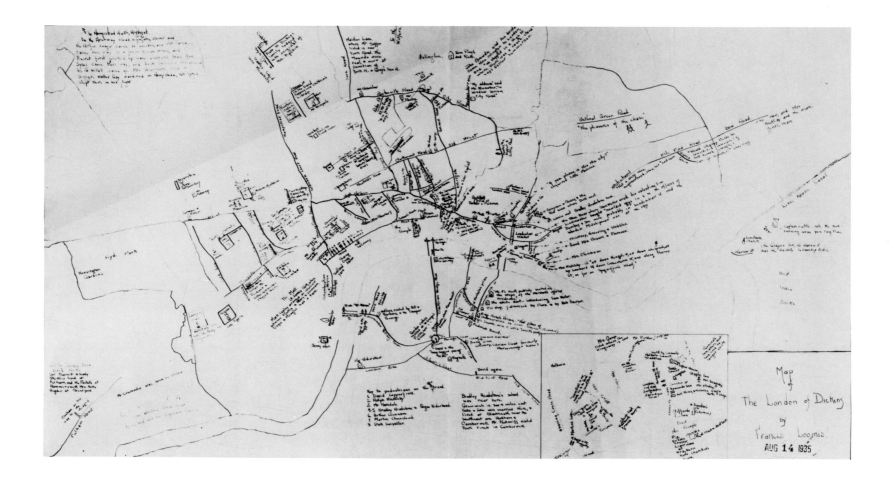

A Tale of Two Cities from the Book by Charles Dickens

EVERETT HENRY
Illustrator

Cleveland: Harris-Seybold, 1957
75 x 64 cm
Color
G5754 .L7E65 1789 .H5

A Tale of Two Cities shows scenes from the 1859 novel set during the French Revolution by English author Charles Dickens. Two maps show London and Paris, the cities in which the novel's action occurs. The central scene depicts the July 14, 1789, storming of the Bastille prison—symbol of the French monarchy's autocratic power—an actual historic event that Dickens describes in the book. Smaller scenes show other key events in the novel's plot, for example, the child crushed by the Marquis's coach, the death of the Marquis, the wedding of Lucie Manette and Charles Darnay, and Sidney Carton taking Darnay's place and going to the guillotine.

Language of the Land

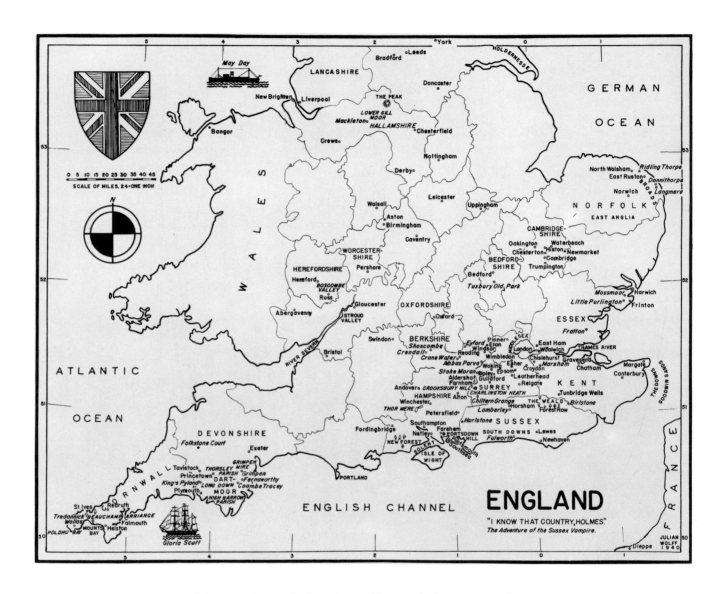

ENGLAND

"I KNOW THAT COUNTRY, HOLMES."
The Adventure of the Sussex Vampire.

JULIAN
WOLFF
1940

ARTHUR CONAN DOYLE

England

JULIAN WOLFF
Illustrator

New York?: J. Wolff, 194
30 x 37 cm
Black and white
G5751 .E65 1940 .W6

This map shows the location of fictional places in southern England mentioned in the Sherlock Holmes stories by Arthur Conan Doyle. Below the title is a quote from the 1927 story *The Adventure of the Sussex Vampire*: "I know that country, Holmes." This map is Part B in a five-part, limited-edition set of Sherlock Holmes maps by Dr. Julian Wolff (1905–1990), long-time president of the Baker Street Irregulars, an organization of Holmes devotees. Other maps in the series are *The World Strictly According to Doyle* (G3201 .E65 1940 .W6), *Europe* (G5701 .1940 .W6), *London* (G5751 .E65 1940 .W6), and *United States* (G3701 .E65 1940 .W6). The maps also appear in "A Sherlockian Gazetteer," in *Baker Street and Beyond* (PR4624 .S55 1957) by Edgar W. Smith. In Smith's book, place names are listed with the Holmes story in which the place appears and an account of what happened there.

Europe

JULIAN WOLFF
Illustrator

New York: J. Wolff, February 1940
31 x 38 cm
Black and white
G5701 .E65 1940 .W6

This map of Europe by Dr. Julian Wolff (1905–1990) is an earlier version of *Europe and the Isles, As Seen from Baker Street: The Sherlock Holmes Map of Europe* (G5701 .E65 1914 .W6). Like its successor, the map shows sites of Sherlock Holmes stories set in Europe. It has less information than the 1948 map and only a quote from a Sherlock Holmes story and coats of arms relating to some of the stories reveal the map as related to the Holmes stories. This map is Part D in a five-part, limited-edition set of Sherlock Holmes maps by Dr. Julian Wolff (1905–1990), long-time president of the Baker Street Irregulars, an organization of Holmes devotees. Other maps in the series are *The World Strictly According to Doyle* (G3201 .E65 1940 .W6), *England* (G5741 .E65 1940.W6), *London* (G5754 .L7E65 1940 .W6), and *United States* (G3701 .E65 1940 .W6). The maps also appear in "A Sherlockian Gazetteer," in *Baker Street and Beyond* (PR4624 .S55 1957) by Edgar W. Smith. In Smith's book place names are listed with the Holmes story in which the place appears and an account of what happened there.

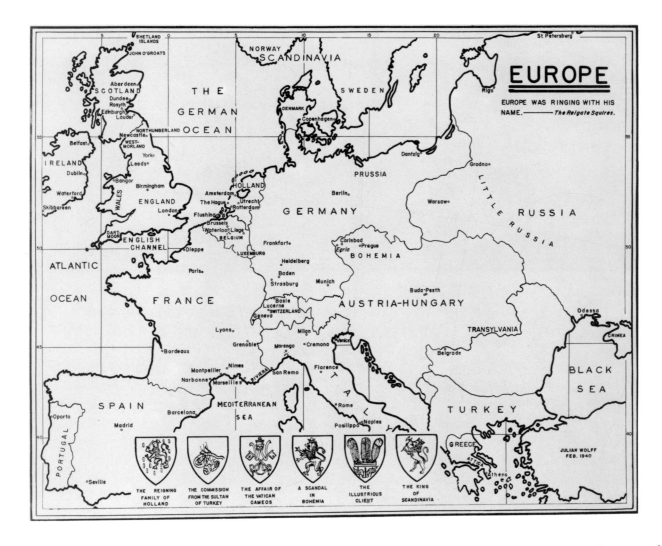

Language of the Land

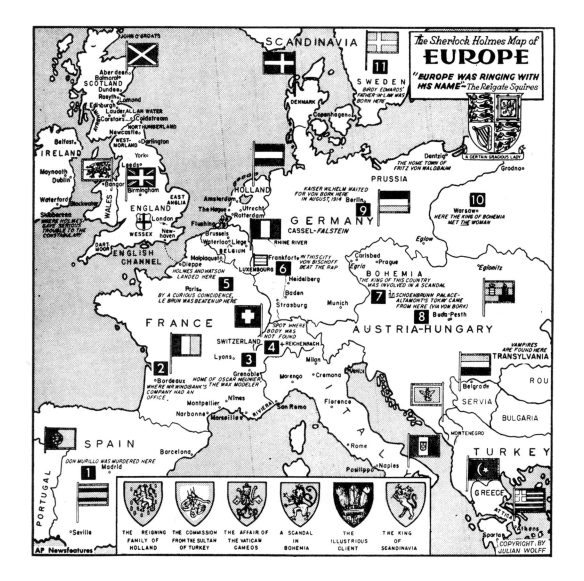

Europe and the Isles, As Seen from Baker Street: The Sherlock Holmes Map of Europe

JULIAN WOLFF
Illustrator

New York: Associated Press Newsfeatures,
     February 24, 1948
55 x 26 cm
Black and white
G5701 .E65 1914 .W6

This map locates sites in the Sherlock Holmes stories by Arthur Conan Doyle that took place on the continent of Europe, among them "The Final Problem," "A Scandal in Bohemia," and "A Study in Scarlet" (1887). Reichenbach, the site of the falls into which Holmes falls in his fight to the death with arch-rival Professor Moriarity, is located with an X. Below the map is an article about it, including an interview with its maker, Dr. Julian Wolff (1905–1990), president of the Baker Street Irregulars, an organization of Holmes devotees, from 1960–1986 and editor of the organization's publication the *Baker Street Journal* (1961–1977). Wolff notes that the map indicates "the locations of many places which are unknown to Messrs. Rand and McNally as well as all their colleagues, although they are extremely interesting to the numerous friends of Sherlock Holmes and Dr. Watson."

London

JULIAN WOLFF
Illustrator

New York?: 1940
22 x 33 cm
Black and white
G5754 .L7E65 1940 .W6

This map of London features sites associated with Sherlock Holmes, the popular detective created by Arthur Conan Doyle. Titles of the stories form the border. An inset map shows the Baker Street area, where Holmes lived at the fictional 221B, and public buildings such as Scotland Yard. Beneath the title is the well-known quote, "Come, Watson, come! The game is afoot" from "The Adventure of the Abbey Grange." The map is Part C in a five-part, limited-edition set of Sherlock Holmes maps by Dr. Julian Wolff (1905–1990), long-time president of the Baker Street Irregulars, an organization of Holmes devotees. Other maps in the series are *The World Strictly According to Doyle* (G3201 .E65 1940 .W6), *Europe* (G5701 1940 .W6), *England* (G5741 .E65 1940 .W6), and *United States* (G3701 .E65 1940 .W6). The maps also appear in "A Sherlockian Gazetteer," in *Baker Street and Beyond* (PR4624 .S55 1957) by Edgar W. Smith. In Smith's book place names are listed with the Holmes story in which the place appears and an account of what happened there.

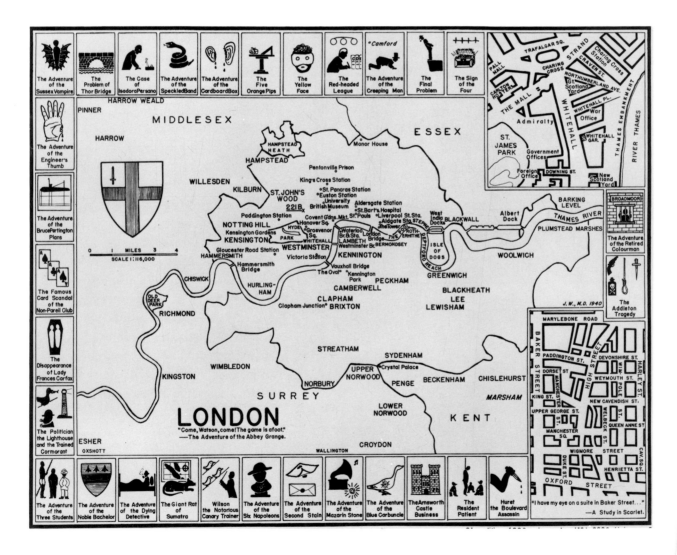

The Sherlock Holmes Mystery Map

MOLLY MAGUIRE
Designer

JIM WOLNICK
Illustrator

Los Angeles: Aaron Blake, 1987
53 x 68 cm
Color *(See color section.)*
G5751 .E65 1987 .A2

Courtesy of Molly Maguire and Aaron Silverman

The Sherlock Holmes Mystery Map enables readers to follow in the footsteps of the famous detective. The central motif shows two crossed magnifying glasses, one containing a map of England and the other one of London, with sites connected with Holmes stories numbered to a key below. The key identifies sites in the Holmes stories, written by Sir Arthur Conan Doyle, from *A Study in Scarlet* (1887) to *The Casebook of Sherlock Holmes* (1927). Images on the map show Holmes and his friend Dr. John Watson on the trail of a mystery and incidents from the books, such as the ferocious Hound of the Baskervilles from the story of that name (1902) and Holmes's fight with his nemesis, Professor Moriarity.

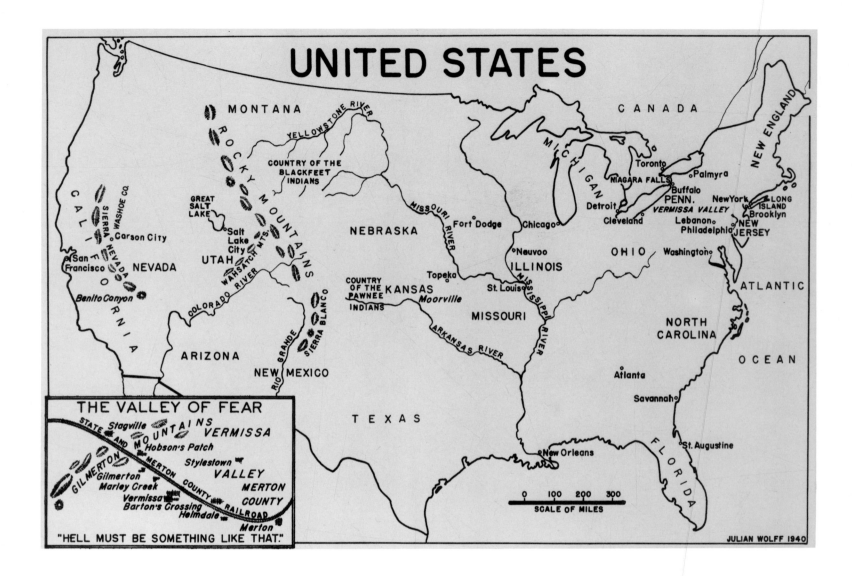

United States

JULIAN WOLFF
Illustrator

New York?: J. Wolff, 1940
20 x 30 cm
Black and white
G3701 .E65 1940 .W6

The *United States* map locates places mentioned in the Sherlock Holmes stories by Arthur Conan Doyle, even though Holmes himself may not have visited them. An inset map shows the "Valley of Fear," from the story of that name. The valley is fictional, but the Appalachian region of Pennsylvania has been proposed as its location. The map is Part E in a five-part, limited-edition series of maps by Dr. Julian Wolff (1905–1990), long-time president of the Baker Street Irregulars, an organization of Holmes devotees. Other maps in the series are *The World Strictly According to Doyle* (G3201 .E65 1940 .W6), *Europe* (G5701 1940 .W6), *England* (G5751 .E65 1940.W6), and *London* (G5754 .L7E65 1940 .W6). The maps also appear in "A Sherlockian Gazetteer," in *Baker Street and Beyond* (PR4624 .S55 1957) by Edgar W. Smith. In Smith's book place names are listed with the Holmes story in which the place appears and an account of what happened there.

Language of the Land

The World Strictly According to Doyle

JULIAN WOLFF
Illustrator

New York?: J. Wolff, 1940
20 x 37 cm
Black and white
G3201 .E65 1940 .W6

*T*he World Strictly According to Doyle locates sites around the world that are related to the Sherlock Holmes stories of Arthur Conan Doyle. At the top is a quote from "The Greek Interpreter": "I hear of Sherlock everywhere." Quotes from other stories are included on inset maps. These maps include India; Switzerland, scene of *The Final Problem*, in which Doyle attempted to kill off Holmes in a battle with his arch-rival Professor Moriarity; and the Island of Uffa, which figures in "The Valley of Fear." This map is Part A in a five-part, limited-edition set of Sherlock Holmes maps by Dr. Julian Wolff (1905–1990), long-time president of the Baker Street Irregulars, an organization of Holmes devotees. Other maps in the series are *Europe* (G5701 . E65 1940 .W6), *England* (G5751 .E65 1940 .W6), *London* (G5754 .L7E65 1940 .W6), and *United States* (G3701 .E65 1940 .W6). The maps also appear in "A Sherlockian Gazetteer," in *Baker Street and Beyond* (PR4624 .S55 1957) by Edgar W. Smith. In Smith's book place names are listed with the Holmes story in which the place appears and an account of what happened there.

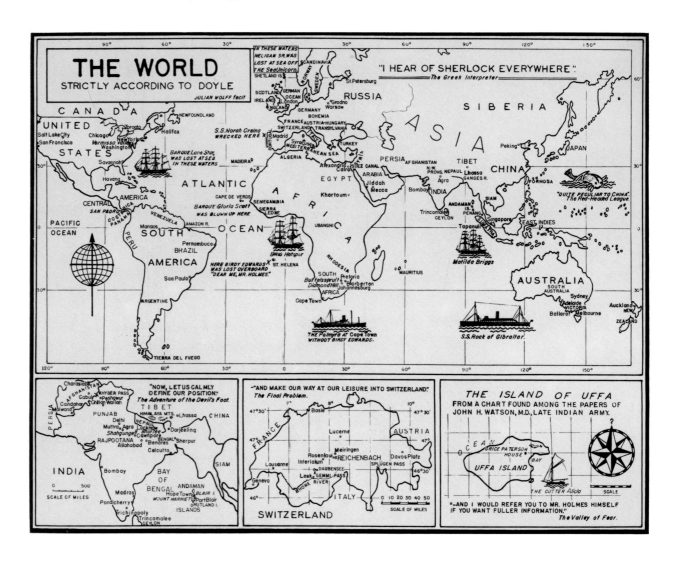

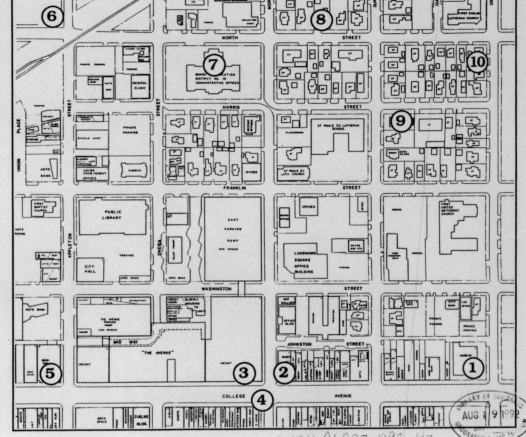

Edna Ferber Walking Tour

1. Outagamie Museum

2. Appleton Post Crescent Office

3. 120 East College Avenue
   Site of Ferber Family Store

4. Site of Interview with Houdini

5. Appleton Opera House

6. Site of Railroad Depot

7. Site of Ryan High School
   (burned down in 1904)

8. 216 North Street
   Ferber Family Home from 1897

9. 320 North Durkee
   Temple Zion

10. 319 Drew Street
    First Ferber Home in Appleton

Prepared by
Tim Hirsch
Department of English
University of Wisconsin-Eau Claire

with help from
Ed Kleckner
Principal Planner
Department of Planning and Development
City of Appleton
&
The Media Development Center
University of Wisconsin-Eau Claire

April 15, 1992

EDNA FERBER

Edna Ferber Walking Tour

TIM HIRSCH
Preparer

Eau Claire: University of Wisconsin-Eau
   Claire, 1992
19 x 22 cm
Black and white
G4124 .A6A85 1992 .H5

Courtesy of Tim Hirsch

This map shows sites in Appleton, Wisconsin, hometown of Edna Ferber, author of the Pulitzer Prize-winning novel *So Big* (1924), *Showboat* (1926), and *Cimarron* (1930). Born in Kalamazoo, Michigan, Ferber moved to Appleton about 1898, when her father opened a store on College Avenue. Ferber graduated from the local high school and worked for a year as the first female reporter on the Appleton *Daily Crescent*. She wrote her first novel, *Dawn O'Hara* (1911), in Appleton. The map locates ten sites associated with Ferber, including her synagogue, school, and family homes and businesses, so that visitors can make a walking tour of them.

IAN FLEMING

The Ian Fleming Thriller Map

MOLLY MAGUIRE
Designer

JOHN ZELNICK
Illustrator

Los Angeles: Aaron Blake, 1987
52 x 69 cm
Color *(See color section.)*
G3201 .E65 1987 .A2

Courtesy of Molly Maguire and Aaron Silverman

Based on the popular tongue-in-cheek adventure novels by Ian Fleming, the *Ian Fleming Thriller Map* features James Bond, Agent 007 of the British Secret Service. The maps shows locations in the British Isles, Europe, North America, the Caribbean, and Japan that Bond visits in his exploits, assignments, and assignations from *Casino Royale* (1953) through *Octopussy* (1965), keyed by number to a list of the Bond books. Research and design for the map were performed by Molly Maguire, who produced a series of literary maps in the 1980s.

JOHANN WOLFGANG VON GOETHE

Karte von Goethes Lebensreise, 1749–1832
(Map of Goethe's Life Journey, 1749–1832)

A. WOELFLE
Illustrator

Munich: Ernst Heimeran Verlag, n.d.
In German
59 x 47 cm
Color
G5701 .E65 1832 .W6

*K*arte von Goethes Lebensreise, *1749–1832* shows important places in the life of Johann Wolfgang von Goethe, Germany's greatest literary figure, most widely known as the author of *Faust*. It also traces his two journeys to Italy between 1786 and 1788. Goethe's account of them remains one of his most-read works and has been translated into English by the noted poet W. H. Auden. In addition to the legend at the bottom right of the map that provides a key to the journeys shown on the map and the years they were made, the map includes two smaller maps on the right and six drawings on the left. The lower small map shows Weimar, where Goethe lived from his mid-twenties until his death, serving as a government official under the area's prince and a chief figure in the cultural life of the city. The numbers on this map designate features of Weimar and are explained by the legend on its left. The upper small map shows the Duchy of Weimar, the small independent state of which the city was the capital, and surrounding areas. The drawings depict places connected to Goethe's life. The top drawing is of the house in Frankfurt am Main in which he was born. The next drawing down depicts his house in Weimar. Below it is Goethe's garden in Weimar, followed by a drawing of his garden house. The next-to-bottom drawing is of a country manor, Schloss Tiefurt, just outside the city of Weimar, which Goethe often visited. A night ride to this manor in April 1779 inspired one of his most famous ballads, *Der Erlkönig* (The Elf King, 1782). The bottom drawing is of the tomb in Weimar that contains the remains of Goethe and Friedrich Schiller, another great figure of German literature.

NIKOLAI GOGOL

Gogolevskie mesta Ukrainy, turistskaia skhema

(Gogol's Ukraine: A Tourist Map)

Moscow: Glavnoe upravlenie geodezii i
    kartografii, 1974
In Russian
48 x 34 cm
Color
G7101 .E635 1974 .R82

Gogolevskie Mesta Ukrainy shows places associated with novelist and short-story writer Nikolai Gogol, a great comic writer and master of Russian prose. His most famous works include the comic play *The Inspector General* (1836) and *Dead Souls* (1842). Gogol was born in Velikie Sorochintsy in the Ukrainian province of Poltava, and his early work reflects the Ukrainian landscape, life, and worldview. The map cover shows a thatched-roofed Ukrainian house. Photographs show a school named for Gogol in the town of Nezhin; the Tarnovsky Palace in Kachanovo, where Gogol visited; the Gogol Literary Memorial Museum in Velikie Sorochintsy; and monuments to Gogol in Kharkov and Poltava. Inset maps show the town of Poltava and an area of the Black Sea coast from Odessa to Evpatoriia. A key identifies places associated with Gogol and records what happened there.

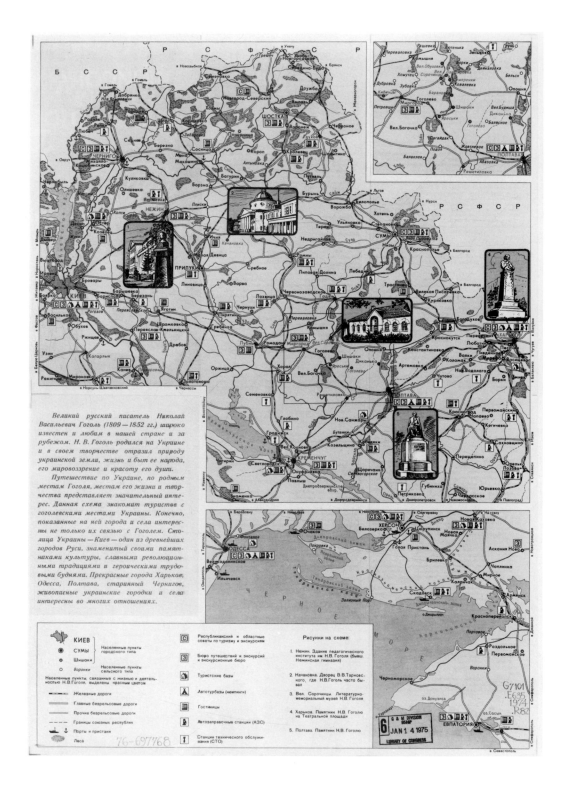

THOMAS HARDY

Map of Dorset Featuring Hardy, 1990

Merle Willis
Designer and Illustrator

Bournemouth, U.K.: Franchise Publishing,
　1990
37 x 57 cm
Color
G5753 .D6 1990 .F7

Part of a larger map produced for the 150th anniversary of the birth of Thomas Hardy, "Thomas Hardy's Wessex" shows the region of southern England where his major novels are set. Hardy first used the name "Wessex," the ancient Saxon name for the area, in his 1874 novel *Far from the Madding Crowd*. Hardy was born three miles east of Dorchester and, except for a few years in London and its suburbs, spent his life in the area. From 1883 to 1928 he lived at Max Gate in Dorchester, the Casterbridge of his novels, including *The Mayor of Casterbridge* (1886). One side of the map shows modern roads in Dorset; the other "Thomas Hardy's Wessex" (shown) is a map of places associated with Hardy. Other area towns that appear in the novels include Christminster (Oxford), Budmouth (Weymouth), and Sandbourne (Bournemouth), where Tess murders Alec d'Urberville in *Tess of the D'Urbervilles* (1891). Text in the bottom margin of the front of the map gives biographical information about Hardy. The map also contains advertisements for hotels, restaurants, and other tourist attractions in the area. Those that have connections to Hardy are indicated.

A Map of the Wessex of Thomas Hardys Novels

J. H. CHILD
Illustrator

Dorchester, U.K.: Dorset County Museum,
ca. 1992
16 x 25 cm
Color
G5752 .W46 .E65 1945 .C4 1993

*Courtesy of the Trustees of the Thomas Hardy
Memorial Collection*

A reproduction of a 1935 map by Miss J. H. Child of Abbotsbury, Dorset, *A Map of the Wessex of Thomas Hardys Novels* shows the region of southern England that forms the setting for the novels of Thomas Hardy. Hardy called his imaginary area "Wessex," the ancient Saxon name for the area bounded by Devon on the east, Berkshire on the west, and the Bristol Channel and the Thames on the north. The fictional names that Hardy gave to actual towns, for example, "Christminster" for Oxford, are indicated in orange. The names of Hardy's novels such as *The Mayor of Casterbridge* (1886), *Tess of the D'Urbervilles* (1891), and *Jude the Obscure* (1895) are listed near the sites in which major events in them occurred. Texts in the margins describe Wessex and give biographical information about Hardy. Coats of arms of the actual cities in the area are depicted in the left and right margins. The original map is in the Dorset County Museum, Dorchester, England.

CYNTHIA HARNETT

London in the Time of King Henry V, 1413–1422

CYNTHIA HARNETT
Illustrator

Minneapolis: Lerner Publications, 1984
42 x 52 cm
Color
G5754 .L7 1422 .H3

*L*ondon in the Time of King Henry V advertises a set of six novels written by Cynthia Harnett. Also an illustrator, Harnett was a pioneer writer of historical novels for children and is noted for her accurate depiction of the lives of ordinary people. Her 1951 novel *The Wool Pack* (reprinted in the United States as *The Merchant's Mark*, 1984) won a Carnegie medal. Taken from Harnett's *The Sign of the Green Falcon* (1984) (British title *Ring Out, Bow Bells!*), a book about an apprentice to Dick Whittington, famous Lord Mayor of Medieval London, this map shows London streets and landmarks of the time of King Henry V (reigned 1413–1422), as well as selected modern buildings, which are shaded in and numbered to a key. Inserts show St. Paul's Cathedral, London Bridge, and the Tower of London as they appeared during Henry's reign. The other novels in the series are *The Great House* (1949), about an architect's family in the time of King William (reigned 1688–1702) and Queen Mary II (reigned 1688–1694); *The Writing on the Hearth* (1971), a story of the Wars of the Roses (1455–1485); *The Merchant's Mark* (1984), featuring a wool merchant's family, set in 1493; *The Cargo of the Madalena* (1984) (British title *The Load of Unicorn*), about early printer William Caxton (1422–1492); and *Stars of Fortune* (1956), the story of the medieval English ancestors of George Washington.

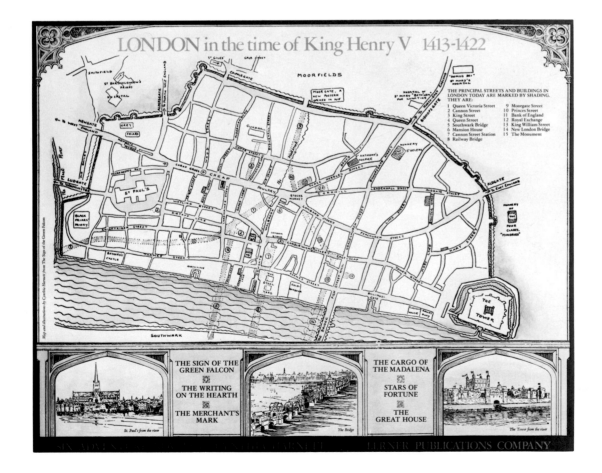

BRET HARTE

The Bret Harte Trail Map, Showing the Land of Romance and Gold Immortalized by Bret Harte and Mark Twain in San Joaquin, Amador, Calaveras, and Tuolumne Counties and Portions of the Counties of Stanislaus, Merced, and Mariposa, All in Central California

A. S. OULLAHAN
Compiler

BUDD AND WIDDOS, CIVIL ENGINEERS
Illustrators

[Stockton, California]: Stockton Chamber
   of Commerce, c. 1922
89 x 149 cm
Blue-line print with colored shadings
G4364 .S9E65 1922 .O91

This map shows the Stockton, California, area. In addition to literary landmarks associated with Bret Harte and Mark Twain, it shows elements of commercial interest, such as citrus-fruit-growing areas and mineral deposits. Numbers on the map are keyed to a list of places that appear in the works of Harte and Twain. One number marks the setting of Twain's 1865 story "The Celebrated Jumping Frog of Calaveras County," and another locates Byrne's Ferry as Poker Flat, scene of Harte's "The Outcasts of Poker Flat" and Roaring Camp, the setting for his "The Luck of Roaring Camp." Fruit-growing and mineral-producing areas are shaded in various colors. The map also exists in a black-and-white version (G4364 .S9E65 1922 .O92) and a smaller, 36 x 59-cm, version (G4364 .S9E65 1922 .O9).

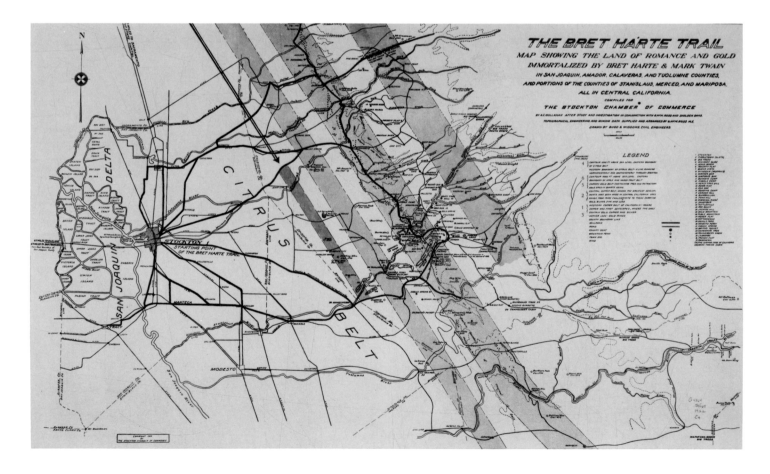

FLORENCE PARRY HEIDE

Kenoska, Home of the Spotlight Club Mysteries

FLORENCE PARRY HEIDE AND
ROXANNE HEIDE
Compilers

Chicago: Albert Whitman, 1978
27 x 42 cm
Black and white
G9930 1978 .H4

This map shows the imaginary town of Kenoska, the setting for a series of books for young people by Florence Parry Heide, in collaboration with Sylvia Van Clief and, later, her daughter Roxanne Heide. In the books three youths—Jay Temple, his sister Cindy Temple, and friend Dexter Tate—form "The Spotlight Club," a detective group that solves mysteries. Books in the series are *The Mystery of the Silver Tag* (1972), *The Mystery of the Missing Suitcase* (1972), *The Hidden Box Mystery* (1973), *Mystery at MacAdoo Zoo* (1973), *Mystery of the Whispering Voice* (1974), *Mystery of the Melting Snowman* (1974), *Mystery of the Bewitched Bookmobile* (1975), *Mystery of the Vanishing Visitor* (1975), *Mystery of the Lonely Lantern* (1976), *Mystery at Keyhole Carnival* (1977), *Mystery of the Midnight Message* (1977), *Mystery at Southport Cinema* (1978), *Mystery of the Mummy's Mask* (1979), *Mystery of the Forgotten Island* (1980), and *Mystery on Danger Road* (1983). A key relates places shown on the map to pivotal events in some of the books.

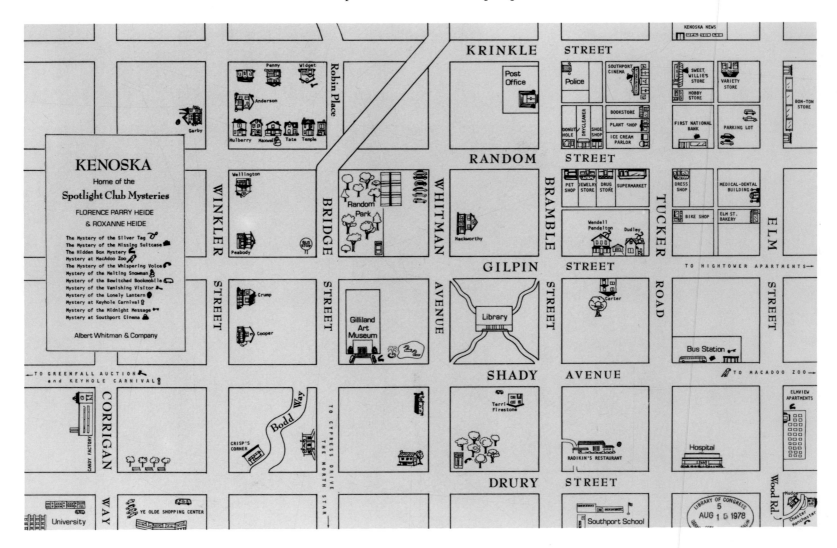

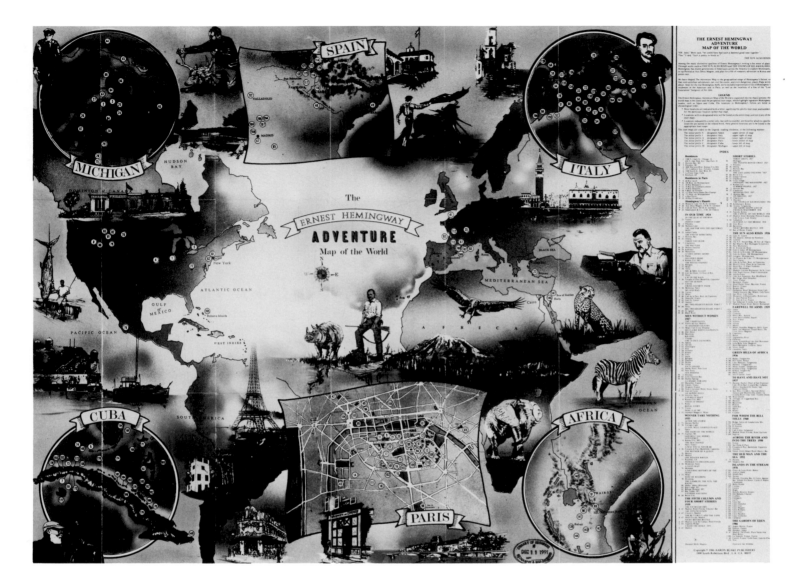

ERNEST HEMINGWAY

The Ernest Hemingway Adventure Map of the World

MOLLY MAGUIRE
Designer

Los Angeles: Aaron Blake, 1986
48 x 57 cm
Color
G3201 .E65 1986 .A2

Courtesy of Molly Maguire and Aaron Silverman

The exotic international settings of Ernest Hemingway's real-life travels and fictional adventures are illustrated in this world map with peripheral insets that highlight signature Hemingway locales, such as Spain, Cuba, Paris, Italy, Michigan, and Africa. In the center is an image of Hemingway as a big-game hunter. The world map and the inset maps are keyed to a numbered index that corresponds to Hemingway's residences and to the places mentioned in Hemingway's literary work from *In Our Time* (1924) to *The Garden of Eden* (1986). The maps also shows places that Hemingway and his circle, dubbed the "Lost Generation," frequented. Research and design for the map were performed by Molly Maguire, who produced a series of literary maps in the 1980s.

HOMER

The Iliad of Homer

Barbara Rogers Houseworth
Illustrator

Normal, Illinois: Educational Illustrators,
   1959
59 x 88 cm
Black and white
G6811 .E65 BC .H6

This map shows ancient sites in Greece and Asia Minor associated with Homer's *Iliad* (ca. 8th c. BC), an epic of the Trojan War. An inset map shows a bird's-eye view of Troy and the Greek camp outside its walls. At bottom is a scene depicting the Greek gods involved in the fray. Another inset gives the map title and shows the Trojan Horse. A series of scenes at left depict key scenes in the epic, such as the death of Hector, the quarrel of Achilles and Agamemnon, and the fight over the body of Patroclus.

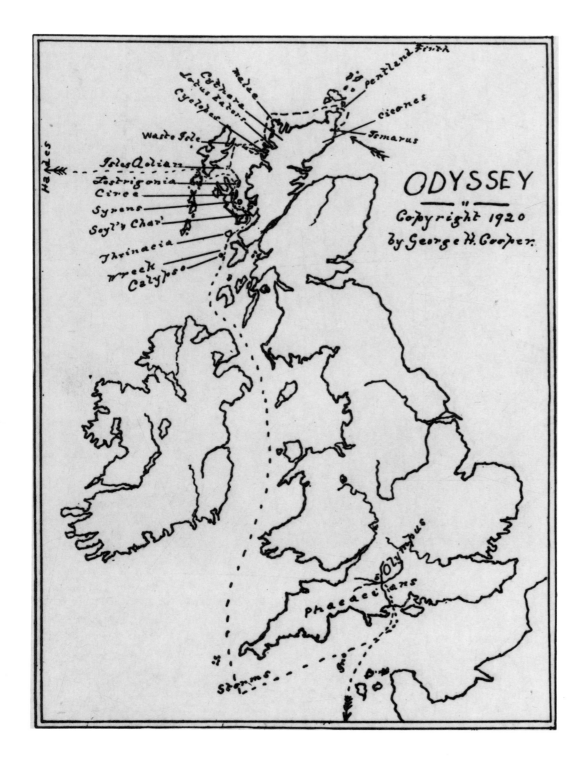

Map of the Odyssey

GEORGE H. COOPER
Illustrator

San Jose, California: George H. Cooper, 1920
21 x 13 cm
Black and white
G5741 .E65 BC .C6

The map shows the route of Odysseus as recounted by Homer in the *Odyssey* (ca. 8th c. BC) as if the story had taken place in the British Isles instead of the Mediterranean. The north coast of Scotland and the islands off it are equated with various locations in Homer's work. The Land of the Phaeacians is located on England's south coast, with Mt. Olympus slightly inland, around Wiltshire.

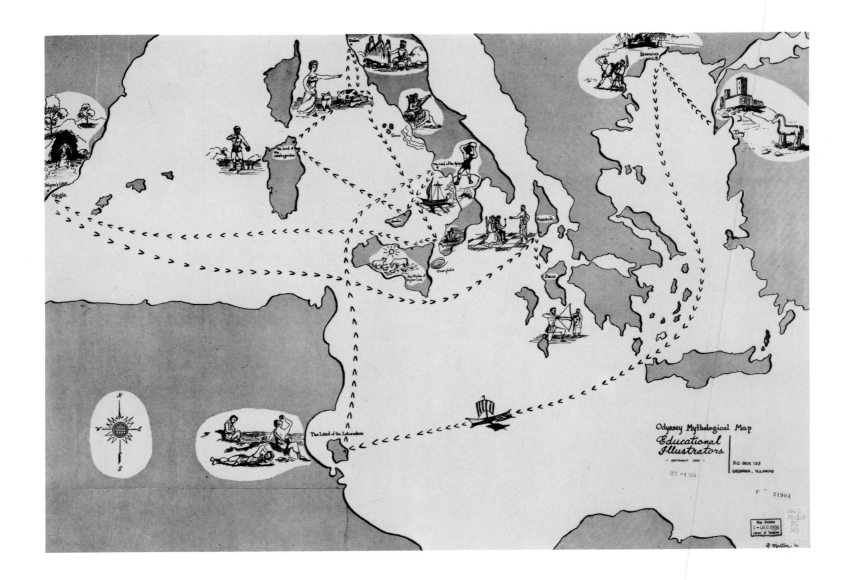

Odyssey Mythological Map

P. Martin
Illustrator

Urbana, Illinois: Educational Illustrators,
   1956
57 x 81 cm
Black and white
G5672 .M4E65 BC .M3

The *Odyssey Mythological Map* shows the route of Odysseus's wanderings in the Mediterranean region from Carthage to western Anatolia during his ten-year voyage home to Ithaca after the Trojan War, as recounted by Homer in the *Odyssey* (ca. 8th c. BC). Places marked include Troy, the Land of the Lotus Eaters, the Home of the Cyclops, Circe's island, Hades, the Land of the Laestrygonians, Calypso's Cave, Scylla and Charybdis, Phaeacia, and Ithaca, Odysseus's home and final destination. Illustrations show the Trojan Horse, the Cyclops, the sorceress Circe and the men she turned to pigs, the Flocks of Hyperion, the Sirens, and other characters and episodes from the epic.

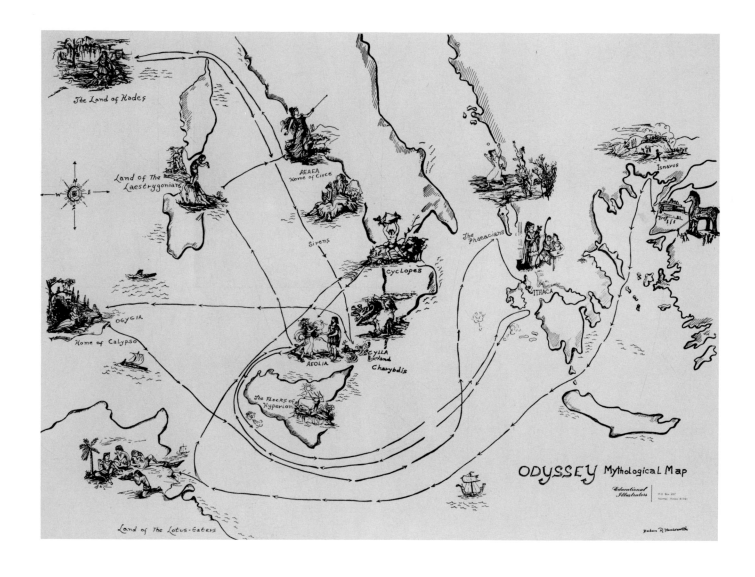

Odyssey Mythological Map

BARBARA R. HOUSEWORTH
Illustrator

Normal, Illinois: Educational Illustrators,
    ca. 1960
55 x 73 cm
Black and white
G5672 .M4E65 BC .H7

This map shows the route of Odysseus's wanderings in the Mediterranean region from Carthage to western Anatolia during his ten-year voyage home to Ithaca after the Trojan War. Characters and episodes from the epic as recounted by Homer in the *Odyssey* (ca. 8th c. BC) are shown in line drawings. Scenes depicted include the Trojan Horse, the Cyclops, the sorceress Circe, and the Land of the Phaeacians.

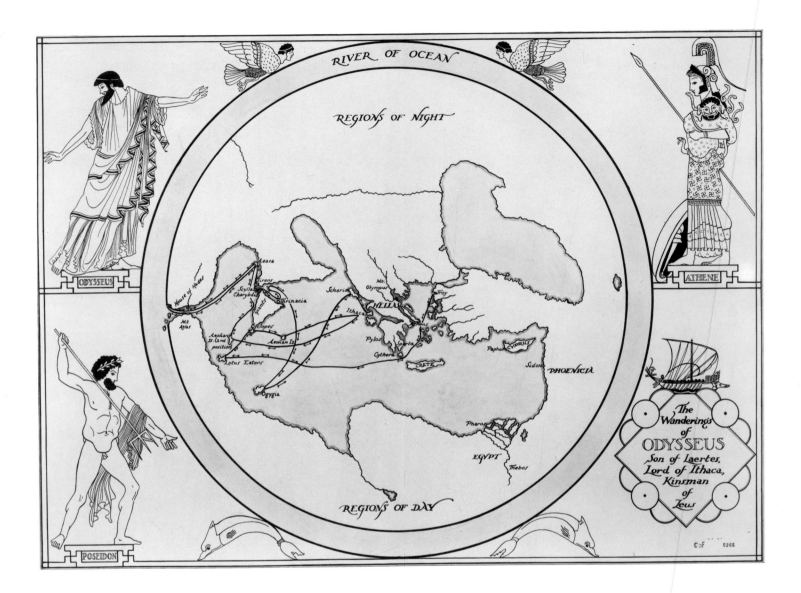

The Wanderings of Odysseus: Son of Laertes, Lord of Ithaca, Kinsman of Zeus

New York: Oxford University Press, ca. 1932
48 x 63 cm
Color
G5672 .M4E65 BC .O9

*T*he *Wanderings of Odysseus* shows the route that Odysseus followed in his return trip from the Trojan War, as recounted by Homer in the *Odyssey* (ca. 8th c. BC). The map's geography is based more on that of the epic than the actual geography of the Mediterranean region. The map area is round, surrounded by the "River of Ocean," and includes "Regions of Day" to the south and "Regions of Night" to the north. Places marked include Troy, the land of the Lotus Eaters, the land of the Cyclops, Calypso's island of Ogygia, the House of Hades, Scylla and Charybdis, and Ithaca—Odysseus's home and final destination. Illustrations show Odysseus, as well as Athene, goddess of wisdom, and Poseidon, god of the sea, both important characters in the story, all drawn in the style of figures on an ancient Greek vase.

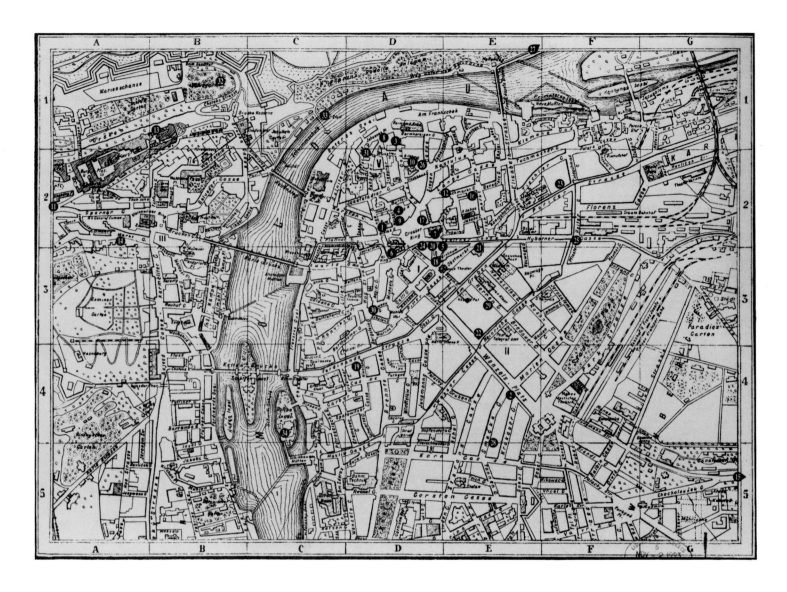

FRANZ KAFKA

Ein Reiseführer durch Franz Kafkas Prag
(Guide to Franz Kafka's Prague)

Prague: Torst Nakladatelství, ca. 1993
In German and English
27 x 37 cm
Black and white
G6514 .P7 E65 1891 .N3

Ein Reiseführer durch Franz Kafkas Prag is based on a map printed in 1891, when Franz Kafka was a young man, and shows Prague's streets with German names. Some street names have changed, and other streets have disappeared over the years. Kafka spent his life in Prague and, although he died from tuberculosis in a sanatorium near Vienna, he is buried with his parents in the city's Jewish cemetery. Kafka received a doctorate in law at the German University in 1906 and for most of his life held a civil service post. Numbers on the map correspond to a key that shows his birthplace, homes, schools, work places, homes of friends, literary salons, cafes, grave, and other places inseparably connected with Kafka's life and work. His most famous works, published posthumously by his friend Max Brod, include *The Trial* (1925), *The Castle* (1926), and *America* (1927).

IAKUB KOLAS.

Na rodinu IAkuba Kolasa, turistskaia skhema

(In the Homeland of IAkub Kolas,
A Tourist Map)

Moscow: Glavnoe upravlenie geodezii i
      kartografii, 1972
In Russian
40 x 34 cm
Color
G7093 .M5E635 1972 .S6

Na rodinu IAkuba Kolasa was produced to honor the ninetieth anniversary of the birth of IAkub Kolas, the pseudonym of Konstantin Mikhailovich Mitskevich. Kolas was a prominent Byelorussian poet, prose writer and dramatist, a leader of Byelorussian Soviet literature, and the founder of the Byelorussian literary language. From 1908 to 1911, he was imprisoned because of his political activities. Kolas was born at Stolbtsy, near Minsk, and the map shows the Minsk area, with an inset of the city itself. Illustrations on the map show the Kolas House Museum in Minsk, a linden tree in front of Kolas's house, and his study. In the house, Kolas's bedroom and study are preserved along with books, photographs, manuscripts, and recordings of him reading his works. A text describes Kolas's life and works and includes tributes from other writers. A road map traces a Minsk-Dzerzhinsk-Stolbtsy-Nikolayevshchina route, and a key locates monuments, museums, and tourist facilities in the area.

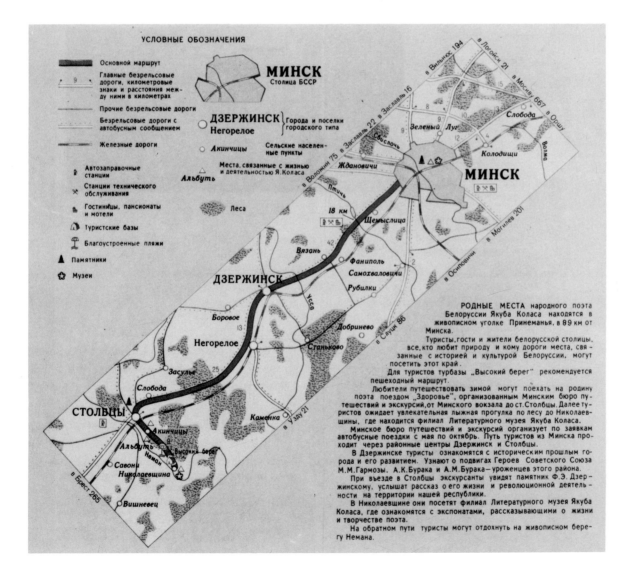

MIKHAIL LERMONTOV

Po lermontovskim mestam Penzenskoi oblasti, turistskaia skhema

(Lermontov in the Penza Region,
A Tourist Map)

Moscow: Glavnoe upravlenie geodezii i
    kartografii, 1982
In Russian
35 x 50 cm
Color
G7063 .P4E635 1981 .S6

Po lermontovskim mestam Penzenskoi oblasti shows places associated with the great Russian romantic poet and novelist Mikhail Lermontov around the cultural and administrative center of Penza, southeast of Moscow. His most famous poems include *The Demon*, *Ismail Bey*, and *The Song of the Czar Ivan Vasilievich*, and his best-known novel is *A Hero of Our Time*. The cover of the map shows a portrait of Lermontov. Other illustrations include the estate of Tarkhany (renamed Lermontovo), where Lermontov spent his childhood and which is now a museum; a photograph of his grave at Lermontova; the chapel where he was married; a statue of him; and an oak tree he planted. The map shows a tourist route between the cities of Belinsky and Kuznetsk. A key locates places on the map associated with Lermontov and other literary figures from the Penza region, such as journalist and novelist Alexander Hertzen. A text provides information about Lermontov's life and work and includes quotations from his poems. A 1983 revision of the map (G7063 .P4E635 1983. S6) is almost identical to this one.

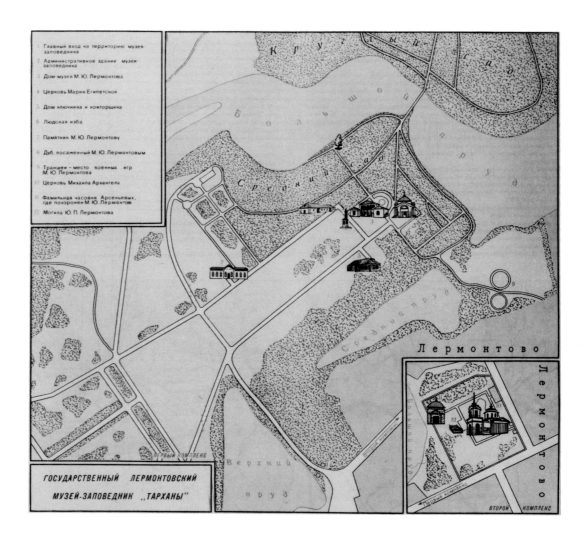

SINCLAIR LEWIS

A Map of Sinclair Lewis' United States as It Appears in His Novels

GEORGE ANNAND
Illustrator

New York: Doubleday, Doran, 1934
33 x 55 cm
Color
G3701 .E65 1934 .D6

A Map of Sinclair Lewis' United States shows sites mentioned in the works of Lewis, who in 1930 became the first American author to win the Nobel Prize for Literature. Pulitzer Prize-winning literary critic Carl Van Doren, who had published a highly commendatory biography of Lewis in 1933, wrote the notes for the map. The map highlights Winnemac, a mythical state bordered by Michigan, Ohio, Illinois, and Indiana which Lewis created as a setting for many of his works. The state's capital is Zenith, home of George F. Babbitt (*Babbitt*, 1922), Samuel Dodsworth (*Dodsworth*, 1929), and Lowell F. Schmaltz (*The Man Who Knew Coolidge*, 1928), and the scene of activities of Dr. Martin Arrowsmith (*Arrowsmith*, 1920) and evangelist Elmer Gantry (*Elmer Gantry*, 1927). Other fictional locations

include Gopher Prairie (identified with Lewis's birthplace, Sauk Centre, Minnesota), home of Carol Kennicott in *Main Street* (1920); Wheatsylvania, North Dakota, where Martin Arrowsmith has a medical practice; and Terwillinger College, Kansas, scene of Elmer Gantry's early triumphs. Insets in the upper corners depict two of Lewis's most memorable characters—George F. Babbitt, the real estate salesman whose name has become synonymous with unthinking conformity, and Carol Kennicott, who flees from the stifling small-town life of Gopher Prairie. A shield at left shows Lewis's Nobel Prize-winning books at top; Milton Daggett, the garage-owner hero of *Free Air* (1919), at left; the towers of Zenith at the bottom; and Istra Nash, an unconventional art student in *Our Mr. Wrenn* (1914) and *The Trail of the Hawk* (1915), at right. The map was issued to promote the thirteen novels Lewis had published between 1914 and 1934.

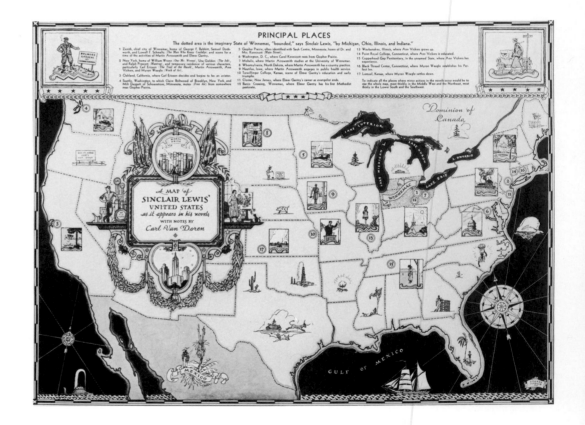

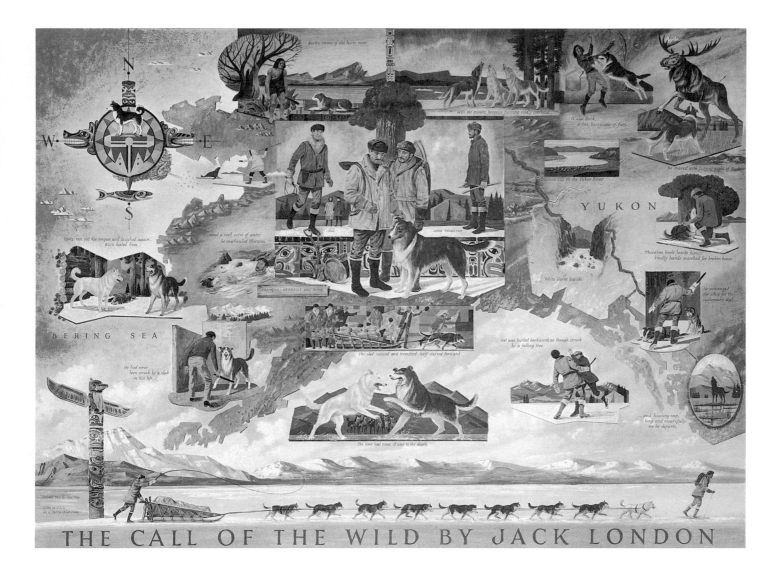

THE CALL OF THE WILD BY JACK LONDON

JACK LONDON

The Call of the Wild by Jack London

PAUL RIBA
Illustrator

Cleveland: Harris-Intertype Corporation,
   1962
46½ x 64 cm
Color *(See color section.)*
G4371 .E65 1962 .R5

The Call of the Wild colorfully portrays scenes from the 1903 novel by Jack London. The map depicts the adventures of Buck, a pampered pet who is kidnaped and turned into a sled dog in gold-rush Alaska before eventually reverting to the wild state of his wolflike ancestors. With its factual basis in London's own adventures during the Klondike gold rush, the novel broke new ground for the adventure tale, moving it away from the unrealistic plots of previous examples of the genre. The novel is also unusual in being told from an animal's viewpoint.

HERMAN MELVILLE

The Voyage of the Pequod from the Book Moby Dick by Herman Melville

EVERETT HENRY
Illustrator

Cleveland: Harris-Seybold, 1956
43 x 61 cm
Color *(See color section.)*
G3201 .E65 1956 .H4

*T*he Voyage of the Pequod depicts episodes from *Moby Dick* (1851) by Herman Melville. Against a monochromatic map of the world, an orange and yellow line traces the route of the ship *Pequod* from Nantucket, Massachusetts, to the South Seas. The central scene shows Captain Ahab swearing vengeance on the white whale Moby Dick. Also depicted are the characters Ishmael, Queequeg, Daggoo, Starbuck, and Moby Dick himself. Insets show Nantucket and scenes of whaling. At the map's bottom is a dramatic rendering of the novel's climax, when the ship sinks during a battle with Moby Dick and all the characters except Ishmael die.

A. A. MILNE *(See p. 279.)*

MARGARET MITCHELL

Atlanta in 1864: To Illustrate Margaret Mitchell's Gone with the Wind

FINLEY FOSTER
Preparer

Cleveland: Western Reserve University
    Press, 1946
39 x 28 cm
Black and White
G3924 .A8E65 1864 .F6

*A*tlanta in 1864 is based on a map drawn by a Confederate officer during the American Civil War. The map includes references to authentic historical locations such as the Governor's Mansion and Georgia Railroad Depot and fictitious places mentioned in Margaret Mitchell's *Gone with the Wind* (1936), such as the houses of Rhett Butler and Ashley Wilkes and Belle Watling's establishment.

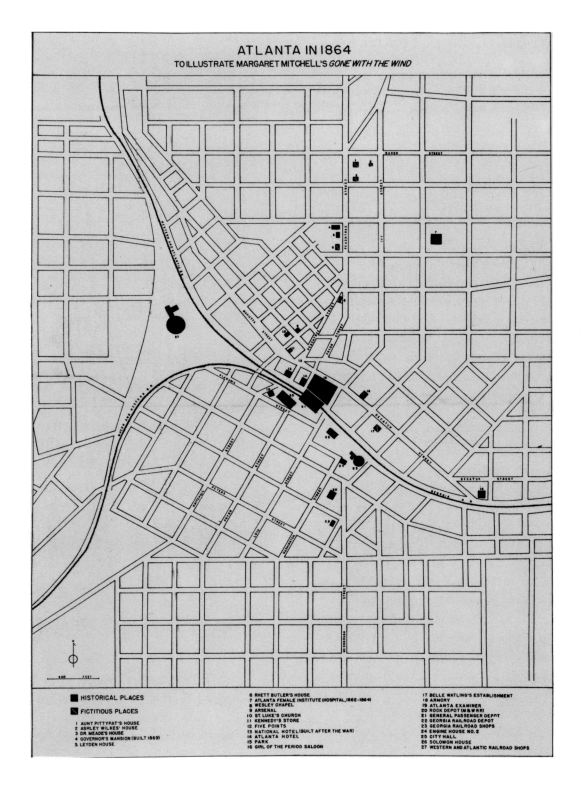

ALEXANDER PUSHKIN

Po Pushkinskim mestam Verkhnevolzh'ia, turistskaia skhema
(Pushkin in the Upper Volga, A Tourist Map)

Moscow: Glavnoe upravlenie geodezii i
kartografii, 1975
In Russian
21 x 33 cm
Color
G7062 .V6E635 1982 .S6

*P*o Pushkinskim mestam
Verkhnevolzh'ia identifies places in
the upper Volga region associated with
the major Russian poet Alexander
Pushkin. Pushkin pioneered the techniques and set the standards for the extraordinary development of Russian literature in the nineteenth century, and
many critics consider him to be Russia's
greatest poet. Pushkin first visited the
Volga region in 1812, when he was
twelve years old and made his last visit in
1836. The map shows the area around
Kalinin (now renamed Tver, as it was in
Pushkin's day), where Pushkin lived and
gathered material for his works. The natural environment of the beautiful
wooded landscape is reflected in *Eugene
Onegin* (published in parts between
1823 and 1830) and other poems. Photographs on the map show sites associated with Pushkin, such as the grave of
A. P. Kern (1800–1879) in Prutnia. On
Kern's grave are the first four lines of a
famous poem that Pushkin wrote to her.
Also shown are the Pushkin Museum,
located in a house in which the poet
lived in Bernovo; Pavloskoe, the estate of

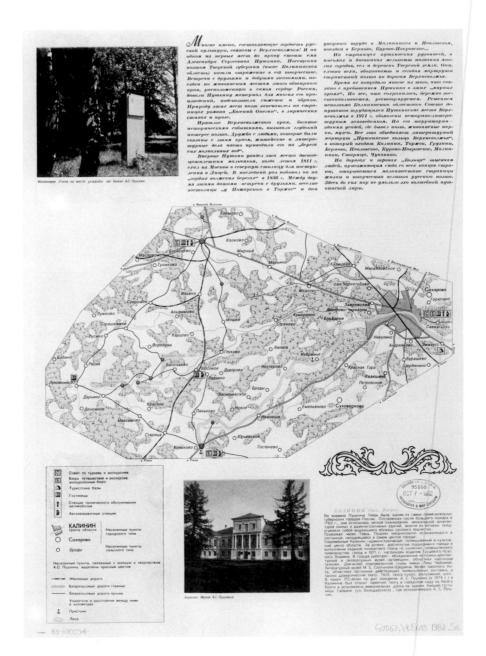

P. I. Vulf, where Pushkin occupied a room, now also a museum; and a plaque on a place
where Pushkin stayed in Malinniki. The map also features quotations from Pushkin's
poems. A 1980 version of the map (G7062 .V6E635 1980 .S6) has different illustrations,
including Staritska, a house where Pushkin stayed in the town of Torzhok, and a room in
the Pushkin Museum in Bernovo. The map is a revision of one issued in 1975 (G7062
.V6E635 1975 .S61).

Pushkinskie mesta Leningrada, turistskaia skhema
(Pushkin in Leningrad, A Tourist Map)

Moscow: Glavnoe upravlenie geodezii i
kartografii, 1980
In Russian
59 x 46 cm
Color
G7004 .L4E65 1980 .S6

*P*ushkinskie mesta Leningrada shows places associated with the Russian national poet Alexander Pushkin. From 1817 to 1820 Pushkin lived in St. Petersburg (Soviet name Leningrad) while working for the foreign office. He returned there in 1826, when he was attached to the court of the tsar. During his youth in the city, he became a member of several small, upper-class political-literary societies, attended theater constantly, and worked on his first romantic narrative poem, *Ruslan and Lyudmila* (1820). Photographs on the map show the Pushkin Statue on Art Square, Pushkin's apartment museum on the quay of the Moika River, and the statue of Peter the Great that inspired Pushkin's poem *The Bronze Horseman* (1837). A key shows sites associated with Pushkin and his works. An inset showing the area surrounding Leningrad is keyed to sites in Pushkin, called Tsarskoye Selo until 1937, when it was renamed for the poet. From 1811 to 1817 Pushkin attended a select lyceum

for noblemen's sons in the town, and the education and friendships he formed shaped his life and writing. A photograph of the school, now the Pushkin Museum, is included on the map. A slightly revised version of the map was issued in 1983 (G7004 .L4E65 1983 .S61).

Pushkinskie mesta Moskovy i Podmoskov'ia, turistskaia skhema
(Pushkin Places in Moscow and the Surrounding Area, A Tourist Map)

L. I. Liubavina
Editor

Moscow: Glavnoe upravlenie geodezii i
    kartografii, 1979
In Russian
54 x 48 cm
Color
G7004 .M7E635 1979 .S6

*P*ushkinskie mesta Moskovy i Pod-
moskov'ia shows places associated
with the major Russian poet Alexander
Pushkin. Because Pushkin pioneered the
techniques and set the standards for the
extraordinary development of Russian literature in the nineteenth century, many
critics consider him to be the greatest
Russian writer. Having spent his childhood in Moscow, Pushkin visited the city
often between 1827 and 1836 and knew
the city's major writers, artists, and musi-
cians. The map features a portrait of
Pushkin and a quotation from a poem in
which he mentions Moscow. Photographs
show the statue of Pushkin in Pushkin
Square; the State Pushkin Museum; the
site of the English Club, to which the poet
belonged; and the palace of Prince
Usupov, where the Pushkin family occupied a wing that no longer exists. A key
identifies street addresses of places associated with Pushkin. An inset map identifies
places associated with the poet in the area
surrounding Moscow, and a key explains
what happened in the various locales.
Slightly modified versions of the map were
published in 1979 (G7004 .M7E65 1979
.S6) and 1985 (G7004 .M7E65 1985 .S6).

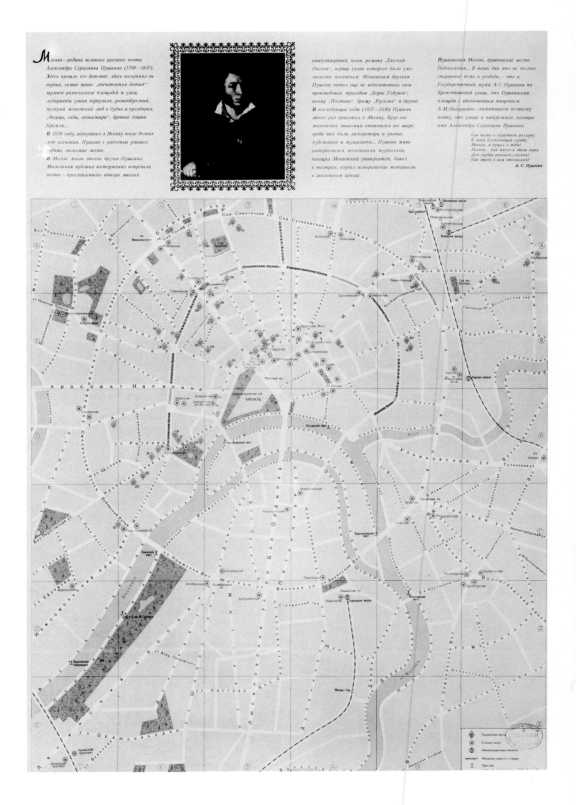

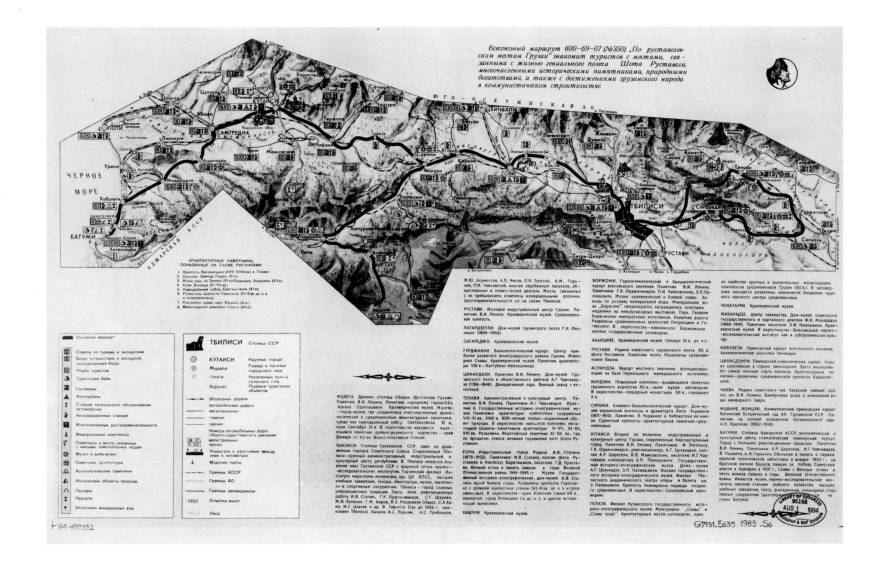

SHOTA RUSTAVELI

Po Rustavelevskim mestam Gruzii:
Turistskii marshrut 600–69–07
(no. 350)
(Around Rustaveli Places in Georgia,
A Tourist Route)

Moscow: Glavnoe upravlenie geodezii i
    kartografii, 1983
In Russian
37 x 54 cm
Color
G7131 .E635 1983 .S6

Po Rustavelevskim Mestam Gruzii shows places associated with the major Georgian poet Shota Rustaveli (12th to 13th c.). Photographs show monuments to Rustaveli in Tbilisi and on the road to Kutaisi, a corner of old Tbilisi, and the Chavchavadze Drama Theatre in Batumi. Inset maps of Tbilisi and Batumi show monuments, museums, theaters, hotels, tourist offices, railroads, and other tourist facilities. A large map on the verso shows a route from Batumi on the Black Sea to Gurdzhaani in the east. Text on the map is arranged by city or town and relates what associations the places have with Rustaveli as well as other cultural figures including Alexander Pushkin, Mikhail Lermontov, A. S. Griboedov, Anton Chekhov, Leo Tolstoy, Maxim Gorky, and Peter Illich Tchaikovsky.

MARI SANDOZ *(See p. 279.)*

SIR WALTER SCOTT

The Tale of Ivanhoe from the Novel by Sir Walter Scott

EVERETT HENRY
Illustrator

Cleveland: Harris-Intertype, 1958
43 x 60 cm
Color
G5752 .M5E65 11—.H

*T*he Tale of Ivanhoe shows scenes from the romantic novel (1819) by Sir Walter Scott. Set in twelfth-century England, the book describes how Wilfred of Ivanhoe champions the lovely Jewish maiden Rebecca and wins the fair Saxon princess Rowena as his bride. Although Scott invented the major characters, he introduced figures from history and legend, such as King Richard the Lionhearted, his wicked brother John, Robin Hood, and Friar Tuck, into a complicated plot that includes elaborate pageantry, suspense, honor, loyalty, and courage. The map captures this spirit and shows episodes from the book, such as the Tournament at Ashby-de-la-Zouche, Ivanhoe dueling with the Templar to vindicate Rebecca, Ivanhoe's marriage to Rowena, and the appearance of the Black Knight, who is Richard the Lionhearted in disguise.

Language of the Land

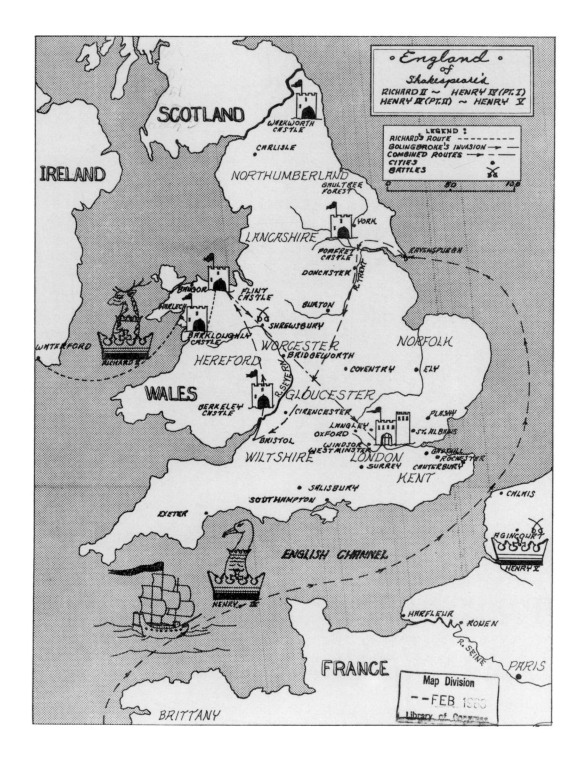

WILLIAM SHAKESPEARE

England of Shakespeare's Richard II, Henry IV (Part I), Henry IV (Part 2), and Henry V

[?] SAMUELS
Illustrator

W. Krumm & B. Brackett, 1963
23 x 18 cm
Blue and white
G5751 .E65 1422 .S3

This map identifies places in England, Ireland, and France that are important to understanding the series of plays covering the history of England from 1398 to 1415 written by William Shakespeare. Routes are shown for the invasion by Henry Bolingbroke that resulted in the deposition of Richard II (reigned 1377–1399) and Bolingbroke's coronation as Henry IV (reigned 1399–1413). Flint Castle, where Richard is captured, and Pontefract Castle, scene of Richard's murder, are located. Sites in France include the location of the Battle of Agincourt, October 25, 1415, where Henry V (reigned 1413–1422) defeated French forces. Under the treaty that followed, he married the daughter of the French king and was recognized as heir to the throne of France.

MAP OF THE ROMAN WORLD IN CAESAR'S DAY

Julius Caesar: A Map of the Roman World in Caesar's Day

BARBARA R. HOUSEWORTH
Illustrator

Normal, Illinois: Educational Illustrators, 1962
59 x 89 cm
Black and white
G6701 .E65 1057 .H6

This map identifies sites in Europe, Africa, and Asia Minor where events depicted in William Shakespeare's *Julius Caesar* took place. A key with numbers gives additional information on the life of Caesar (100–44 BC). Around the borders of the map are eight illustrations, with accompanying quotes, of scenes from the play including Caesar's assassination (III, i) and Mark Antony's "Friends, Romans, countrymen" speech (III, ii).

Map of Scotland Illustrating Shakespeare's Macbeth

Barbara Rogers Houseworth
Illustrator

Normal, Illinois: Educational Illustrators,
  1957
79 x 59 cm
Black and white
G5771 .E65 1057 .H6

The his map relating to William Shakespeare's *Macbeth* identifies sites in Scotland and northern England, such as Cawdor Castle, Dusninane, and Birnam Wood, that are mentioned in the play. Around the border are illustrations of twelve scenes from the play, such as Macbeth's meeting with the three witches (I, iii), Macbeth seeing the ghost of Banquo (III, iv), and Lady Macbeth's sleepwalking scene (V, i). Quotations from the scenes accompany the illustrations.

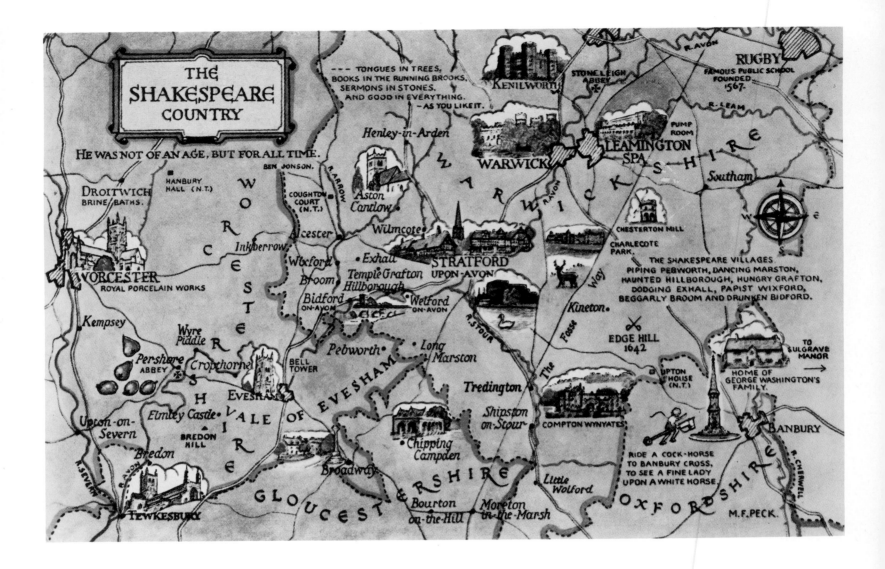

The Shakespeare Country

M. F. Peck
Illustrator

Sevenoaks, Kent, U.K.: J. Salmon, Ltd.,
    c. 1950
9 x 14 cm
Color
Ethel M. Fair Collection 687

Copyright© J. Salmon, Ltd., Sevenoaks, England.
Reprinted by permission

The *Shakespeare Country* postcard shows the Cotswolds area of England around Stratford-upon-Avon, hometown of William Shakespeare. The area includes parts of the counties of Warwickshire, Oxfordshire, Gloucestershire, and Worcestershire. For Stratford, the map features images of the cottage at Wilmcote where Shakespeare's mother Mary Arden lived; Shakespeare's birthplace; Holy Trinity Church, site of his baptism and burial; and the Royal Shakespeare Theatre. The map also includes a list of local villages that have Shakespeare associations. Landmarks in other nearby cities such as Worcester, Tewkesbury, and Warwick are also shown. The card includes a quote from Shakespeare's *As You Like It*, and the famous tribute to Shakespeare "He was not of an age, but for all time" by Shakespeare's contemporary playwright and poet Ben Jonson.

Shakespeare's Britain

Lisa Biganzoli
Preparer

Washington, D.C.: National Geographic
    Society, 1964
62 x 47 cm
Color
G5741 .E65 1544 .B5

Courtesy of the National Geographic Society

Produced in honor of Shakespeare's
400th birthday, *Shakespeare's Britain*
is based on a famous map of Shakespeare's time, "The Kingdome of Great
Britain and Ireland," from the atlas *Theatre of the Empire of Great Britaine*
(1611) by John Speed (1552?–1629).
Places with Shakespearean associations
are marked and the names of the plays
associated with them are printed on
banners. Other symbols locate towns,
abbeys, battlefields, castles, forests, and
heaths. A table lists Shakespeare's plays
with English settings. Insets show a
bird's-eye view of London, based on a
sixteenth-century map that shows the
Globe Theatre, and Shakespeare's hometown, Stretford upon Auen (Speed's
spelling).

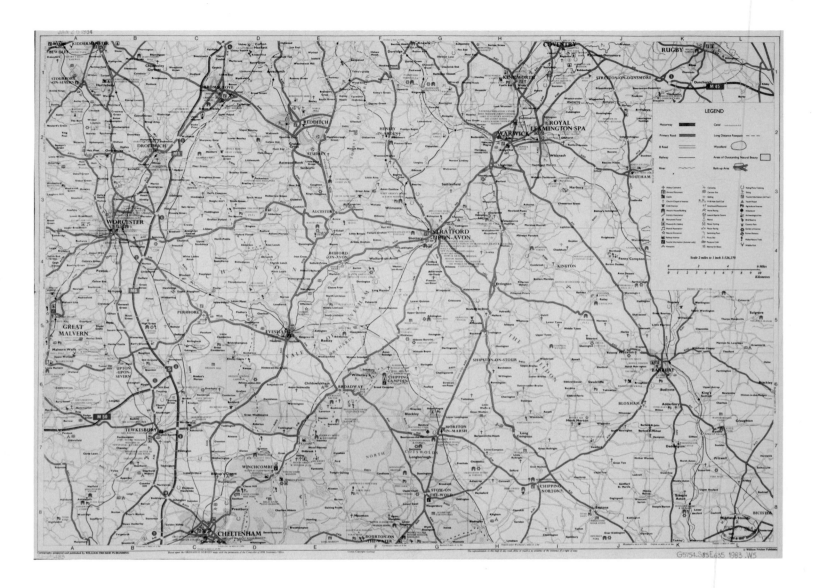

G5754.S85E635 1983 .W5

Shakespeare's Country: Map and Guide of Places to Visit

Prestbury, Cheltenham, Gloucestershire:
    William Fricker, 1983
42 x 61 cm
Color
G5754 .S85 .E635 1983 .W5

This map shows the area of the English Midlands around Stratford-upon-Avon, hometown of William Shakespeare, from Coventry and Rugby in the north to Great Malvern and Cheltenham in the east, and Bourton-on-the-Water in the south. The legend shows abbeys, castles, ancient monuments, churches, historic houses, and places having literary associations, An inset map of Stratford, showing the principal sites associated with Shakespeare, appears on the verso, which also has photographs of properties of the Shakespeare Birthplace Trust and other sites of interest in the town. A text describes Shakespeare's life and his associations with Stratford.

Language of the Land

Stratford on Avon

[United Kingdom?]: J. Ross Brown, 1908
59 x 74 cm
Color *(See color section.)*
G5754 .S85 .E65 1908 .B7

Rather than portraying Shakespeare's characters or the settings of the works, *Stratford on Avon* is a cartographically accurate bird's-eye map of the hometown of William Shakespeare as it was in 1908. Because of its connection with Shakespeare, since the eighteenth century Stratford-upon-Avon has been a popular tourist destination. This map is designed to help tourists find the town's sites. Insets on the map show the principal Stratford landmarks such as the poet's birthplace; Holy Trinity Church, site of his baptism and burial; Clopton Bridge; and the old Memorial Theatre, which burned in the 1930s.

JOHN STEINBECK

The John Steinbeck Map of America

MOLLY MAGUIRE
Designer

JIM WOLNICK
Illustrator

Los Angeles: Aaron Blake, 1986
43 x 55 cm
Color
G3701 .E65 1986 .A2

Courtesy of Molly Maguire and Aaron Silverman

*T*he *John Steinbeck Map of America* features popular images from Steinbeck's novels such as *Tortilla Flat* (1935), *The Grapes of Wrath* (1939), and *The Pearl* (1947). The outline of the map shows the route of *Travels with Charley* (1962), and the central portion consists of detailed street maps of the California towns of Salinas and Monterey, where Steinbeck lived and set some of his works. Numbers on the maps are keyed to lists of events in the books. A portrait of the author appears in the upper right corner. Research and design for the map were performed by Molly Maguire, who produced a series of literary maps in the 1980s.

ROBERT LOUIS STEVENSON

Treasure Island from the Book by Robert Louis Stevenson

Everett Henry
Illustrator

Cleveland: Harris-Seybold, 1954
43 x 61 cm
Color
G9930 1954 .H4

*T*reasure Island (1883), the classic adventure novel by Robert Louis Stevenson, began with a map. Housebound by bad weather, Stevenson amused himself and his young stepson by drawing a map of an imaginary island, with piratical place names and clues to buried treasure. Thereafter, Stevenson invented a story to fit the map. Based on Stevenson's map, this map shows Treasure Island, with landmarks such as Skeleton Island, Spyglass Hill, Rum Cove, and Ben Gunn's cave. An inset map shows the Atlantic Ocean, across which the ship *Hispaniola* sails from Bristol, England, to the West Indies, where the island is located. Characters such as Long John Silver, with his parrot Cap'n Flint; Billy Bones; and Captain Smollett are shown in scenes from the novel.

HENRY DAVID THOREAU

A Thoreau Gazetteer

ROBERT F. STOWELL
Author

Calais, Vermont: The Poor Farm Press, 1948
Various sizes
Black and white
Muriel H. Parry Collection 635

A Thoreau Gazetteer is a collection of maps intended to enable readers of Henry David Thoreau to follow the journeys that Thoreau wrote about in his books. The maps included are: I. *A Week on the Concord and Merrimack Rivers* (1849), associated with the book of that name; II. A *Concord* map by Herbert Gleason printed in the 1906 Houghton Mifflin edition of Thoreau's *Journals*; III. A topographic contour map of Concord surveyed in 1886 by the United States Geologic Survey; IV. An 1846 map of Walden Pond drawn by Thoreau; V. A Cape Cod map drawn by Thoreau; VI. The Maine Woods, as they were when Thoreau journeyed there in the 1850s and wrote about them; VII. A map based on several drawings by Thoreau in a folder in the Free Library of Concord and used to illustrate "A Yankee in Canada" in *Excursions* (1893); and VIII. A map of the journey to Minnesota (shown) that Thoreau made from May to July 1861, some description of which is given in the *Journals*. The maps are collected in a folder along with a five-page descriptive guide that supplies information on the maps and their relation to Thoreau's work.

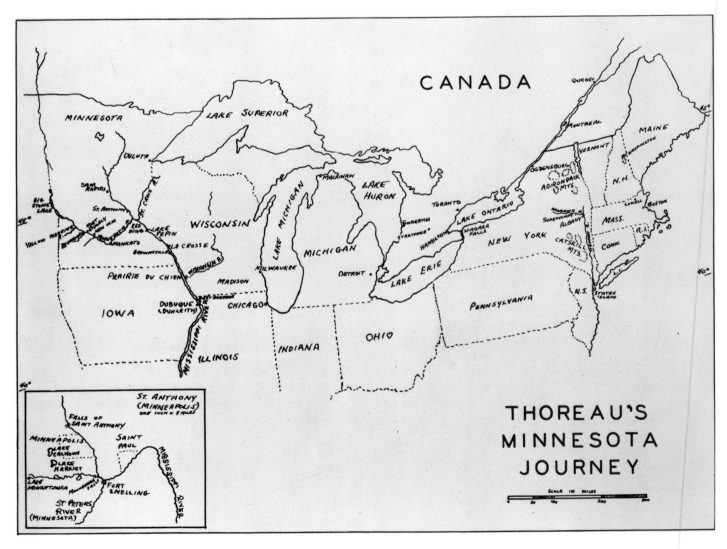

Thoreau's Rivers

Mary Gail Fenn
Compiler

Geneseo, New York: Thoreau Society, 1973
69 x 56 cm
Black and white
G3762 .C65E65 1973 .F4

Courtesy of Mary Gail Fenn

*T*horeau's Rivers (Thoreau Society booklet no. 27) shows the area of Massachusetts around Concord, Sudbury, Lincoln, Wayland, and the Assabet River valleys, where Henry David Thoreau spent most of his life. It locates places mentioned in Thoreau's *Journals*, written in the 1850s and 1860s, and includes an alphabetical list of those places, dates on which the places are mentioned, and coordinates to the map.

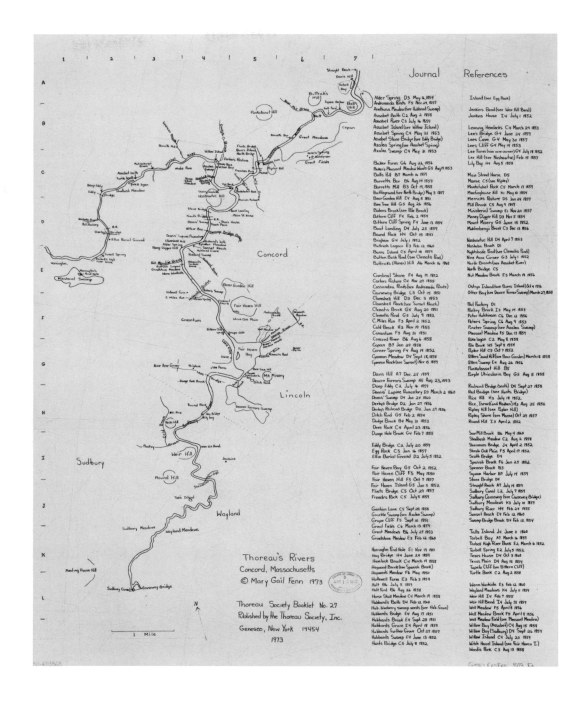

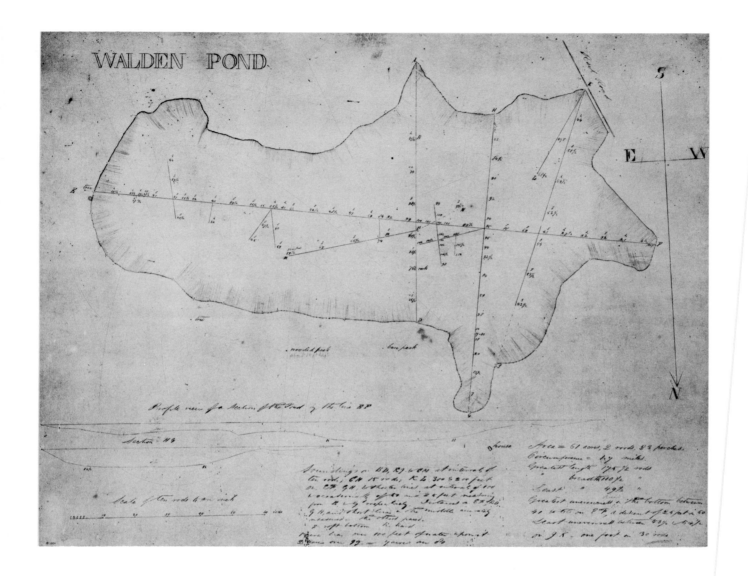

Walden Pond

HENRY DAVID THOREAU
Illustrator

Boston: Charles E. Goodspeed & Co., 1954
41 x 53 cm
Color
G3762 .W3 1846 .T5 1954

*W*alden Pond reproduces a drawing of Walden Pond by Henry David Thoreau in the collection of the Concord, Massachusetts, Free Library, which owns a folder donated by Thoreau's sister Sophia that contains a number of Thoreau's holograph land surveys and drawings. The map shows a profile of the pond and the depths as shown by soundings. Landmarks such as trees and railroad around the pond are also shown. At the bottom are Thoreau's statistical notes on the pond. Although it has been omitted in many modern editions, a similar map appeared in the first edition of *Walden* (1854). The map is an integral part of the narrative, and modern surveys have attested to its accuracy. It reflects Thoreau's keen interest in cartography.

J[OHN] R[ONALD] R[UEL] TOLKIEN

A Map of Middle-Earth

Pauline Baynes
Illustrator

[London]: George Allen & Unwin, Ltd., 1970
74 x 51 cm
Color
G9330 1970 .B3

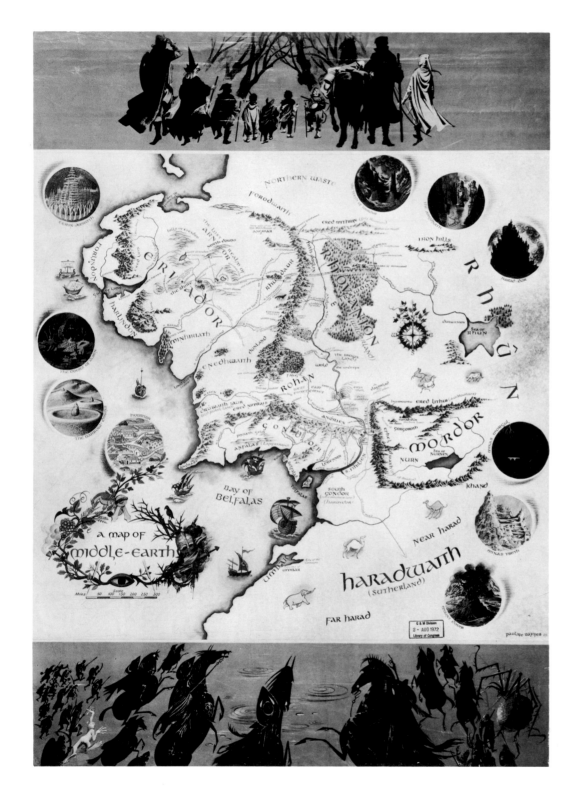

A Map of Middle-Earth, based on the cartography of J. R. R. Tolkien and his son C. J. R. Tolkien, shows places mentioned in J. R. R. Tolkien's *Lord of the Rings* trilogy. Insets around the edge of the map show Cerin Amroth, where Aragorn and Arwen were betrothed in the Elvish Kingdom; the doors of Durin; the Barrow-Downs, inhabited by evil spirits; Hobbiton; the Teeth of Mordor; the Argonath or Gates of the King; Barad-dur Minas Morgul; Minas Tirith; and the volcano Mount Doom, which dominates the sinister land of Mordor. An illustration at the top of the map shows the company of the Ring, consisting of the hobbits Frodo, Sam, Merz, and Pippin; the dwarf Gimbi; the elf Legolas; and the men Aragorn and Boromir, all free peoples, on their journey. An illustration at the bottom portrays the forces of evil, consisting of orcs, trolls, and gollum, arrayed against them.

Middle Earth

M. BLACKBURN
Illustrator

New York: Bruin, Inc., ca. 1966
71 x 71 cm
Color
G9930 1966 .B5

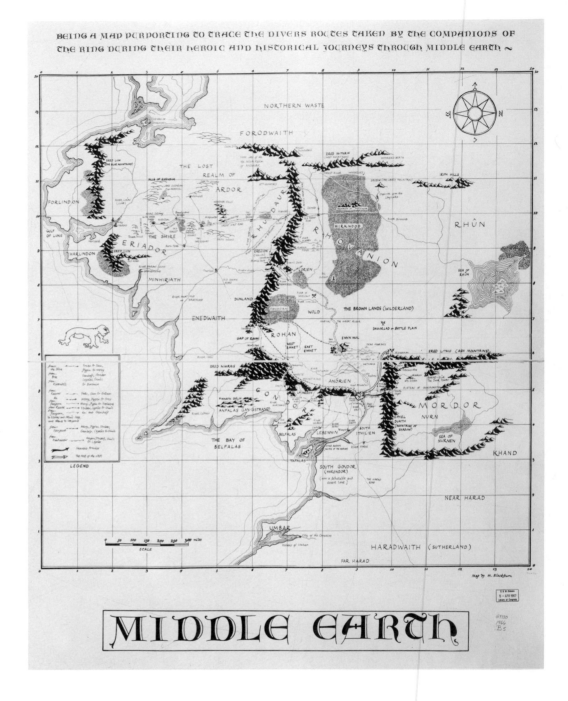

*M*iddle Earth is based on information in J. R. R. Tolkien's *Lord of the Rings* trilogy (1955)—consisting of *The Fellowship of the Ring, The Two Towers,* and *The Return of the King.* Authorized by Houghton Mifflin, Tolkien's American publisher, the map traces the routes taken by the companions of the Ring during their journeys through Middle Earth, an imaginary world inhabited by dwarves, dragons, and hobbits—small, semihuman creatures. A legend is keyed to lines on the map showing routes taken by various characters. The action of the books involves a quest for a powerful magic ring that corrupts whoever wears it and must be destroyed. The map shows landmarks of Middle Earth such as Mirkwood, an area of marshes and fens; Gondor, a powerful kingdom; and Mordor, literally a black land, dominated by the volcanic Mt. Doom, which reflects the sinister nature of its ruler, Sauron. The One Ring was cast into the Cracks of Doom, causing a final eruption.

Road Map, Third Age, Middle Earth

R[ichard] Caldwell, 1978
59 x 90 cm
Color
G9930 1978 .C8

*R*oad Map, Third Age, Middle Earth, based on the highly popular works of J.R.R. Tolkien, shows fictional landmarks from his *Lord of the Rings* trilogy (1955)—consisting of *The Fellowship of the Ring, The Two Towers,* and *The Return of the King.* In the books, the Third Age is a time of upheavals, battles, escapes, and migrations. The map shows landmarks such as Mirkwood, an area of marshes and fens; Gondor, a powerful kingdom that extended its territory during this age; and Mordor, a land dominated by the volcanic Mt. Doom, which reflects the sinister nature of its ruler, Sauron. The Third Age covers the first defeat of Sauron to the War of the Rings, where Sauron suffered his second defeat. It is also known by elves as the "Fading Years" because it represents the end of their dominance of the land and the beginning of the power of humankind.

LEO TOLSTOY

Moskva-IAsnaia Poliana, turistskaia skhema
(Moscow-Yasnaya Polyana, A Tourist Map)

Moscow: Glavnoe upravlenie geodezii i
    kartografii, 1973
In Russian
49 x 35 cm
Color
G7004 .I34 .2M8A3 1973 .S6

Moskva-IAsnaia Poliana shows the 110-mile route from Moscow to Yasnaya Polyana, the ancestral estate and birthplace of Leo Tolstoy. The route goes by places of interest connected with other writers, for example, Anton Chekhov, whose house it passes, and Alexander Pushkin, and includes information on these places and writers. Tolstoy, who was deeply attached to his home, once said, "Without my Yasnaya Polyana, it would be hard for me to imagine Russia." While living there he wrote his masterpieces *War and Peace* (1865–1869) and *Anna Karenina* (1875–1877), as well as the philosophical tracts that occupied his last years. He also opened a village school for the peasant children on the estate, where he practiced his progressive theories of education. An inset map shows the grounds of Yasnaya Polyana, with a key to the places tourists can visit, including the house museum, literary museum, and Tolstoy's grave. Photographs show these places and the interior of the house. Text on the map provides information on Tolstoy's life and work. The map is apparently a revision of a 1971 version that is not in the Library of Congress collections.

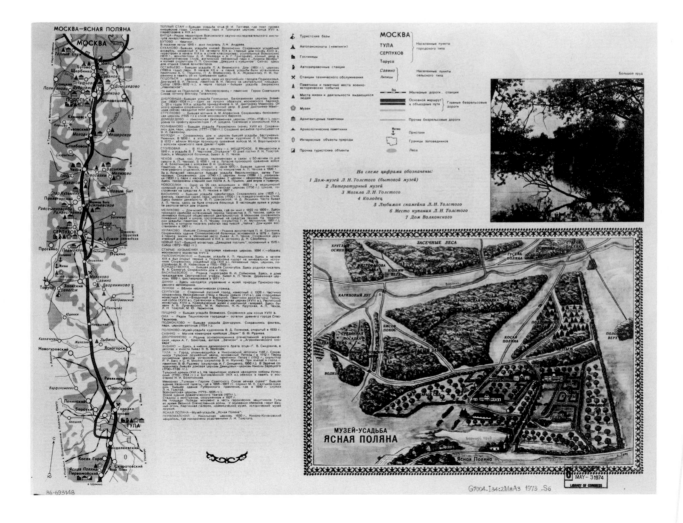

Moskva-IAsnaia Poliana, turistskaia skhema

(Moscow-Yasnaya Polyana, A Tourist Map)

Moscow: Glavnoe upravlenie geodezii i
    kartografii, 1976
In Russian
41 x 53 cm
Color
G7006 .I34 .2M8A3 1976 .S6

*M*oskva-IAsnaia Poliana shows the 110-mile route from Moscow to Yasnaya Polyana, the ancestral estate and birthplace of Leo Tolstoy. The route passes places of interest connected with other writers, for example, Anton Chekhov and Alexander Pushkin, and includes information on these places and writers. Tolstoy, who was deeply attached to his home, once said, "Without my Yasnaya Polyana, it would be hard for me to imagine Russia." While living there he wrote his masterpieces *War and Peace* (1865–1869) and *Anna Karenina* (1875–1877), as well as the philosophical tracts that occupied his last years. He also opened a village school for the peasant children on the estate, where he practiced his progressive theories of education. An inset map shows the grounds of Yasnaya Polyana, with a key to the places tourists can visit, including the house museum, literary museum, and Tolstoy's grave. Photographs show these sites and the interior of the home. Text on the map provides information on Tolstoy's life and work. The map is a revision of a 1971 map not in the Library

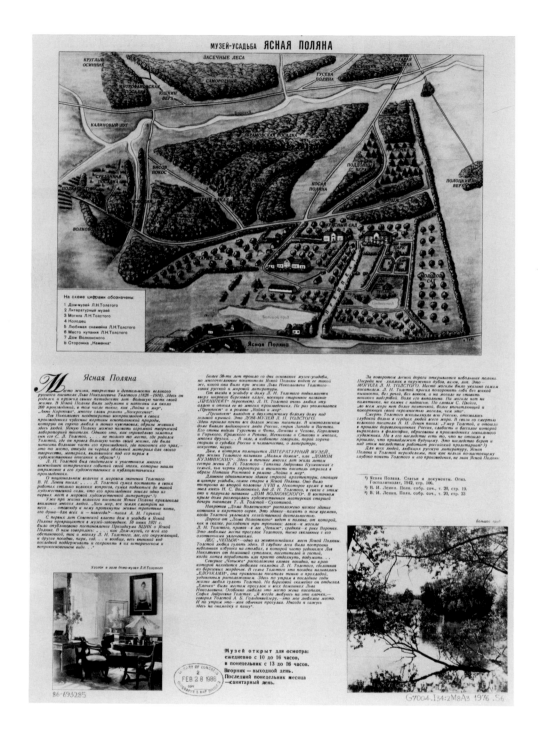

of Congress collections and a 1973 revision (G7006 .I34 .2M8A3 1973 .S6) that the Library does own. Slightly revised versions of the map were also issued in 1978 (G7006. I34 .2M8A3 1978 .S6) and 1980 (G7006. I34 .2M8A3 1980 .S6).

MARK TWAIN
(Samuel Clemens, see also Bret Harte)

The Adventures of Huckleberry Finn from the Book by Mark Twain

Everett Henry
Illustrator

Cleveland: Harris-Intertype, 1959
76 x 54 cm
Color *(See color section.)*
G4042 .M5E65 185–.H4

Against a map of the Mississippi River, *The Adventures of Huckleberry Finn* map presents scenes from Mark Twain's 1884 novel that portrays pre-Civil War life along the Mississippi and the moral complexities of a boy's growing up. The map's central image shows Huck and Jim, the escaped slave whom he befriends, on the raft that takes them down river. They are rehearsing scenes from Shakespeare with the King and the Duke, two con men who accompany the main characters on part of the trip. An inset map shows Missouri, Illinois, Kentucky, Tennessee, Arkansas, Louisiana, and Mississippi, the states in which the novel's action occurs. Episodes from the book depicted include the Grangerford-Shepherdson feud, the Boggs-Sherburn duel, the King's Royal Nonesuch performance, and Huck's and Tom Sawyer's plots to free Jim. Important characters such as Pap Finn, Miss Watson, Aunt Sally, and Uncle Silas also appear.

Language of the Land

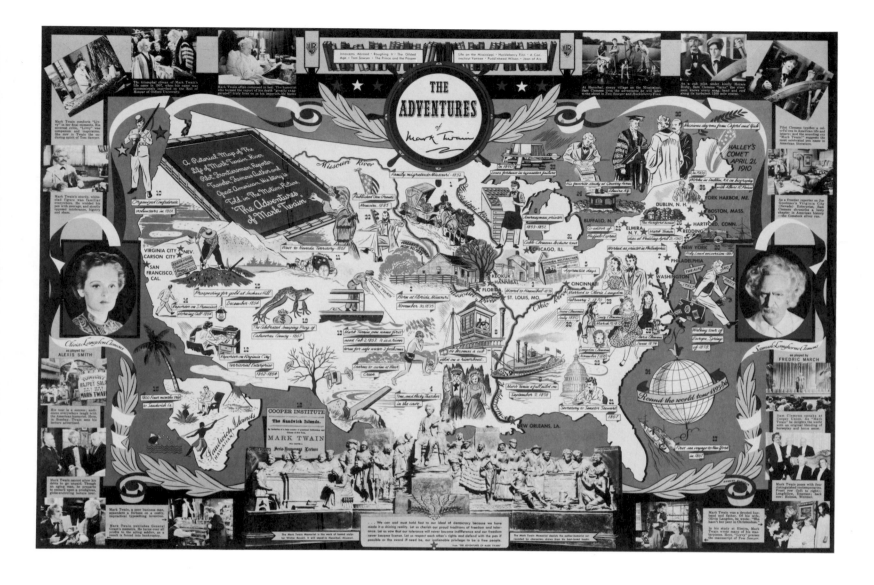

The Adventures of Mark Twain

Hollywood: Warner Brothers, 1944
55 x 78 cm
Color
Ethel M. Fair Collection 282

Subtitled "A Pictorial Map of the Life of Mark Twain—River Pilot, Frontiersman, Reporter, Traveller, Famous Author, and Great American," this map was produced in conjunction with a 1944 Warner Brothers film starring Frederic March (1899–1975). The central image is a map of the United States with places important to Twain's life and work. Hawaii, which he visited in 1866, is also shown. At the center is a list of Twain's major works, including *The Innocents Abroad* (1869), *Roughing It* (1872), *The Adventures of Tom Sawyer* (1876), and *The Adventures of Huckleberry Finn* (1884). Around the left and right borders are key scenes from the film. At the bottom center is a photo of the Mark Twain Memorial in his hometown, Hannibal, Missouri. By Walter Russell (1871–1963), the sculpture depicts Twain surrounded by characters from his books. Produced during World War II, the map features a patriotic quote from the film and an admonition to "Buy More War Bonds and Stamps."

Here Took Place the Adventures of Tom Sawyer from the Book by Mark Twain

EVERETT HENRY
Illustrator

Cleveland: Harris Seybold, 1953
64 x 48 cm
Color
29 x 61 cm
G9930 1953 .H4

*T*he *Adventures of Tom Sawyer* map presents scenes from the classic 1876 novel by Mark Twain, which portrays a boy's life in a small town before the Civil War. The book draws on Twain's boyhood in Hannibal, Missouri, which was the model for the book's St. Petersburg. At the bottom of the map is a bird's-eye view of St. Petersburg from the Mississippi River, showing the river and Jackson's Island. The upper part of the map depicts a street layout of the town, locating such landmarks as the church and the houses of Tom, Becky Thatcher, and the Widow Douglas. An inset at upper left locates Hannibal. Episodes from the book depicted include the famous fence white-washing, Tom's and Huck's attendance at their own funeral, Tom and Becky lost in Injun Joe's Cave, and the boys' digging for pirate treasure.

OWEN WISTER

The Virginian from America's First "Western" Novel, Written by Owen Wister

EVERETT HENRY
Illustrator

Cleveland: Harris-Intertype, 1962
43 x 61 cm
Color
G4261 .E65 1890 .H4

*T*he Virginian (1902) by Owen Wister was one of the first and most influential of a long line of novels romanticizing life in the West and establishing the cowboy as a folk hero. Against an outline of the Dakotas, Wyoming, Nebraska, and Idaho, this map highlights scenes from the classic novel, such as the card game with Trampas during which the Virginian delivers his famous line, "When you call me that, smile." An inset map shows the states where the events in the novel take place, with Wyoming, the main locale, highlighted.

VIRGIL (VERGIL)

Aeneae Navigatio
(Voyages of Aeneas)

Boston: Cummings, Hilliard, and Company,
  ca. 1826
20 x 26 cm
Black and white
G5672 .M4 .E65 BC .C8

Aeneae Navigatio appears to be a fold-out map from a book about the adventures of Aeneas. It traces Aeneas's voyages after the Trojan War as recounted by Virgil in the *Aeneid* (30–19 BC). The map shows the eastern Mediterranean region from Anatolia to Italy, with parts of North Africa. An inset map shows the coast of Italy around Rome, where Aeneas eventually settled.

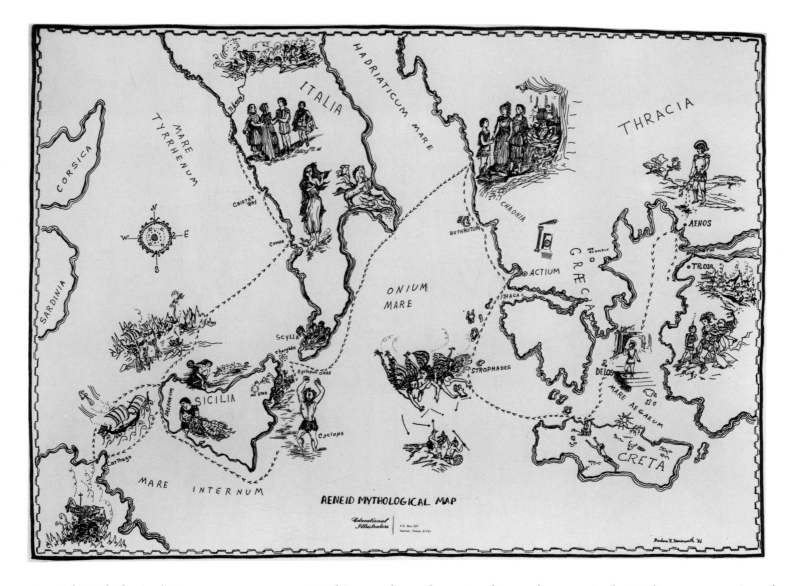

Aeneid Mythological Map

A. R. Houseworth
Illustrator

Normal, Illinois: Educational Illustrators,
1956
52 x 72 cm
Black and white
G5672 .M4 .E65 BC .H6

This map shows the route of Aeneas's voyage in the Mediterranean region after the Trojan War as recounted by Virgil in the *Aeneid* (30–19 BC). Line drawings show scenes from the epic, such as the Greek sacking of Troy, from which the Trojan prince Aeneas flees with his son Ascanius while carrying his father Anchises on his back; Dido, queen of Carthage, burning on her funeral pyre after killing herself at Aeneas's departure; and the arrival of Aeneas in Italy, where he became an ancestor of the Romans.

Carte du Voyage d'Enée, et de tous les lieux qui font nommez dans les oeuvres de Virgile, pour bien entendre cet auteur

(Map of the Voyages of Aeneas, and all the places that are named in the works of Virgil, to understand that author well)

A. Peyrounin, Illustrator Paris:
    P. Mariette, 1705
36 x 50 cm
Color
G5672 .M4E65 BC .D8 Vault

Carte du Voyage d'Enée, traces Aeneas's voyage in the Mediterranean region after the Trojan War as recounted by Virgil in the *Aeneid* (30–19 BC). Originally published as plate 91 in J. LeClerc's *Atlas antique* (1705), the map shows the northern Mediterranean from Sardinia to western Anatolia, with dotted lines of the hero's route from Troy to Italy. At the bottom of the map are drawings of some of Aeneas's ships (shown as eighteenth-century vessels), with references to events of the epic, such as twelve vessels that were separated from Aeneas's fleet in a tempest. A note says that the map was designed by the Val Géographe according to the research and memoirs of Michel de Marolles, Abbé of Villeloin.

WILLIAM WORDSWORTH

Wordsworth's Lake District: An Illustrated Map and Guide

RAM ASSOCIATES
Designer

Windermere, Cumbria, United Kingdom:
    Cumbria Tourist Board, 1987
28 x 40 cm
Color
G5752 .L2E65 1987 .R3

Courtesy of the Cumbria Tourist Board

Prepared by the Cumbria Tourist Board and the Wordsworth Trust, this map features the English Lake District, with places numbered to a key. Sites associated with Romantic poet William Wordsworth are one of the major tourist attractions in Cumbria, and the map supplies information useful to those wanting to visit them. Around the map's edges are detailed descriptions with illustrations of places important in the life and career of the poet. Illustrations include Wordsworth's birthplace at Cockermouth; Rydal Mount, his home from 1813 to 1850; and an 1839 portrait of Wordsworth and his wife Mary. On the reverse is a lengthy biography of Wordsworth. Also given are brief biographical sketches of important people in the poet's life: his sister Dorothy Wordsworth and fellow writers Samuel Taylor Coleridge, Robert Southey, and Thomas De Quincey, all of whom lived for a time in the Lake District. Reprinted in 1995, the map is also available in Japanese.

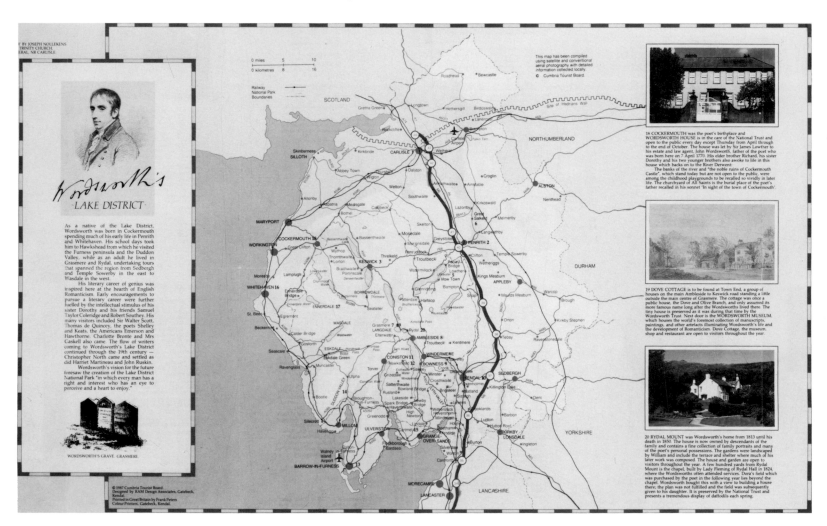

AUSTIN TAPPAN WRIGHT

The Country of Islandia

ROBERT GRAVES
Illustrator

n.d.
24 x 32 cm
Black and white
Ethel M. Fair Collection 59

The map of Islandia shows the imaginary country created by Austin Tappan Wright in his posthumously published book of the same name. Wright, a law professor at the University of California who wrote *Islandia* (1942) as a hobby, also produced a complete history of the fictional southern hemisphere continent of Karain, of which the constitutional monarchy of Islandia is the southern and temperate part. The map is supposedly based on those in the notebooks of John Lang, who goes to Islandia in 1908 as the first American consul. *Islandia* describes Lang's experiences in the country, a primarily agricultural society where neither coffee nor tobacco is used and the number of foreigners allowed at any one time is limited to 100. Mark Saxton also used the country as the setting for a series of sequels: *The Islar* (1969), *The Two Kingdoms* (1979), and *Havoc in Islandia* (1982). Islandia is further described in *An Introduction to Islandia: Its History, Customs, Laws, Language, and Geography* (1942) by Basil Davenport and in Alberto Manguel and Gianni Guadalupi, *The Dictionary of Imaginary Places.* (see Map Collections section). The map may have been distributed to bookstores to promote *Islandia*.

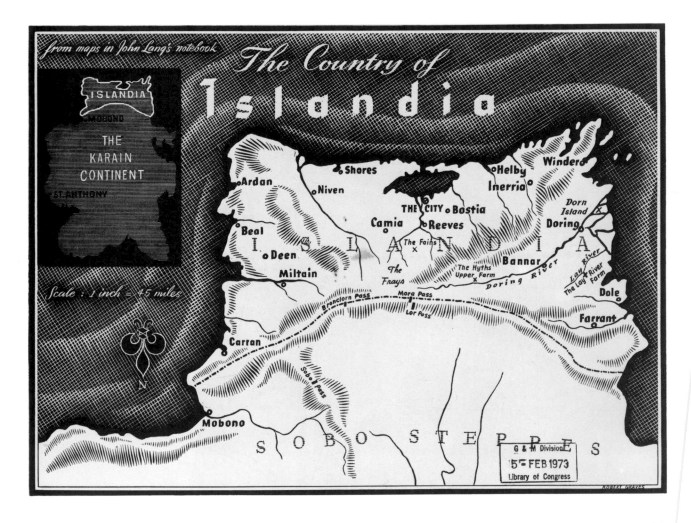

STARK YOUNG

The Country of So Red the Rose by Stark Young

ARTHUR ZAIDENBURG
Cartographer

New York: Charles Scribners and Sons,
    ca. 1934
82 x 43 cm
Color
G3981 .E65 193– .Z3

*T*he Country of So Red the Rose map shows the Mississippi setting of the novel *So Red the Rose* (1934) by Stark Young. Like the later and better-known *Gone with the Wind* (1936), for which its success paved the way, *So Red the Rose* portrays Southern life during the Civil War. Its plot relates the story of two large and interconnected plantation families, the McGehees of Montrose and the Bedfords of Portobello. One of the best-selling novels of its time, the book was made into a 1935 motion picture starring Randolph Scott, Margaret Sullivan, and Robert Cummings. This map showing characters and events from the novel and the locations associated with them was probably a promotional vehicle produced by the novel's publishers.

Imaginary Worlds, Folklore, Myths, Fairy Tales, and Nursery Rhymes

"It was not on any map. Real places never are."

Herman Melville
Moby Dick

FICTIONAL PLACES

Ambridge

ROBERT JONES
Illustrator

Newton Abbot, Devon, U.K.: David and
    Charles, 1986
46 x 70 cm
Color
G9930 1986 .J6

*A*mbridge records the fictional area of England that is the setting for "The Archers," a British radio program about rural life that began production in 1951. An archetypal small village of about 360 inhabitants in the fictional English county of Borsetshire, Ambridge is located six miles south of the also imaginary town of Borchester, seventeen miles from the imaginary large town of Felpersham, and approximately two hours from London by train. Ambridge is surrounded by a number of farms that are home to characters in the program. A key at the left of the map describes these farms and the characters who live there. An enormously popular serial, "The Archers" inspired several novels, including *Ambridge Summer* (1975) by Keith Miles.

Islandia *(See Austin Tappan Wright)*
Kenoska *(See Florence Parry Heide)*
Middle Earth *(See J [ohn] R[onald] R[uel] Tolkien)*
Never Land *(See James M. Barrie)*
Oz *(See L. Frank Baum)*
Poictesme *(See James Branch Cabell)*
Treasure Island *(See Robert Louis Stevenson)*

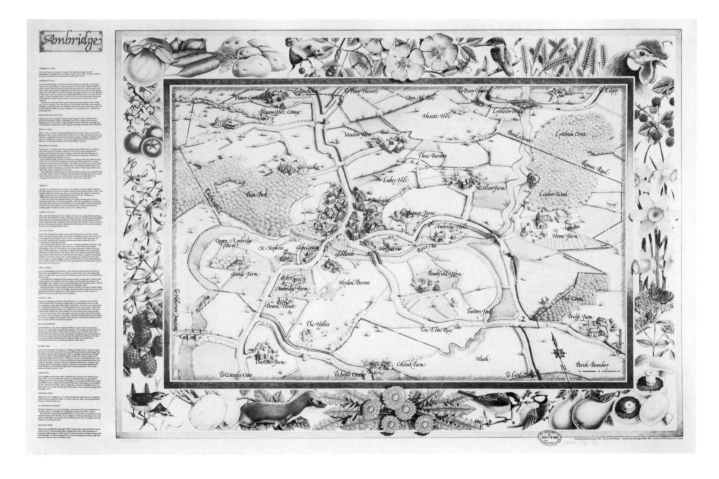

EUROPE

The All Mother Goose Panorama

LUXOR PRICE
Illustrator

New York: Frederick A. Stokes Company,
    1923
63 x 128 cm
Color
Ethel M. Fair Collection 718

*T*he All Mother Goose Panorama
shows characters from nursery
rhymes. Old King Cole (shown) is en-
throned in the center, with Mother
Goose above him. Other nursery-rhyme
characters prominently featured include
Humpty Dumpty, Hey Diddle Diddle,
Little Jack Horner, Simple Simon, Jack
Sprat, Jack Be Nimble, Little Miss Muffet, and the Lion and the Unicorn.

An Ancient Mappe of Fairyland, Newly Discovered and Set Forth

Bernard Sleigh
Illustrator

London: Sidgwick & Jackson, ca. 1920
43 x 177 cm
Color *(See color section.)*
G9930 1920 .S5

Txhe highly detailed *Ancient Mappe of Fairyland* depicts hundreds of motifs from many European fantasy traditions—fairy tales, nursery rhymes, Arthurian legends, children's books, and Celtic, Norse, and Greco-Roman mythology. The various mythological traditions appear in zones from left to right across the map. Surrounded by rainbows at the middle of the top is Valhalla, home of Wotan and the gods of Norse legend. Medieval Arthurian legends are represented by the Isle of Avalon and the Holy Mountain Monsalvat. A text entitled *A Guide to the Map of Fairyland* by Bernard Sleigh (G9930 .S5 1920) gives background information about the map and contains a list of its many literary sources, which include Shakespeare, *The Arabian Nights*, Hans Christian Andersen, and the Brothers Grimm.

Sir Richard repays the Prior

Here Took Place the Adventures of Robin Hood and His Merry Men from Tales of Sherwood Forest

Everett Henry
llustrator

Cleveland: Harris-Seybold 1955
48 x 65 cm
Color
G5752 .S46 .E627 119– .H4

*H*ere Took Place the Adventures of Robin Hood shows scenes from the Robin Hood tales, part of English medieval folklore. The background of the map shows the parts of the English counties of Derbyshire, Lincolnshire, and Nottinghamshire where the tales took place. The central image shows Robin and his Merry Men entertaining King Richard the Lionhearted, who visited the outlaw band disguised as a friar, pardoned them, and took them into his service. Scenes from other tales include the first meeting of Robin and his chief lieutenant Little John, Will Scarlet meeting Robin, Robin's nemesis the Sheriff of Nottingham trying to hang Robin's man Will Stutely and the dying Robin shooting his last arrow after being betrayed. At the top of the map is a large scene of Robin winning the famous Royal Archery contest at Finsbury Fields.

Language of the Land

The Land of Make Believe

The Land of Make Believe

Jaro J. Hess
Illustrator

Grand Rapids, Michigan: Jaro J. Hess, 1930
25 x 36 cm
Color
G9930 1930 .H4

*T*he Land of Make Believe is a colorful bird's-eye view of places mentioned in nursery rhymes, fairy tales, and other children's stories. Nursery rhymes located include the house that Jack built, the home of the old woman who lived in a shoe, and Mother Hubbard's house. Fairy tale locations include Sleeping Beauty's castle, Bluebeard's castle, and Cinderella's house. Children's stories include *Peter Pan* (1904) by James M. Barrie, *The Water Babies* (1863) by Charles Kingsley, and *Peter Rabbit* (1900) by Beatrix Potter. Illustrations of many of the characters from these tales are also shown.

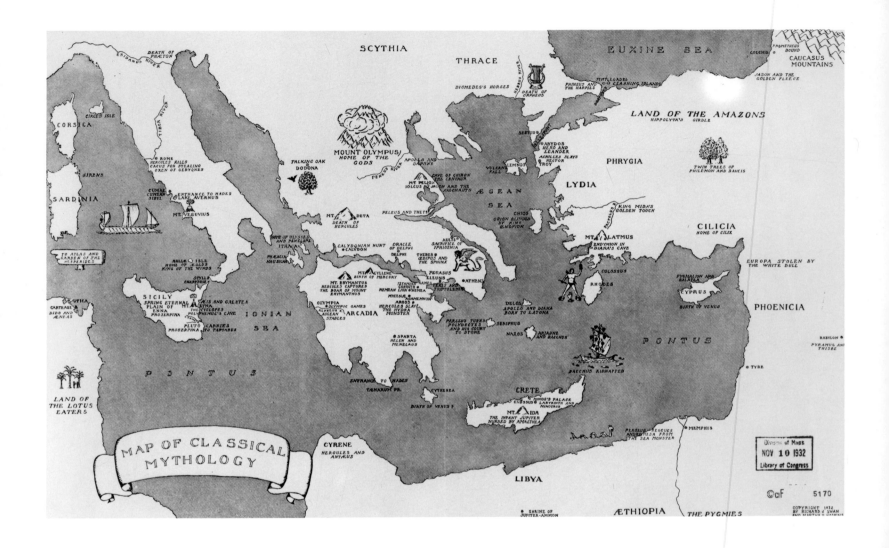

Map of Classical Mythology

Richard J. Swan and Martha H. Hoskins,
    1932
28 x 43 cm
Black and white
G5672 .M4E627 BC .59

The *Map of Classical Mythology* locates places in the eastern Mediterranean Sea mentioned in Greek and Roman myths and literature. Among those mentioned are the Land of the Amazons, warrior women; Crete, site of King Minos's Palace and the labyrinth of the minotaur; Carthage, home of Queen Dido in the Aeneid; Delphi, site of the famous oracle; Ithaca, home of Odysseus; and Thebes, home of Oedipus.

Language of the Land

Folklore and Legends of Our Country

UNITED STATES

Folklore and Legends of Our Country

[?] SOLTESZ
Illustrator

New York: Esso Standard, 1960
61 x 90 cm
Color
G3701 .E62 1960 .G41

Produced for classroom use, *Folklore and Legends of Our Country* illustrates a number of characters from American folklore, history, and literature. Literary characters include the Headless Horseman from "The Legend of Sleepy Hollow" (1820) by Washington Irving, Natty Bumppo and Chingachgook from the "Leather-stocking Tales" by James Fenimore Cooper, Evangeline, from the 1847 poem of that name by Henry Wadsworth Longfellow, Brer Rabbit, Brer Fox, and Brer Bear from the Uncle Remus stories by Joel Chandler Harris, and the celebrated jumping frog of Calaveras County from Mark Twain's 1865 story. State boundaries are outlined, but no place names or character names are given. Alaska and Hawaii appear as insets. The verso of the map contains a wealth of information about folklore, including a reading list. A separate key identifies the sixty-five characters on the map and provides a descriptive paragraph about each.

Paul Bunyan's Pictorial Map of the United States, Depicting Some of His Deeds and Exploits

R. D. HANDY
Illustrator

Duluth, Minnesota: R. D. Handy, 1935
50 x 75
Color
Ethel M. Fair Collection 468

On an outline map of the forty-eight contiguous states are shown the exploits of Paul Bunyan, whom the map labels as "America's only folklore character." A mythical hero of the American frontier lumber camps, Paul Bunyan has become a symbol of size, strength, ingenuity, and exaggeration. At the bottom of the map is a large figure of Paul, along with smaller figures of other characters in the Bunyan legend—Sourdough Sam, the cook; Shot Gunderson, the foreman; Johnny Inkslinger, the bookkeeper; Big Ole, the blacksmith; and Chris Crosshaul, the straw boss. Illustrations with explanatory text show key incidents in the legend—the Great Lakes, which Paul dug as a watering hole for his giant blue ox, Babe; the Allegheny and Rocky mountains, formed when Paul was deepening the Mississippi River; Paul digging the Puget Sound; pancakes being cooked on a griddle so big that boys with slabs of bacon on their feet skate around greasing it; and Paul fighting a sea serpent using a frozen swordfish as a weapon.

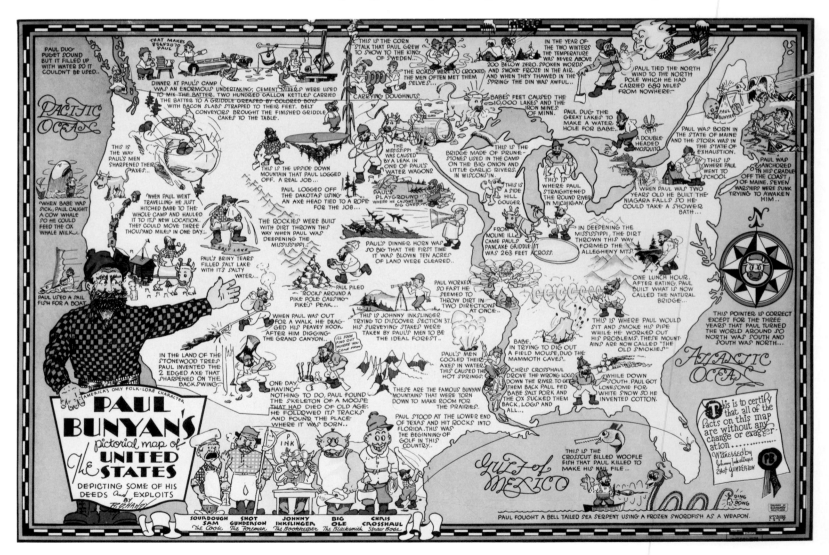

A Storyteller's Map of American Myths

JAMES LEWICKI
Illustrator

LILLIAN LEWICKI
Assistant Illustrator and Researcher

From "Ballads and Tales of the Frontier,"
 Life Magazine, August 22, 1960, pp. 58–59
35 x 77 cm
Color
Muriel H. Parry Collection 499

Courtesy of Mrs. James Lewicki

A Storyteller's Map of American Myths, a fold-out that appeared as part of a *Life* magazine article, is a map of the forty-eight contiguous states showing folklore characters in their most familiar locales. A detail of the Eastern United States is shown. Some of the illustrations depict historical characters who became legendary, such as Blackbeard (Edward Teach, d. 1718), Davy Crockett (1786–1836), Billy the Kid (William H. Bonney, 1859–1881), Wyatt Earp (1848–1929), Sacajawea (ca. 1784–1884), and Pocahontas (ca. 1595–1617) and Captain John Smith (1580–1631). Other characters, for example, Paul Bunyan and his blue ox Babe, are entirely legendary. The magazine article depicts many of the characters on the map in large illustrations and gives a detailed, state-by-state explanation of the legends. Artist James Lewicki (1917–1980), aided by his wife Lillian, conceived and executed this map, which was the culmination of his five-part series on "Folklore in America," published in *Life* issues of August 31 and November 2, 1959, and January 25, April 11, and August 22, 1960.

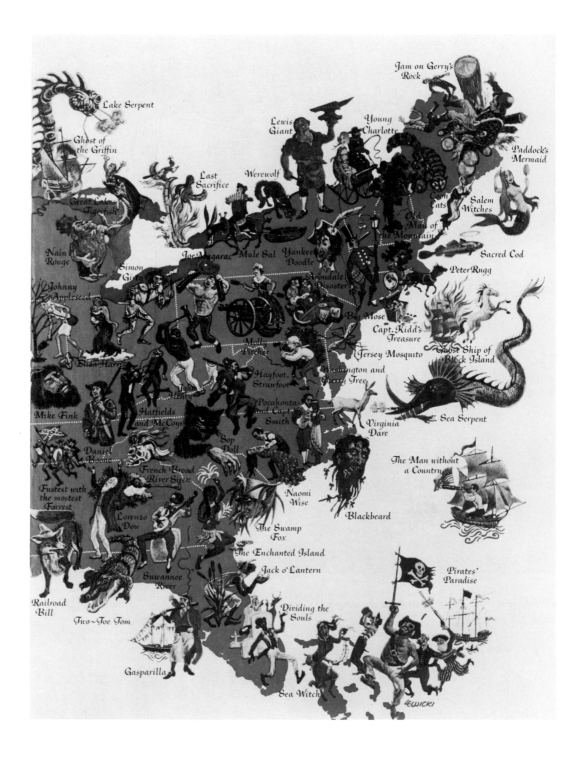

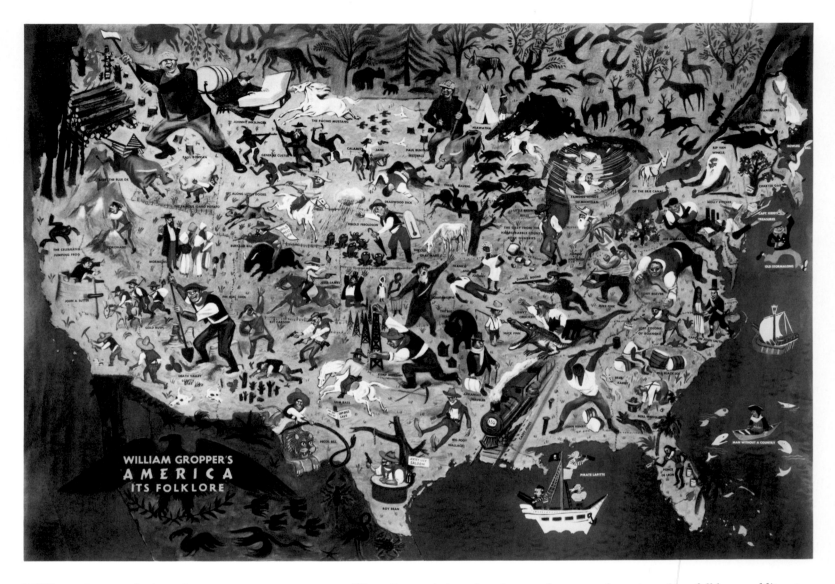

William Gropper's America: Its Folklore

William Gropper, 1946
57 x 83 cm
Color
Muriel H. Parry Collection 500

William Gropper's America pictures characters from American folklore and literature. Although most of the characters are legendary figures such as Paul Bunyan and John Henry, a number of the illustrations depict characters from formal literature. Examples include Huck Finn, from *The Adventures of Huckleberry Finn* (1884) by Mark Twain; the celebrated jumping frog of Calaveras County (1865) from Twain's story of that name; Evangeline, from the poem (1847) by Henry Wadsworth Longfellow; and the man without a country from the poem (1863) by Edward Everett Hale. An advocate for the poor and disadvantaged, artist William Gropper (1897–1977) contributed to radical journals and visited the Soviet Union. In 1953, this map attracted the attention of Senator Joseph McCarthy, who denounced all of Gropper's art as communist-directed, anti-American propaganda and objected to distribution of the map by U.S. government agencies.

The following maps are not illustrated.

A. A. MILNE

The 100 Acre Wood

E. H. SHEPARD
Illustrator

From Bowen Pearse, "In the Land of
  Winnie the Pooh." *British Heritage,* 15,
  no. 2, February-March 1994, pp. 44–45.
16 x 23 cm
Color
G9930 1994 .S5

*T*he 100 Acre Wood appeared in a *British Heritage* magazine article designed to encourage tourists to visit the area associated with the Winnie the Pooh books by A. A. Milne. The wood is actually a part of Ashdown Forest, near Hartfield in East Sussex, thirty-five miles south of London. The map identifies places in the books, such as the Bee Tree and the houses of characters such as Owl, Pooh Bear, Kanga, and Piglet. The map is by E. H. Shepard (1879–1976), illustrator of Milne's Pooh books.

MARI SANDOZ

The Old Jules Home Region

New York: J. F. Carr, 1965
57 x 44 cm
Black and white
G4191 .E65 1965 .S3

*T*he Old Jules Home Region shows areas of South Dakota and Nebraska that are the setting for the book *Old Jules* (1935) by Mari Sandoz. The book traces Sandoz's father's attempts to survive as a frontier farmer after settling in the Niobrara River area of northwestern Nebraska in 1884. One key on the map designates places of historical importance in the area before Jules Sandoz arrived from Switzerland. Another locates places mentioned in the book, such as farms he homesteaded and the homes of his children.

Literary Atlases and Other Compilations

"Imagination is as good as many voyages—and how much cheaper."

George William Curtis
(1824–1892)

GENERAL

An Atlas of Fantasy

J[EREMIAH] B[ENJAMIN] POST
Author

Baltimore: Mirage Press, 1979
G3122 .P6 1979

*A*n *Atlas of Fantasy* was written by J. B. Post, map librarian at the Free Library of Philadelphia, from which most of the maps were reproduced in black-and-white illustrations. Literary maps depict places described in A. A. Milne's Winnie the Pooh books, John Bunyan's *The Pilgrim's Progress* (1678), Jonathan Swift's *Gulliver's Travels* (1726), Jules Verne's *The Mysterious Island* (1874), Robert Louis Stevenson's *Treasure Island* (1883), Thomas More's *Utopia* (1516), and Austin Tappan Wright's *Islandia* (1942). Anthony Trollope's Barsetshire, A. Conan Doyle's Baskerville Hall, William Faulkner's Jefferson and Yoknapatawpha counties, J. R. R. Tolkien's Middle Earth, C. S. Lewis's Narnia, and James Branch Cabell's Poictisme are also illustrated. Short descriptions accompany each map.

The Dictionary of Imaginary Places

ALBERTO MANGUEL AND
GIANNI GUADALUPI
Authors

San Diego, New York, and London:
    Harcourt Brace Jovanovich, 1987
GR650 .M36 1987

*W*ritten in the matter-of-fact style of a nineteenth-century gazetteer, *The Dictionary of Imaginary Places* gives information on more than 1200 places described in literature and legend from the time of Homer to the present. The geography, history, and inhabitants of these worlds are described in detail. Localities excluded include heavens and hells, places in the future, places outside planet Earth, and pseudonymous places such as Thomas Hardy's Wessex and William Faulkner's Yoknapatawpha. Also excluded are actual sites that can be visited and mapped, for example, the London of A. Conan Doyle's Sherlock Holmes. The book features more than two hundred illustrations and maps of places such as Laputa, from *Gulliver's Travels* (1726) by Jonathan Swift; the Land of Oz, from works by L. Frank Baum; and Never Land, from *Peter Pan* (1904) by J. M. Barrie. The book contains an alphabetical index of authors and titles related to the works in which the places appear. This expanded version of the 1980 edition (G650 .M36 1980), includes a section of new entries, including Spoon River, an imaginary New England town created by Edgar Lee Masters, and the abbey where Umberto Eco set *The Name of the Rose* (1980).

A Literary and Historical Atlas of Africa and Australasia

J[OHN] G[EORGE] BARTHOLOMEW
Compiler

London: J. M. Dent, 1913
G2446 .S1B3 1913

A Literary and Historical Atlas of Africa and Australasia was created to provide geographical background for readers of the "Everyman's Library" book series published by J. M. Dent. Most of the maps show the boundaries of countries in Africa or Asia at various periods or locate historical events. One section contains maps that relate to literature, including places in the South Seas where Robert Louis Stevenson lived. At the end of the book is an alphabetically arranged gazetteer of places shown on the maps, with explanations of their literary and historic interest.

A Literary and Historical Atlas of America

J[OHN] G[EORGE] BARTHOLOMEW
Compiler

London: J. M. Dent, 1911
G1101 .S1 .B3 1911

A Literary and Historical Atlas of America was created to provide geographical background for readers of the "Everyman's Library" book series published by J. M. Dent. Most of the maps show the boundaries of cities or countries in the Americas at various periods or locate historical events. One section contains maps that relate to literature, including Boston; Concord, Massachusetts, sites connected with Ralph Waldo Emerson, Nathaniel Hawthorne, and Henry David Thoreau; and "Virginia in American Fiction." At the end of the book is an alphabetically arranged gazetteer of places shown on the maps, with explanations of their literary and historic interest.

A Literary and Historical Atlas of Europe

J[OHN] G[EORGE] BARTHOLOMEW
Compiler

London: J. M. Dent, 1910
G 796 .S1 .B3 1910

A Literary and Historical Atlas of Europe was created to provide geographical background for readers of the "Everyman's Library" book series published by J. M. Dent. Most of the maps show the boundaries of countries and empires at various periods or locate historical events. One section contains maps that relate to English literature, including the Lake District, the route of the pilgrims in Geoffrey Chaucer's *The Canterbury Tales* (ca. 1387–1400), and places associated with the works of Robert Burns, Walter Scott, and Charles Dickens. Some maps pertain to specific books, such as Scott's *Ivanhoe* (1819) and Charles Reade's *The Cloister and the Hearth* (1861). Notes below the map indicate the titles of the related "Everyman's Library" books. At the end of the volume is an alphabetically arranged gazetteer of places shown on the maps, with explanations of their literary and historic interest. The volume was revised in 1923 and 1930 and reprinted several times up to 1941 (G1796 .S1 .B3 1941). New material includes a map of London in the time of Queen Elizabeth I (reigned 1558–1603).

Literary Maps for Young Adult Literature

MARY ELLEN SNODGRASS
Compiler

RAYMOND M. BARRETT, JR.
Cartographer

Englewood, Colorado: Libraries Unlimited, Inc., 1995
G1046 .A65 .S6 1995

Literary Maps for Young Adult Literature contains maps relating to thirty-five literary works involving a journey that might be read by high school students. Each book entry pairs a plot summary with a geographic overview, a detailed itinerary, labeled black-and-white maps, and suggestions for further reading. Books featured include Mark Twain's *The Adventures of Huckleberry Finn* (1884), Jules Verne's *Around the World in Eighty Days* (1872), Richard Wright's *Black Boy* (1937), Jack London's *The Call of the Wild* (1903), and J. D. Salinger's *The Catcher in the Rye* (1951).

A Mapbook of English Literature

John Briscoe D'Auby,
Robert Lathrop Sharp, and
Murray Eugene Borish
Compilers

New York: Henry Holt, 1936
PR 109 .B7 1936

A Mapbook of English Literature consists of sixteen black-and-white maps supplying geographical background for students about places where English literature was created, where authors lived, and where they set their scenes. Individual maps include biographical and literary maps for England, Wales, and southern Scotland for the periods before 1660, 1660 to 1800, and 1800 to 1936; maps of London from 1400 to 1666, 1666 to 1800, and 1800 to 1900; the environs of London from 1800; The Lake Country; Wessex, the Hardy Country; Oxford and Cambridge, with lists of the colleges and the principal writers who studied at them; Western and Central Europe, annotated with facts relating to British literature; and Ireland. Detailed legends on the maps indicate the literary significance of the locales. An index lists authors, places, and titles, with coordinates to the map.

SPECIFIC AUTHORS

Patrick O'Brien

Harbors and High Seas: An Atlas and Geographical Guide to the Aubrey-Maturin Novels of Patrick O'Brian

Dean King with, John B.
Hattendorf, William Clipson,
and Adam Merton Cooper
Illustrators

New York: Henry Holt, 1996
PR6029 .B55 Z73 1996

Harbors and High Seas is a guide to places mentioned in seventeen novels by Patrick O'Brian. The novels, from *Master and Commander* (1969) to *The Commodore* (1995), describe the travels of two fictional adventurers of the early nineteenth century—Jack Aubrey and Stephen Maturin. The atlas consists of an introduction discussing trade routes of the time around the Napoleonic Wars (1803–1815) and other background information on seafaring as well as maps of the British Isles in 1812. These maps are followed by chapters on each of the novels, with plot details, maps of places visited by the characters, and descriptions of those places. Some chapters offer illustrations of places and quotations about them taken from books of the time in which the novels are set. This atlas is a sequel to *A Sea of Words: A Lexicon and Companion for Patrick O'Brian's Seafaring Tales* (PR6029 .B55 Z74 1995), published in 1995.

J[ohn] R[onald] R[uel] Tolkien

The Atlas of Middle Earth

Karen Wynn Fonstad
Compiler

Boston: Houghton Mifflin, 1981
G3122 .M5 F6 1981

The Atlas of Middle Earth contains maps relating to the imaginary world of Middle Earth that is the setting for J. R. R. Tolkien's *Lord of the Rings* (1955) trilogy—consisting of *The Fellowship of the Ring*, *The Two Towers*, and *The Return of the King*—as well as *The Hobbit* (1937) and *The Silmarillion* (1977). Groupings include sections for the First, Second, and Third ages, regional maps, and maps specifically relating to events in *The Hobbit* and other books in the *Lord of the Rings* trilogy. Thematic maps describe the land forms, climate, vegetation, population, and languages of Middle Earth. Each map is accompanied by detailed notes about topography as described in the books and the events with which the map is associated. In 1991 a revised version (G3122 .M5 F6 1991) was published to incorporate new data revealed in the *History of Middle-Earth* series (1980–), edited by Tolkien's son Christopher (b. 1924).

Journeys of Frodo: An Atlas of
J. R. R. Tolkien's The Lord of the Rings

Barbara Strachey
Compiler

New York: Ballantine Books, 1981
G 3122 .M5 .S7 1981

Journeys of Frodo contains fifty-one maps covering the journey to Mordor of the hobbit Frodo in J. R. R. Tolkien's *Lord of the Rings* (1955) trilogy—*The Fellowship of the Ring, The Two Towers,* and *The Return of the King.* It is intended to help readers of the books envision the country of Middle Earth through which the route passes and to keep track of each day's adventures. The maps are based on Tolkien's own drawings and maps on the endpapers of the books. Major events in the books are marked on the maps, along with references to the book and title of the chapter in which the event occurs. Each map is accompanied by detailed notes about topography as described in the books and the events with which the map is associated.

Afterword

The Center for the Book in the Library of Congress was established in 1977 to stimulate public interest in books and reading. In sponsoring dozens of projects through the years, the Center for the Book has found that educating people about their own literary heritage—linking local writers to familiar places and regional traditions—has been an especially popular and effective means of promoting books and reading. Today most of the Center's thirty-four state affiliates sponsor programs that honor and promote their state's writers and literary heritage.

The Library of Congress's collection of literary maps, probably the largest such collection in existence, is a wonderful educational resource. This realization is at the root of the Center for the Book's "Literary Heritage of the States" project which, in turn, led to this book.

A three-year education and reading promotion project funded by a generous grant from the Lila Wallace-Reader's Digest Fund, "Literary Heritage of the States" started in 1993 with *Language of the Land: Journeys into Literary America,* an exhibition at the Library of Congress of selected literary maps from the Library's collections. The project continued through 1995 with a traveling version of the *Language of the Land* exhibition that was seen in sixteen states under the sponsorship of different state centers for the book—each affiliated with the Center for the Book in the Library of Congress. The first traveling exhibit site was Currigan Exhibition Hall in Denver, Colorado (September 1–October 30, 1993); the last site was the California Library and Courts Building in Sacramento (May 21–July 15, 1995). The exhibit then became part of the Library's traveling exhibit program and was seen at several different sites around the country.

The grant from the Lila Wallace-Reader's Digest Fund also supported programming at each of the Center for the Book traveling exhibit sites. Programs included readings by regional authors, radio and television broadcasts, a film series, literary heritage projects in eight different schools; four symposia, and six special events honoring local and regional authors.

The development and publication of more than a dozen new literary maps also was supported by the "Literary Heritage of the States" project. Many of them are in this book.

The Center for the Book wishes to express its appreciation to the Lila Wallace-Reader's Digest Fund for supporting the project and to its Library of Congress partners, the Interpretive Programs Office and the Geography and Map Division, for their help and enthusiasm.

John Y. Cole
Director, Center for the Book

Index

Numbers in bold face indicate pages with map images.

Language of the Land